MW00962201

Preface

It is with sincere humility and a grateful heart that I present this collection of research papers dedicated to the defense of Hebraic Christian Monotheism—the cornerstone of Oneness Pentecostal faith. The following papers were originally written during the years of 1996 through 2006 and represent both undergraduate and graduate material. I have taken this opportunity to revise these works in an attempt to correct errors and insure accuracy; however, if you encounter grammatical or theological errors, please feel free to contact me and provide feedback, as this can only help sharpen my understanding.

The following studies are not presented in the chronological order they were penned. Rather, I have chosen to arrange them in a format more conducive to the subject matter. For example, Volume 1 contains a selection of studies that focus on the Hebraic foundations of Oneness Pentecostalism. These are presented in 'stair-step' fashion so that each independent study builds upon another. This is intentional as I believe this will facilitate one's study of the material; however, I am also cognizant of possible redundancy. Please keep in mind that each study was originally a paper written for a specific theological class. Hence one may encounter the same passage or line of argumentation that is presented in another study. Yet, I encourage you to carefully examine the apparent redundancy because—in reviewing this material I discovered that oftentimes the subject is presented from a different theological angle and to a lesser or greater extent elaborated on.

I have been in active full time ministry for over 25 years in both pastoral and evangelistic work. The first 7 years of full time ministry was in a Trinitarian Pentecostal organization but in 1994 I was asked to surrender my credentials because of my *'re-baptism'* in the name of Jesus Christ. I continued my affiliation with this organization until I was excommunicated in 1998 due to my refusal to recant my views relative to baptism and the nature of God. From 1998 until 2005, while furthering my education, I served as an independent pastor in Tennessee, North Carolina and Georgia. In 2005 I became affiliated with the Church of Our Lord Jesus Christ of the Apostolic Faith and endorsed in the military chaplaincy in 2007.

I have been married to Missy for over 25 years and we have 5 children: Aaron, Fayeth, Danielle, Jeremiyah and Jonathan and one grandchild Elizabeth Katherine. I am fully committed to the principles of the faith outlined in the following studies and I pray you will be strengthened as a result of them

James D. Hogsten

2013

Introduction

This volume contains five studies, which examine the Hebraic foundation and fundamental teachings of Oneness Pentecostalism. The first study is an investigation of Hebraic Monotheism and seeks to show that *the Hebrew understanding of strict monotheism* is not in conflict with Biblical Christianity. The second study focuses on the second-century transmutation of the church from Hebraic theological contours of thought to Hellenism —and the effect of this *shift* on the doctrine of God.

The third study utilizes the second-century writings of Ignatius and demonstrates the theological position of 'Praxeas' finds historicity in these epistles. Although no attempt is made to show Ignatius *embraced* Patripassianism, it does demonstrate that his view of God has a greater affinity to the teaching of Praxeas than the apologists—typified by Tertullian and Hippolytus. In fact, this study challenges Tertullian's accusation that Praxeas is a *"pretender of yesterday,"* who has no claim to doctrinal historicity in the early church.

The fourth study in this volume addresses the fundamental teachings of the Oneness Pentecostalism in light of the previous studies. Often labeled as a *'heretical cult,'* this work attempts to demonstrate the Oneness view of God and baptism in Jesus name is consistent with the pristine Christian faith. Additionally, it seeks to prove the Oneness movement is not an aberrant form of Christianity and therefore is undeserving of the label 'heresy.' This study examines areas of *continuity* and *discontinuity* between the Oneness faith and the majority of Christendom and in areas of divergence, the Oneness rationale is provided to enable the reader to better comprehend the Oneness perspective. It is hoped this research will show that—*at worst*—Oneness Pentecostals should be classified as heterodox and—*at best*—should be commended for reflecting the faith of the original Apostolic church.

The final study explores the rationale and historical precedence for the use of the monadic formula of water baptism by Oneness Pentecostals. Often called the *new issue* by both supporters and detractors, the use of monadic formula of Jesus' name in baptism is not a recent innovation but is historically and theologically grounded in the Christocentric and restorationist impulse of the nineteenth century. This study does not disparage the significance of the revival of Jesus name baptism in 1913-1914, but attempts to show the historical framework for this teaching was already embedded among groups which sought to promulgate the principle of primitivism. In fact, it is argued that Jesus name baptism was the logical evolution for a Movement that understood themselves as the eschatological people of God walking in the 'evening light' of the restored church.

TABLE OF CONTENTS

James D. Hogsten

I

Hebraic Monotheism:

A Deficient Form of

Monotheism?

Introduction
Presuppositions—the Theological Starting Point

Despite sincere efforts to examine the Bible objectively, everyone has presuppositions that impact and influence their hermeneutics. This is especially true when addressing issues of doctrinal development in ecclesiastical history. There are a variety of nuances affecting one's perception of this subject—yet, most positions can be classified under two major assumptions: namely, the '*evolving of the faith*' theory or the '*abandonment of the faith*' theory.[1] The former ideology, is espoused by Roman Catholicism, mainline Evangelicals and most *post-modern* Pentecostals and maintains that:

> ...the churches' traditional teachings were emergent rather than defined and only codified in general councils in the fourth and fifth centuries.[2]

> ...dogmatic statements of the Church...have been crystallized only in our own day. The fact is, however, that practically all the elements of ecclesiology have been the object of theological development...and proclamation through the centuries.[3]

In this view the process of doctrinal development is not seen as problematic because:

> ...it was not necessary in the earlier period to make the proper logical deductions from the axioms provided by Scripture...In other words, controversies had not raised questions to be answered and the implications of the worship and faith of the Church had not been fully recognized.[4]

Consequently, those who support this position believe there is little benefit in questioning the *process* or *outcome* of early

---

[1] The second study of this book provides a more detailed treatment of these positions. Suffice to say—these 'labels' are not "*official*" but merely descriptive of ecclesiological themes found in the history of the church.

[2] Ronald A. Wells, <u>History Through the Eyes of Faith</u> (San Francisco, CA: Harper Collins, 1989), 42.

[3] Michael Schmaus, <u>Dogma 4: The Church its Origin and Structure</u>, (London, England: Sheed & Ward, 1972), 69.

[4] Peter Toon, <u>The Development of Doctrine in the Church</u>, (Grand Rapids, MI: Eerdmans, 1979), xii.

ecclesiastical doctrinal struggles, for they are God's method for bringing the community of faith to a unified orthodoxy.

In contrast, those espousing the latter view argue that the New Testament church organically deteriorated subsequent to the death of the Apostles—and eventually apostatized from the faith *'once delivered unto the saints.'* Advocates of this position contend that the *"...idea of an evolving or formulating faith holds no credence with the New Testament."*[5] Although this position does not deny the possibility of *'healthy development'* in the church—it recognizes the truth of the *'law of corruption'* wherein:

> ...things are better at first, and then deteriorate, that freshness and purity wear off; that deflections arise and that the inclination from the strict line, one made, widens with insensible but fatal steadiness, in a word, the tendency of things to degeneracy...[6]

Development or *deterioration* is possible in any institution—yet, those embracing the *'abandonment of the faith'* theory argue the New Testament writers *prophetically warned of an apostasy.* Thus, they believe any doctrine boasting of a late development must be viewed with suspicion—as it might have contributed to the apostasy. While not as pervasive in post-modern Christendom, this view was the <u>dominant</u> understanding of the Protestant reformation and early Pentecostalism.[7]

Because of their antithetical nature—each theory generates a distinct epistemology—resulting in a radically different approach as to how they view the *process* and *outcome* of doctrinal struggles within the post-apostolic church. Indeed, both positions are rooted in assumptions shaping their hermeneutic—a fact that continues

---

[5] Thomas Weisser, *Was the Early Church Oneness or Trinitarian? Symposium on Oneness Pentecostalism* (Hazelwood, MO: Word Aflame, 1986), 59.

[6] J.B. Mozley, <u>The Theory of Development: A Criticism of Dr. Newman's Essay on the Development of Christian Doctrine</u>, 1847 (reprint BiblioBazaar, 2009), 6-7.

[7] Some would argue—in varying degree—the entire Reformation was predicated on a belief that the church departed from the pristine faith.

to be evident between those embracing the ecclesiastical doctrine of the Trinity and those advocating a Hebrew-Christian or 'Oneness' view of God. Both camps sincerely desire truth, appeal to Scripture as the touchstone of faith and attempt to find support for their view in pre-Nicene writings. Yet, despite some similarity, two diverse positions emerge with respect to God's nature and His identity in Jesus Christ.

The remainder of this study seeks to examine the nature of God in light of Biblical monotheism from a Hebraic-Christian perspective. Admittedly, not every theological nuance related to this subject is treated in these pages. However, every effort is made to analyze the major arguments used by those who support the concept of eternal intra-personal relationships within God against the Hebrew-Christian understanding. It is the hope of this writer that one will discover that the Hebraic-Christian view of Monotheism—espoused by Oneness Pentecostalism—is not inconsistent or at variance with the Scriptural portrayal of God.

Hebraic Monotheism in the Old Testament

The Oneness Pentecostal understanding of God begins with a Hebraic comprehension of God's *numerical* or *absolute* oneness. Thus, there is **one** God with no eternal hypostatic distinctions in His nature. Although, God is **not** viewed as a plurality of divine eternal persons—He has "...*a plurality of manifestations, roles, titles, attributes or relationships to man...these are not limited to three.*"[3]

This perception of Monotheism is a continuation of God's revelatory self-disclosure bequeathed *to* and promulgated *by* the nation of Israel—the original recipients of monotheism.

> Monotheism also, the cornerstone of Judaism, remains, as in the Bible, the religious doctrine that there is one God and no other, or, if it must be expressed abstractly, the doctrine of the *soleness* of God, in contradiction to polytheism, the multiplicity of gods. There is no assertion or implication of the unity of God in the metaphysical sense...[4]

The classic expression of Judaic and Christian Monotheism is expressed in Deuteronomy 6:4-9, which begins with the words: *"Hear Israel Yahweh our God Yahweh one."*[5]

This text, referred to as the '*Shema,*' is arguably the most important text regarding the nature of God within Judaism.[6] In fact, no other Old Testament passage impacts the daily life of Jewish believers worldwide like the Shema.

---

[3] David K. Bernard, <u>The Oneness of God</u> (Hazelwood, MO: Word Aflame, 1983), 294.

[4] George Foot Moore, <u>Judaism,</u> 3 vols., (Peabody, MA: Hendrickson, 1997), 1:360-361.

[5] Gilbrant Thoralf, ed., *The Old Testament Study Bible: Deuteronomy*, vol. 4, <u>The Complete Biblical Library</u> (Springfield, MO: World Library Press, 1996), 76. The translation of Deuteronomy 6:4 is based on the interlinear. All other Scriptural quotes are from the King James Version unless otherwise noted.

[6] J. A. Thompson, *Deuteronomy: An Introduction and Commentary* in <u>Tyndale Old Testament Commentaries</u> (Downers Grove, IL: Intervarsity, 1974), 121. The word "Shema" is taken from the first word in Deuteronomy 6:4 "HEAR."

> The *Shema* is an affirmation of Judaism and a declaration of
> faith in one God. The obligation to recite the *Shema* is separate
> from the obligation to pray and a Jew is obligated to say *Shema*
> in the morning and at night (Deut. 6:7).[7]

Jewish and Oneness theology maintains that an understanding of
this passage is critical to a correct apprehension of God's nature.
In fact, they believe this verse advocates a *strict form of Monotheism*
that precludes the idea of eternal distinctions within God's being.

The theological function of the Shema in ancient and second
temple Judaism was to affirm the absolute **oneness** of God and
enjoin the exclusive worship of the God who is **one**. Thus, the
Shema emphasized exclusive <u>Monotheism</u> and <u>Monolatry</u>:

> Their self-conscious monotheism was not merely an
> intellectual belief about God, but a unity of belief and praxis,
> involving the exclusive worship of this one God...Monolatry
> (the worship of only the one God) as the corollary of
> monotheism (belief in only the one God) is an important aspect
> of Jewish monotheism...[8]

Unfortunately, many within post-modern Christendom distort
or challenge the message of *'numerical oneness'* affirmed by the
Shema—inserting theological formulations into the text. For
example, Millard Erickson argues the word '<u>one</u>,' אֶחָד (echad) in
Deuteronomy 6:4 is a <u>*united*</u> and not a <u>*solitary*</u> one—citing Genesis
2:24 *"...and they shall be <u>one</u> (echad) flesh"* to substantiate his claim.[9]

Those who embrace Hebrew-Christian Monotheism reject such a
view for three primary reasons. First, there is no evidence that
anyone prior to the second-century interpreted the Shema's use of
echad as a *united* **one** instead of a <u>*numerical*</u> **one**. Indeed, such a

---

[7] Shira Schoenberg, *"the Shema,"* i n <u>Jewish Virtual Library</u> internet
resource <u>www.jewishvirtuallibrary.org</u>., 2012.

[8] Richard Baukham, <u>Jesus and the God of Israel</u>, (Grand Rapids, MI:
Eerdmans, 2008), 5. The 'Shema' served the same function in the early
Apostolic Church which is evident in the Gospels and in the Epistles
(*i.e. Mk. 12:29; 1Cor. 8:4; Eph. 4:6 etc..*).

[9] Millard J. Erickson, <u>God in Three Persons: A Contemporary
Interpretation of the Trinity</u> (Grand Rapids, MI: Baker, 1995), 174.

view places unnecessary strain on Deuteronomy 6:4—reading second and third century doctrinal formulations *into the text*. Thus, rather than a legitimate hermeneutic based upon sound exegesis, this view is an *interpolation* that actually obscures the theological message of the Shema.

Second, the Hebrew word אֶחָד (echad) is a <u>cardinal numeral</u>; thus, its <u>inherent</u> meaning is **one**—not *'compound unity.'*[10]

> אֶחָד...a cardinal number in contrast to more than one...an ordinal number, as the first in a series involving time, space, or set...[11]
>
> one, same, single, first, each, once...this word occurs 960 times as a noun, adjective, or adverb, as a cardinal or ordinal number, often used in a distributive sense.[12]
>
> The primary meaning for 'echadh' is "one." However, as a numerical adjective, it can mean "only" and "solitary..."[13]

Third, interpreting echad as a *'compound unity'* results in a number of Scriptural inconsistencies—demonstrating the fallacy of this position.

> And the LORD God caused a deep sleep to fall upon Adam, and he sleep; and he took **one of his ribs** [אַחַת מִצַּלְעֹתָיו] and closed up the flesh instead thereof (Genesis 2:21).

The word rendered 'one' in the above verse is the feminine form of *echad—the same used in Deuteronomy 6:4.* Yet, the use of 'echad' does not indicate God removed a *rack* of Adam's ribs. Rather, this verse uses the <u>numeral one</u> to show that God took a singular rib

---

[10] Gregory A. Lint, *The Old Testament Hebrew-English Dictionary: Aleph-Beth* in <u>The Complete Biblical Library</u> (Springfield, MO: World Library Press, 1996), 145. I examined 10 translations and **not one** translated the Hebrew word <u>echad</u> as *'united'* in Deuteronomy 6:4.

[11] J. Swanson, <u>Dictionary of Biblical Languages with Semantic Domains: Hebrew (Old Testament)</u>, electronic edition, Oak Harbor: Logos Research, 1997.

[12] R. Laird Harris, edt. <u>Theological Wordbook of the Old Testament</u>, (Chicago, IL: Moody, 1980) electronic edition, Oak Tree Software Inc.

[13] Bruce E. Willoughby, *"A Heartfelt Love: An Exegesis of Deuteronomy 6:4-19,"* in <u>Restoration Quarterly</u>, 20 (Wenham, MA: Gordon College, 1977), 78.

from Adam and used it to fashion Eve. Yet, this is not the only verse of Scripture demonstrating 'echad' has no inherent meaning of plurality.

> And the LORD turned a mighty strong wind which took away the locusts and cast them into the Red Sea; there remained not **one** (אֶחָד) locust in all the coasts of Egypt. (Exodus 10:19).
>
> And the LORD said unto Moses, Yet will I bring **one** (אֶחָד) plague more upon Pharaoh...(Exodus 11:1).
>
> ...ye shall eat unleavened bread, until the **one** (אֶחָד) and twentieth day of the month at even (Exodus 12:18)
>
> **One** (אֶחָד) law shall be to him that is homeborn, and unto the stranger that sojourneth among you (Exodus 12:49).

The above verses employ the word 'echad;' yet, in none of these verses does 'echad' signify an inherent plurality. Indeed, in each case: *one locust* (Ex. 10:19); *one plague* (Ex. 11:1); *one and twentieth day* (Ex. 12:18) and *one law* (Ex. 12:49)—**one** simply means **one**! Of course, this is consistent with the Old Testament's use of echad in an absolute *numerical* sense—and raises serious questions as to the validity of the claim that 'echad' expresses the idea of a *composite* or *compound* one.[14]

There **are** verses where *echad* must be understood as a *collective* or *compound unity.* However, this is **not** based upon the use of the cardinal numeral אֶחָד *echad*. Rather, in each case—the *context* and use of *collective nouns* govern the collective interpretation of the text.

> Therefore shall a man leave his father and his mother, and shall cleave unto his wife: **and they** shall be one flesh (Genesis 2:24).
>
> And they came unto the brook of Eschcol, and cut down from thence a branch with **one cluster** of **grapes**...(Numbers 13:23).

Clearly, a <u>collective</u> or <u>compound</u> oneness is advocated in the above verses; yet, this understanding is **not** determined by the use of the cardinal numeral *echad*. Rather, Genesis 2:24 is interpreted collectively based on the Hebrew plural verb translated "<u>they</u>" in

---

[14] Several other verses affirm the numerical use of echad (*i.e. Genesis 22:2; Exodus 25:19 Leviticus 16:5; Numbers 14:15; Job 9:3; Ps 89:36 etc...*).

reference to the <u>man</u> and his <u>wife</u>. Likewise, in Numbers 13:23, the compound view of 'one' is governed by the *collective nouns* '<u>cluster</u>' and '<u>grapes</u>' and **not** the numeral echad. In other words, the **only** reason 'echad' is interpreted as a compound unity in Genesis 2:24 and Numbers 13:23 is that 'one' is used in reference to *collective nouns*—**not** because the numeral *one* means something other than *one*.

In truth—the reason some insist the use of 'echad' in the Shema (Deuteronomy 6:4) must be understood collectively is based on the theological bias that there are intra-personal distinctions in the Godhead. Thus, they allow a doctrinal bias to <u>govern</u> their hermeneutic of the text—instead of allowing <u>the text</u> and <u>how</u> it was understood by the original recipients to <u>inform</u> their view of the text. Some object to this by insisting that if Moses intended to convey the *numerical oneness* of God—he would have used the word יָחִיד (*yachid*) which refers to an '*absolute one*.'[15]

It is true 'yachid' <u>can</u> express the idea of '<u>*only one*</u>' and is usually used this way in the sense of a unique or only child; however, the fundamental meaning of *'yachid'* is to *"be united."*[16]

> only unique child, pertaining to a child very special...and in that sense unique...in some contexts this child may be numerically the only child...lonely, alone pertaining to being in a solitary place.[17]
> to be united...with...to join with...to come together[18]

Interestingly, the verbal adjective yach<u>id</u> (יָחִיד) forms the root of the adverb יַחַד (yach<u>ad</u>)–which means:

---

[15] Wade H. Phillips, <u>God the Church and Revelation,</u> (Cleveland, TN: White Wing, 1986), 160-161.

[16] Brown, F., Driver, S. R., & Briggs, C. A., יָהִיד, <u>Enhanced Brown-Driver-Briggs Hebrew and English Lexicon</u> (electronic ed.) (402). Oak Harbor, WA: Logos Research Systems, 2000.

[17] Swanson, יָהִיד.

[18] Ludwig Koehler and Walter Baumgartner, יחד, in <u>The Hebrew and Aramaic Lexicon of the Old Testament,</u> (Leiden, The Netherlands, 2000) electronic edition.

unitedness...in union together—together of community in action, place or time...[19]

properly a unit, i.e. (adverb) unitedly: alike, at all (once), both, likewise, only, altogether, withal.[20]

Join, be united i.e., enter into an association with a person or group (Gen 49:6; Isa 14:20); unit.[21]

The above definitions explicitly reveal that—*far from being an absolute or numerical one*—the verbal adjective yach<u>id</u> (יָחִיד) and the adverb יַחַד (yach<u>ad</u>) express the concept of '<u>unity</u>.' Therefore, these words—rather than the numeral אֶחָד echad—have an inherent sense of *unity in plurality*. In fact, the words 'unity' and 'unite' are translated from the verb יַחַד (yach<u>ed</u>) and the adverb yach<u>ad</u> (יָחִיד) not the cardinal numeral אֶחָד 'echad.'

> Teach me thy way O LORD; I will walk in they truth: **unite** (yach<u>ed</u>—יַחֵד) my heart to fear thy name (Psalm 86:11).
>
> Behold, how good and how pleasant it is for brethren to dwell together in **unity** (yach<u>ad</u>—יַחַד) (Psalm 133:1).[22]

The Hebrew language does not support the claim that *yachid* is a better word to use when expressing *numerical oneness*. In truth, Scripture consistently uses forms of *'yachid'* (*i.e. yached; yachad*) to emphasize a *unity in plurality*. Furthermore—since these words are **not** cardinal or ordinal numbers—the Biblical writers purposely and correctly used the numerical adjective אֶחָד (echad) to express Yahweh's absolute or numerical oneness.

Despite the linguistic evidence—some continue to assert *yachid* more accurately conveys the idea of numerical oneness. To bolster this position—it is argued that, in his <u>Thirteen Principles of Faith</u>, Jewish philosopher Moses Maimonides (1135-1204) intentionally

---

[19] Brown-Driver-Briggs, יַחַד.

[20] James Strong, יַחַד in <u>Strong's Hebrew and Chaldee Dictionary of the Old Testament</u>, electronic edition, Oak Tree Software.

[21] Swanson, יַחַד.

[22] Adrian Schenker edt., <u>Biblia Hebraica Stuttgartensia</u> (Stuttgart, Germany, Deutsche Bibelgeselschaft, 1983) electronic edition with Westminster Hebrew Bible Morphology. Hereafter BHS.

uses *yachid* when expressing God's oneness because he knew the numeral *echad* is inherently plural.[23]

> ...Moses Maimonides (1135-1204), the greatest medieval Jewish philosopher, chose when drawing up the thirteen principles or articles of faith...he used not <u>echad</u>, from the Shema, but <u>yachid</u>! Obviously, the word <u>echad</u> **lacked the philosophical precision** necessary **to teach the God is one Person only**.[24]

Even **if** Moses Maimonides substituted *yachid* in place of *echad*, this does not negate the fact that:

1. The basic meaning of יָחִיד (*yachid*) is '*united*,' a fact confirmed in every reputable Hebrew Lexicon.
2. That Scripture employs the verbal and adverbial form of יָחִיד (*yachid*) to emphasize *unity in plurality. (Psalm 86:11; 133:1)*.
3. The word יָחִיד (*yachid*) is **not** a cardinal or ordinal numeral.

Actually, Maimonides **does** use the word יָחִיד (*yachid*) in his work entitled "<u>The Thirteen Principles of Faith</u>." However, he **NEVER** uses יָחִיד (*yachid*) to express God's numerical oneness or when quoting the Shema. In fact, this word is **only** used in reference to God's **unity**.

> I believe with perfect faith that the Creator, blessed be his name, is a <u>Unity</u> [one] יָחִיד, and that there is no <u>unity</u> יָחִיד in any way manner like unto his, and that he alone is our God, who was, is, and will be.[25]

יָחִיד (*yachid*) is used twice in this article to express the unity of God—not his numerical oneness. Moreover, there is no indication Maimonides substitutes יָחִיד (*yachid*) in place of אֶחָד (*echad*) when quoting the Shema (Deut. 6:4) or addressing God's numerical oneness. In fact, in his magnum opus, <u>The Mishneh Torah</u>—the *Mitzvot Aseh (positive commandments)* declares:

---

[23] Phillips, 159-160.

[24] Eric V. Snow, <u>A Zeal For God Not According to Knowledge</u> (Lincoln, NE: 2005), 556. Emphasis mine.

[25] Joseph H. Hertz trans. <u>The Thirteen Principles of Faith of Maimonides</u>, in <u>The Authorized Daily Prayer Book</u>, rev. ed. (New York, NY: Bloch Pub, 1948), 248-255.

To unify [*yachid*—לִיַחֲדוֹ] Him, as [Deuteronomy 6:4] states: "God is our Lord, God is one [*echad*—אֶחָד].

לִיַחֲדוֹ שֶׁנֶּאֱמָר ה אֱלֹהֵינוּ הי אֶחָד[26]

In the above section—Maimonides uses *yachid* to express the idea of **'unify'** and *echad* when expressing God's *numerical oneness* as revealed in Deuteronomy 6:4. In fact, throughout the Mishneh Torah—Maimonides always uses *echad* when emphasizing God's numerical oneness!

> This God is one. [אֶחָד] He is not two or more, but one,[אֶחָד][27]
>
> They all answered and said: "Listen, Israel, God is our Lord, God is One [אֶחָד] i.e., listen to us, Israel, our father, God is our Lord, God is one [אֶחָד][28]

These verses are only a small portion of those in the Mishneh Torah where Maimonides uses *echad* to express God's numerical oneness. Thus, Maimonides' use of *yachid* to emphasize **unity** and *echad* when conveying a **numerical absolute** is consistent with Scripture, every reputable Hebrew Lexicon and strict Hebrew Monotheism.

Actually, the argument regarding Maimonides is built on a false assumption—that is apparently designed to garner Old Testament support for a doctrine unknown to the children of Israel and the New Testament church! In fact, if the charge against Maimonides were true it would be evident among post-modern Jews—many of whom follow the rabbinic tradition of Maimonides—and in so doing **always** use *echad* when reciting Shema—and **never** *yachid!*

> Rabbinic tradition based on a radical monotheism, the interpretation of Maimonides (12th century), and the Jewish response to the Christian theology of the Trinity, translate Yhwh Elohenu Yhwh **echadh,** "The Lord our God, the Lord is One." It is a statement of the oneness and unity of God.[29]

---

[26] Eliyahu Touger, trans., etd. The Mishneh Torah (English-Hebrew), Moznaim publication, online edition, www.chabad.org.

[27] Ibid., *Hilchot Yesodei Hatorah, chapter one Halacha 7.*

[28] Ibid., *Kri'at Shema, chapter one Halacha 4.*

[29] Willoughby, 77. Emphasis mine.

The Old Testament—as well as ancient and second temple Judaism affirm that *echad* is understood as a cardinal numeral in reference to God's nature. Moreover, the New Testament supports this interpretation as well.

> And Jesus answered him, The first of all the commandments is, Hear, O Israel; the Lord our God **is one** Lord (Mark 12:29).

Like the Septuagint rendering of Deuteronomy 6:4—the Gospel of Mark records Jesus' quote of the Shema using the Greek word ἑις (heis) to express God is one. Like the Hebrew *echad*—this Greek word is primarily:

> a numerical term 'one' a single person or thing, with focus on quantitative aspect...a single entity, with focus on uniformity or quality.[30]

Proof the Jewish scribe believed Jesus' affirmation of the Shema was congruent with the *Hebrew understanding of God's oneness* is evident in his response.

> And the scribe said unto him, Well, Master, thou has said the truth: for there is <u>one God</u>; and there is <u>none other</u> but he (Mark 12:32).

The Jewish scribe did not interpret Jesus' declaration of God's oneness to be indicative of hypostatic distinctions in the Godhead. Rather, he believed Jesus was affirming the numerical oneness of God!

> ἐπ ἀληθείας εἶπας ὅτι εἷς ἐστιν καὶ οὐκ ἔστιν ἄλλος πλὴ αὐτοῦ (lit. upon truth you have said that one is and not is another except him) [Mark 12:32].[31]

Three important grammatical features in this verse—explicitly reveal neither Jesus nor the scribe used the word "one" to convey the idea of compound or collective oneness in God's nature.

---

[30] Fredrick William Danker, ἑις, in <u>A Greek-English Lexicon of the New Testament and other Early Christian Literature</u>, third edition, (Chicago, IL: University of Chicago, 2000), electronic edition.

[31] Maurice A. Robinson and William G. Pierpont, edt. in <u>The New Testament in the Original Greek: Byzantine Textform 2005</u>, electronic edition.

A. The conjunction ὅτι (<u>that or namely that</u>) functions in a declarative sense in this verse, for the scribe is emphasizing or 'recasting' Jesus statement—like that of *'active listening.'*[32]

B. After using ὅτι the scribe affirms that Jesus spoke 'upon truth' when he declared: εἷς ἐστιν (<u>one is he</u>). Both the numerical adjective and the context reveals the scribe's use of 'one' is in the absolute sense of *"one, in contrast to more than one"*[33]

C. This view is strengthened by the words: καὶ οὐκ ἔστιν ἄλλος πλὴν αὐτοῦ (<u>and **not** is another except him</u>). The use of the negative particle οὐκ (not) is especially noteworthy because it:

> denies the reality of an alleged fact. It is the clear-cut, point-blank negative, objective, final...the force of οὐ is sometimes very powerful, like the heavy thud of a blow.[34]

The use of the negative particle οὐκ in this verse is a denial that ἔστιν ἄλλος (there is another). The Greek word '<u>another</u>' *"pertains to that which is other than some other entity...pertains to that which is different in type or kind..."*[35] This word is followed by πλὴν (except) a *"...of contrast, implying the validity of something irrespective of other considerations,"*[36] coupled with the third person masculine pronoun αὐτοῦ (him). In short, the scribe clearly believed Jesus supported the Hebrew understanding of monotheism without qualification or suggestion that God was something other than numerically and solitarily...one!

Mark 12:28-34 is important because it is a testament as to *how* God's oneness expressed in the Shema was viewed within Second Temple Judaism. This passage also provides insight into Jesus' understanding of Deuteronomy 6:4—especially when examining the dialogue between Jesus and the scribe. Clearly, Jesus knew the

---

[32] Daniel B. Wallace, <u>Greek Grammar Beyond the Basics</u>, (Grand Rapids, MI: Zondervan, 1996), 456.

[33] Johannes P. Louw and Eugene A. Nida edts., εἷς, in <u>Greek-English Lexicon of the New Testament Based on Semantic Domains</u>, (New York: NY: United Bible Societies, 1989), electronic edition.

[34] A. T. Robertson, <u>A Grammar of the Greek New Testament in the Light of Historical Research</u>, (Nashville, TN: Broadman, 1934), 1156.

[35] Danker, ἄλλος.

[36] Louw & Nida, πλήν.

scribe interpreted his statement 'God is one' as an affirmation of strict Hebrew Monotheism. Interestingly, Jesus did not 'qualify' or offer clarification and correction to the scribe—but commended his response!

> And when Jesus saw that he answered <u>discreetly</u>, he said unto him, Thou art not far from the kingdom of God (Mark 12:34).

The Greek word translated "discreetly" carries the idea of *wisely* or *sensibly*. Thus according to the text—the scribe's <u>*comprehension*</u> of the Shema **and** his *grasp* of <u>Jesus' answer</u> is **wise!**[37] Of course, <u>if</u> the Shema actually teaches God is a *unity in plurality*—then the scribe's answer is **not wise** and Jesus perpetuates his error by allowing the scribe to believe He embraces the same '<u>*misguided*</u>' view of Deuteronomy 6:4.

Some may argue this is an assumption; yet, it is one based on the *character* and *conduct* of Jesus. Indeed, the Gospels record several instances where Jesus corrects the misguided beliefs of the scribes and Pharisees (*i.e. Matt. 23:1-39*); their faulty interpretation of Scripture (*i.e Matt 22:23-32*); **and** their *misperceptions* of <u>His beliefs</u> (*i.e. John. 8:13-30*). Yet, even if Jesus offered no clarification or correction to the scribe—one certainly would not expect him to commend the scribe—if he was deceived or misunderstood Jesus' statement!

Mark 12:28-34 clearly reveals Jesus affirmed the <u>**Jewish view**</u> of Shema—and there is no debate that their comprehension of God precluded eternal distinctions in his nature. Even if one argues their understanding is deficient—this is no justification for using *echad* to 'prove' an intra-plurality in God. In fact, any hermeneutic that postulates such a position is guilty of allowing preconceived ideas regarding God's plurality to influence their treatment of this text

---

[37] Barclay M. Newman Jr., **νουνεχῶς,** in <u>A Concise Greek-English Dictionary of the New Testament</u>, (Stuttgart, Germany: United Bible Society, 1971), electronic edition.

Hebraic Monotheism in Light of אֱלֹהִים (Elohim)

The Hebrew concept of strict or absolute monotheism is often challenged on the basis of the Hebrew word אֱלֹהִים (*Elohim*). This word is translated 'God' over 2500 times in the Old Testament.[38] Yet, because it is **plural** in construction but used to describe the **singular** God of Israel—some believe this indicates there is an intra-plurality of eternal persons in God's nature.

> Most conservative Christians hold that the plural is representative of the multiple Godhead, and is an earlier reflection of the Trinity.[39]
>
> The plural form of the noun for the God of Israel אֱלֹהִים (*elohim*), is sometimes regarded as an intimation of a trinitarian view.[40]

Those embracing Hebrew-Christian monotheism acknowledge Elohim is a plural word—however, they bifurcate with respect to the *meaning* or *significance* of this plurality. In fact, they argue it is impossible to use Elohim to substantiate the doctrine of hypostatic distinctions in God based on the historical, linguistic and literary use of Elohim in Scripture.

Historically, there is no *internal* or *external* evidence suggesting the writers of Scripture understood Elohim to indicate there is an eternal ontological plurality in God. In fact, this view is a post-apostolic innovation that coincides with late second and early third century doctrinal developments of the church. Hence, this idea is rooted in speculative theology—not genuine exegetical work.

Linguistically, the idea Elohim indicates an intra-plurality in God completely ignores other similar peculiarities of the Hebrew language. For example, the word 'water' מַיִם (*mayim*) is a plural

---

[38] Larry Pierce., ed. *Hebrew and Greek Lexicon Aids.*, electronic edition., The Online Bible Millennium Edition (Ontario, Canada: The Online Bible Foundation, 2003).

[39] Lint., *Aleph-Beth.*, 245.

[40] Millard J. Erickson, Christian Theology, (Grand Rapids, MI: Baker, 1998), 353.

word but is used in a singular sense and often with singular nouns—i.e. *"bottle of water"* (Genesis 21:14).[41] Scripture does not offer a rationale as to *why* this word is plural—yet, no one interprets the 'plurality' of this word as proof of hypostatic distinctions in water. In short, although composed of two-parts Hydrogen and one part Oxygen—no one argues the plurality of this Hebrew word is a *Divine intimation* of this truth!

Likewise, the Hebrew word "face" פָּנִים (*paniym*) is a plural word but **always** used *"as a singular."*[42] Like "water," no reason is given as to *why* "face" is plural. Yet, no scholar argues the plurality of 'face' is an implication of hypostatic distinctions—even when used with the Hebrew word "Elohim" (*i.e. Gen. 33:10*). Rather, 'face' is simply understood as a plural word with a singular meaning and there is **no** *veiled significance* attached to this word.

Elohim אֱלֹהִים is the plural form of EL אֵל both of which are translated 'God' in the Old Testament. The plural form is also used to designate rulers, judges and divine ones, such as angels,[43] but when used to denote the God of Israel—it is always singularly understood. Thus, many scholars maintain Elohim is an *abstract* or *intensive plural* that should not be treated as a literal plural.

> ...the attachment of the plural ending serves, as it often does in the Semitic languages, which have various peculiar uses different from modern grammatical notions, to express the idea of greatness, supremacy, and the like.[44]

> Its plural form may mean it had polytheistic...overtones at one time. Yet its use in the OT for Israel's God (always with singular verbs) probably means that the plural has reference to intensification or absolutization or exclusivity (say, God of gods).[45]

---

[41] Pierce, word number 04235.

[42] Strong's, פָּנִים, word number 6440.

[43] Brown-Driver-Briggs, אֱלֹהִים.

[44] The New International Encyclopedia, *Elohim*, in Wikisource, The Free Library, Dec. 2012, http://en.wikisource.org.

[45] Terence E. Fretheim, אֱלֹהִים, in New International Dictionary of Old Testament Theology & Exegesis, Willem A. VanGemeren, edt., (Grand

Even some Trinitarian scholars—question the validity of using Elohim to support the doctrine of the Trinity.

> This is a generic name used to refer to other gods as well...The plural form is commonly interpreted, however, as an indication of majesty or intensity rather than of multiplicity within God's nature.[46]

> *ᵉlohim* is usually considered an abstract, intensifying, majestic or dominical plural...In any case, the singular sense of the plural form is so uncontested for the OT that it used the word throughout without limitation (suspicion of polytheism).[47]

> The plural ending is usually described as a plural of majesty and not intended as a true plural when used of God. This is seen in the fact that the noun אֱלֹהִים is consistently used with singular verb forms and with adjectives and pronouns in the singular.[48]

Some may argue these explanations are also *assumptions*; yet, they differ, in that, they have a valid linguistic basis, rather than imposing post-apostolic theological views on the Hebrew word. Of course, the most accurate way to discover how Elohim should be interpreted is by examining the way this word is used in Scripture. In so doing, one can easily demonstrate the fallacy of using Elohim to 'prove' ontological distinctions in the Godhead.

Literarily, Scripture uses the plural forms of EL (*Elohim or Elohe*) to describe the singular God of Israel *as well as* the major deities of various pagan nations.

> ...the ark of the **God** (אֱלֹהֵי) of Israel shall not abide with us: for his and is sore upon us, and upon Dagon our **god** (אֱלֹהֵי) (1Sam 5:7).

> ...thus saith the LORD, the **God** (אֱלֹהֵי) of Israel...they have forsaken me, and have worshipped Ashtoreth the **goddess** (אֱלֹהֵי) of the Zidonians, Chemosh the **god** (אֱלֹהֵי) of the

Rapids, MI: Zondervan, 1997)., electronic edition.

[46] Erickson, 353.

[47] W. H. Schmidt, אֱלֹהִים, in <u>Theological Lexicon of the Old Testament</u> Jenni & Westermann edt., electronic edition.

[48] Jack B. Scott, אֱלֹהִים in <u>Theological Wordbook of the Old Testament</u>, R. Laird Harris edt., (Chicago, IL: Moody, 1980), electronic edition.

Moabites, and Milcom the **god** (אֱלֹהֵי) of the children of Ammon (1Kings 11:31, 33).

> ...the children of Israel...went a whoring after Baalim, and made Baalberith their god (אֱלֹהִים) And the children of Israel remembered not the LORD their God (אֱלֹהֵי)...(Judges 8:33-34).

Notice that 1Sam. 5:7 and 1Kings 11:31,33 uses the plural word אֱלֹהֵי (Elohe) to designate the God of Israel—**and** the false gods of the heathen nations. Yet, in Judges 8:33-34 אֱלֹהֵי (Elohe) is used to denote the God of Israel—while אֱלֹהִים (Elohim) designates the pagan god 'Baalberith'.

If the plural forms of 'EL' (*Elohim, Elohe*) are indicative of an intra-plurality in God's nature, consistent hermeneutics demand the same understanding when these words are used to describe pagan deities. Yet, there is **no evidence** to suggest the worshipers of these false gods believed they were comprised of ontological eternal distinctions. Chemosh, was the *principle* national or ethnic god of the Moabites,[49] while Dagon and Ashtoreth—were gods in the pantheon of the Philistines.

> We know of only three Philistine deities, all with Semitic names: Dagon, Ashtoreth, and Baal-zebub. Dagon was the principal Philistine god...Dagon is said to have been Baal's father.[50]

The use of Baal-berith (the lord of the covenant) in Judges 8:33-34, refers to the local deity worshipped in Shechem after Gideon's death.[51] The Bible often speaks concerning the cult of Baal using various name, but:

> These names do not denote various gods with the epithet 'lord,' but local venerations of the same West Semitic storm and fertility deity called simply Baal, 'Lord...' he is a war god and

---

[49] Gerald L. Mattingly, *Moabites*, in Peoples of the Old Testament World, (Grand Rapids, MI: Baker, 1994), 329.

[50] David M. Howard Jr., *Philistines*, i n Peoples of the Old Testament World, (Grand Rapids, MI: Baker, 1994), 246-247.

[51] M.G. Easton, *Baal-berith*, i n Easton's Bible Dictionary (Nashville, TN: Thomas Nelson, 1897), electronic edition.

fertility deity who consorts with Anat (is later equated with Astarte).[52]

It is significant that God inspired the Biblical writers to identify the pagan deities with the **same plural word** used to denote the God of Israel! Since the gods of the surrounding nations were not considered transcendent beings—the word Elohim does not suggest ontological similarities between Yahweh and the pagan gods. This means 'Elohim' is **not** a *subtle reference* to hypostatic distinctions—but is an *intensive plural* denoting the **principle deity** of a given nation (*i.e. the God of Israel, Yahweh; god of the Philistines, Dagon*).

Two other passages are worth examining in this regard, both of which show Elohim should not be interpreted as a true plural or understood as an intra-plurality of God.

> ...and fashioned it with a graving tool, after he had made it **a molten calf**: and they said, these by thy gods אֱלֹהֶי, O Israel, which brought thee up out of the land of Egypt. And when Aaron saw it, he built an altar before it; and Aaron made a proclamation and said, To morrow is a feast to the LORD יהוה...they have made them **a molten calf** and have worshipped it, and have sacrificed thereunto and said these by thy gods אֱלֹהֶי, O Israel, which have brought thee up out of the land of Egypt (Exodus 32:4-5, 8).

In this passage Aaron fashions **one** calf—identified with the plural form of 'EL.' According to the text—the **singular calf** represents Yahweh—the God of Israel. Hence, the plural form of 'EL' is not used to indicate a plurality in the Godhead, but to emphasize the **one calf** symbolizes the principle God of Israel—Yahweh!

Unlike 'Yahweh', the personal covenant name of God—Elohim is a generic word that designates the gods of heathen nations **and** the God of Israel. Hence, the literary use of this word is that of an *intensive plural* when referencing a singular deity and a true plural when describing *multiple gods (i.e. 2Kings 18:33; 19:12; Psalm 96:5).*

---

[52] Bruce K Waltke, בַּעַל in <u>Theological Wordbook of the Old Testament</u>, (Chicago, IL: Moody, 1980), electronic edition.

Yet, this word **never** denotes hypostatic distinctions in God and such an assertion is not based on sound hermeneutic principles.

Some may argue the *implication of plurality* is valid <u>only</u> when Elohim is used for Israel's God; yet, there is no exegetical or linguistic justification for such a position. Furthermore, if Elohim denotes a *plurality of persons*—the reverse **must be true** when 'EL' is used. In other words, 'EL' must be only **one hypostasis** of the hypostases within Elohim. Of course, Scripture actually uses אֵל (EL) and אֱלֹהִים (Elohim) interchangeably—in reference to God.

> ...the LORD יהוה appeared to Abram, and said unto him, I am the Almighty God אֵל (EL); walk before me, and be thou perfect. And Abram fell on his face and God אֱלֹהִים (Elohim) talked with him, saying...(Genesis 17:1, 3).

If Elohim denotes multiple hypostatic distinctions in God—this passage is problematic for—*according to Genesis 17:1*—Yahweh appears to Abram, identifying himself as 'EL' (*one hypostasis?*). Yet, in Genesis 17:3 'Elohim' is the speaker (*multiple hypostases?*). Does this passage suggest *one person of God* spoke with Abram in the first verse and—*unbeknown to Abram*—was joined by additional *persons* in verse three? Of course not—Yahweh is the only God who speaks to Abram in Genesis 17:1-3; thus, showing that 'EL' and 'Elohim' are used interchangeably to describe Yahweh.

The fallacy of interpreting 'Elohim' as an indication of multiple hypostases is even more evident in the following verses.

> ...who hath told it from that time? Have not I the LORD יהוה? And there is no God אֱלֹהִים (Elohim) else beside me; a just God אֵל (EL) and a Saviour; there is none beside me. (Isaiah 45:21).
>
> Remember the former things of old: for I am God אֵל (EL), and there is none else; I am God אֱלֹהִים (Elohim) and there is none like me (Isaiah 46:9).

This writer realizes no one interprets אֵל (EL) as a singular distinction of God. However, if אֱלֹהִים (Elohim) is plural <u>because</u> of an intra-plurality in God's nature—it is only consistent to interpret 'EL' as one hypostasis of God. Of course, in the above verses this would be confusing because both forms are used in the same verse. In Isaiah 45:21, Yahweh speaks as "Elohim" and then as "EL." Likewise, in Isaiah 46:9 Yahweh claims to be 'EL' saying 'I am <u>God</u> 'EL' and there *is none else*' and then identifies himself as 'Elohim' saying 'I am <u>God</u> (Elohim)and there *is none like me*.'

In truth, there is no confusion in the above passages—especially when one realizes "El" and "Elohim" are used interchangeably when referring to the God of Israel. Thus, whatever *raison d'être* one gives for the plural form of Elohim it <u>must</u> be consistent with its use in Scripture.[53] This being the case, rather than interpreting the plural word אֱלֹהִים (Elohim) as an indication of God's intra-plurality—it is more hermeneutically consistent to conclude this is an *intensive plural* identifying the principle God of Israel, Yahweh.

---

[53] Robertson McQuilkin, <u>Understanding and Applying the Bible</u> (Chicago, IL: Moody, 1992), 116.

Hebraic Monotheism in Light of God's Relationality

Recent discussions concerning God's nature center around the idea that Yahweh's relationship with humanity flows out of His eternal *intra-personal* relationships. In fact, some argue absolute or strict monotheism is incompatible to the Christian view of God as loving and relational.

> ...the very notion of an undifferentiated, unrelated unity...is an unintelligible notion. Pure unity is equivalent to 'nothingness,' and is therefore neither picturable nor conceivable...the notion that God is in his essence alone, that apart from and before creation God exists in *total solitude*, is completely incompatible with the Christian understanding that God is essentially love or even essentially personal.[54]

This position is the basis of what is commonly known as the *'Social Trinity'* doctrine, which teaches:

> ...that the one divine Being eternally exists as three distinct centers of consciousness, wholly equal in nature, genuinely personal in relationships, and each mutually indwelling the other.[55]

'Social Trinitarianism' has a robust history—taking ideas from Latin and Greek views of God.[56] Historically, there seems to be no **uniform** doctrine of the Social Trinity—rather, there are a variety of models under the umbrella of Social Trinitarianism—each of which stress particular aspects of this doctrine. Yet, despite minor differences—each school of thought emphasizes the intra-personal relationality of God, believing that:

> ...an understanding of the Trinity must begin with the fellowship of a plurality of persons, understood as three

---

[54] Gregory A. Boyd, Oneness Pentecostals & the Trinity (Grand Rapids, MI: Baker, 1992), 191.

[55] J. Scott Horrell, *"Toward a Biblical Model of the Social Trinity: Avoiding Equivocation of Nature and Order"* i n Journal of the Evangelical Theological Society, 47/3 (Louisville, KY: Evangelical Theological Society, 2004), 399-421.

[56] A detailed analysis of historical Social Trinitarianism (i.e. *Augustine's Lover and Beloved; the Cappadocian Fathers; Bart and Moltmann etc...*) is not possible here. Yet, contemporary models of Social Trinitarianism contain elements of these historic schools of thought.

centers of conscious activity...the biblical concept of God's triunity as the community and fellowship among three equal persons...[57]

Supporters argue this Divine societal "community" is rooted in the reciprocality of '*love*' mutually shared *in* and *by* the distinct centers of consciousness within the Deity.

> The Godhead is a complex of persons. Love exists within the Godhead as a binding relationship of each of the persons to each of the others.[58]

> the Father Loves the Son; the Son reciprocates that love, and this love between the Father and the Son is the Holy Spirit."[59]

Those promulgating this doctrine argue that '<u>love</u>' is more than an attribute of God—rather, <u>God is love</u> (1John 4:8); thus, love is an essential and **eternal** component of God's being.[60] Moreover, because 'love' is a relational term requiring a *subject* and *object,* this necessitates distinct hypostases in the nature of God.

> ...God being love virtually requires that he be more than one person. Love, to be love, must have both a subject and an object. Thus, if there were no multiplicity in the person of the Godhead, God could not really be love prior to this creation of other subjects. For love to be genuine, there must be someone whom God could love and this would necessarily be more than mere narcissism.[61]

Hebrew Christian monotheists agree that God is relational and that 'love' is an eternal and essential component of His being. Yet, they reject the claim that God's relationality is incompatible or inconsistent with strict monotheism. Their critique of the doctrine

---

[57] Norman Metzler, *The Trinity in Contemporary Theology: Questioning the Social Trinity*, in <u>Concordia Theological Quarterly</u>, 67:3/4 (Fort Wayne, IN: Concordia Theological Seminary, July/October 2003), 270-287.

[58] Millard J. Erickson, <u>God In Three Persons: A Contemporary Interpretation of the Trinity</u>, (Grand Rapids, MI: Baker, 1995), 221.

[59] Stanley J. Grenz, <u>Theology for the Community of God</u> (Grand Rapids, MI: Eerdmans, 1994), 72.

[60] Boyd, 191. It is true 1John 4:8 says θεὸς ἀγάπη ἐστίν (God love is); yet the same Greek construction is used in the LXX rendering of Exodus 34:14, which says θεὸς ζηλωτής ἐστιν (God jealous is).

[61] Erickson, <u>God in Three Persons</u>, 221.

of the Social Trinity begins with the charge that this model of God is rooted in philosophy and not the Bible—which is the **primary** means of revelation. Moreover, they argue the Biblical revelation that God *is love* does **not** demand an ontological intra-plurality in the Godhead—therefore, based on the flawed foundation of Social Trinitarianism—it must be deemed false and rejected.

Both Jewish and Oneness theologians maintain that Scripture equally affirms God's <u>absolute oneness</u> and His <u>relationality.</u> In fact, the Bible reveals the Nation of Israel embraced both of these truths <u>without reservation</u>—believing they were genuinely *loved* by Yahweh—the God who is solitarily **one.**

> The LORD did not set his love חָשַׁק (chashaq) upon you, nor choose you because ye were more in number than any people; for ye were the fewest of all people: But because the LORD loved אָהֲבַת (ahavat) you....(Deuteronomy 7:7-8).
>
> When Israel was a child, then I loved אֹהֵב him and called my son out of Egypt (Hosea 11:1).

The above verses use two words to describe God's love—the first of which is *chashaq*, signifiying *"a deep inward attachment..."*[62] The second word is *ahavat*, which is often linked to the covenant.

> Yahweh's love is one of the most important bases of the covenant...Its personal quality...and the figure of marriage point behind and beneath the covenant to its motive and origin in the innermost personal being of Yahweh. His love is part of the mystery of his personality.[63]

The Nation of Israel clearly understood they were beneficiaries of Yahweh's <u>love</u> and that <u>His love</u> was the basis of the Sinaitic covenant (Exodus 19:20). Yet, Scripture never intimates a belief that God's *love* necessitates an eternal *intra-personal* relationship in His being! In fact, one could rightly argue the greatest weakness of Social Trinitarianism is a <u>lack of</u> **Scriptural support**. In fact, this

---

[62] Leonard J. Coppes, חָשַׁק in <u>Theological Wordbook of the Old Testament</u>, electronic edition.

[63] P. J. Els, אָהֲבַת, in <u>New International Dictionary of Old Testament Theology & Exegesis</u>, electronic edition, 1997.

model of God actually seems to elevate Yahweh's *relationality* at **the expense** of Biblical monotheism.

In truth, the foundational premise of 'Social Trinitarianism' is logically and Biblically unsustainable. This is especially evident considering **other** eternal Divine relational attributes necessitating a *subject-object reciprocal relationship*. Indeed, if the subject-object nature of love demands intra-personal relationships in God's being—the same is true of **all subject-object relational** attributes.

> And the LORD passed by before him, and proclaimed, The LORD, The LORD God, <u>merciful</u> and <u>gracious</u>, <u>longsuffering</u> and abundant in goodness and truth (Exodus 34:6).

There is no argument that 'love' eternally belongs to the Lord and is an essential component of His identity, but the same is true of ALL his relational attributes. Does this mean the so-called *'community of God'* <u>experienced</u> and <u>expressed</u> mercy, compassion and longsuffering intra-personally? This seems strange, especially when one realizes "longsuffering" is a translation of two Hebrew words that convey the idea of *postponing one's anger*.[64] Yet, this is even more difficult to sustain when addressing other attributes that *'philosophically'* <u>demand</u> a subject-object relationship.

> For thou shalt worship no other god: for the LORD, whose name is **jealous**, is a **jealous** God (Exodus 34:14).
> For the LORD thy God **is** a consuming fire, even a **jealous** God (Deuteronomy 4:24).

The Hebrew word 'jealous' (קַנָּא) is not referring to positive zeal but *"...expresses a very strong emotion whereby some quality or possession of the object is desired by the subject"*[65]

> Any association with self-centered pettiness...is absent in the context of the manifestation of the קִנְאָה of God...God's 'jealousy' ...does not tolerate anyone else next to him in the covenant...The notion of the קִנְאָה of God is, therefore, of

---

[64] Brown-Driver & Briggs.

[65] Coppes, קָנָא.

importance in assessing the question whether, and if so to what extent Israel's religion was monotheistic.[66]

Even discounting self-centered pettiness—one still wonders <u>how</u> the so-called "community" of God could mutually express and experience intra-personal *jealousy* within the Godhead! Moreover, what about other attributes that are relationally experienced such as wrath or anger? Surely, no one would suggest these were displayed between the hypostatic distinctions of God! Yet, this is the dilemma faced by those who use a philosophical construct as the primary basis for their model of God.

In contrast, Jewish and Hebraic-Christian monotheists affirm Yahweh's relationality and love. Yet, they maintain the Biblical model of God begins with an understanding that HE is <u>Holy</u> and *all other attributes, to include love,* flow out of His Holiness.

> ...holiness is...the sum of the attributes, the essence of Deity, the goodness of God...God alone is holy in himself...Holiness is not one divine quality among others, even the cheifest, for it expresses what is characteristic of God and corresponds precisely to his deity...the holiness of God is....also the continuous background to the message of love in the New Testament.[67]

The importance of understanding God's holiness as the sum total of **all** His communicable and noncommunicable attributes is evident in the Scriptural emphasis placed on the Holiness of God. Indeed, the Bible uses the title '*Holy One*' in reference to Yahweh over forty times and—while God is love—the angelic hosts to not extoll Him with the words "*Love Love Love*," but declare He is "*Holy Holy Holy*." In fact, the Lord Himself uses the term HOLY as a self-description of **who or what He is.**[68]

---

[66] Hendrick G. L. Peels, קִנְאָה, in <u>New International Dictionary of Old Testament Theology & Exegesis</u>, electronic edition.

[67] W. T. Purkiser, <u>Exploring Christian Holiness</u>, Vol. 1., (Kansas City, MO: Beacon Hill, 1983), 27-28.

[68] Leviticus 11:44-45; 19:2; 20:7, 26; 22:32; Isaiah 29:23; Ezekiel 36:20-22; 39:7, 25 etc...

In this light, it becomes apparent that all attributes used of God will have to be prefaced by the qualification of God's holiness. We have noted...that the unique character of God in Christian theology is love. But love is susceptible to being reduced to human sentimentality. Therefore, even the central declaration of Christian faith about God must be qualified as 'holy love.'[69]

Placing God's love in the context of His holiness is more <u>Hebraic</u> than <u>Hellenistic</u> and more <u>Biblical</u> than <u>philosophical</u>. It also avoids the pitfalls associated with a *humanizing* perception of 'love' within God that is so evident in the Greek philosophical view. Most importantly, using Hebraic-Biblical concepts—one can develop a construct for comprehending God's love that does not conflict with or exceed the revelation of Scripture.

A Biblical construct for understanding God's love is discovered by recognizing that God demands His people display *selfless, altruistic* love that is **not** dependent on reciprocation.

...but thou shalt love thy neighbour **as thyself**: I am the LORD (Leviticus 19:18).

...Thou shalt love thy neighbour **as thyself** (Matthew 19:19).

For all the law is fulfilled in one word, even in this; Thou shalt love thy neighbour **as thyself** (Galatians 5:14).

If ye fulfill the royal law according to the scripture, Thou shalt love thy neighbour **as thyself**, ye do well (James 2:8).

So ought men to love their wives as their own bodies. He that loveth his wife **loveth himself**...For no man ever yet hated his own flesh...(Ephesians 5:28-29).[70]

Some have misunderstood the intent of such passages, believing they teach that relational love is grounded in 'self-love.'

Accepting and loving yourself is a precondition to being in a healthy, reciprocal relationship. However, the oft-recited advice (*you can't love anyone else until you love yourself*) has it backwards: **Before you can LET YOURSELF BE LOVED by another, you must first accept and love yourself.**[71]

---

[69] H. Ray Dunning, <u>Grace Faith & Holiness</u>, (Kansas City, MO: Beacon Hill, 1988), 194.

[70] See also Matthew 22:39; Mark 12:31,33; Luke 10:27; Romans 13:9.

[71] Dr. Tara J. Palmatier, *"Healthy Self-love: The Foundation of Good Relationships,"* at A Shrink For Men, <u>www.shrink4men.wordpress.com</u>,

The verses previously cited certainly presuppose 'self-love;' yet this is not what God is commanding nor is this to be the basis of our love to one another.

Self-love is actually the natural state of <u>fallen humanity</u> and thus, represents a <u>*perversion*</u> of the *imago Dei (the image of God)* Therefore, in reality, the command to love *"thy neighbor as thyself"* sets forth the idea of loving another as God loves—altruistically and without reciprocation.

> It should not need to be said that the commandment of self-love is alien to the New Testament commandment of love, and has grown up out of a wholly different soil form that of the New Testament...Self-love is man's natural condition, and also the reason for the perversity of his will...when love receives this new direction, when it is turned away from one's self and directed to one's neighbor, then the natural perversion of the will is overcome. So far is neighborly love from including self-love that it actually excludes and overcomes it.[72]

This is important because it reveals the flaw of any system using the dynamics of human love—as the basis for grasping God's love. Indeed, in the natural—all forms of love are in some sense motivated <u>by the object loved</u> and therefore love is rooted in:

> ...some form of need in the lover and a corresponding attractiveness in the object or person loved that at least offered the possibility of meeting that need. By contrast, God's agape was not generated by the potentiality of its object to meet a need in God. It arose out of the fulness of the Divine being. It is disinterested love, concern for the well being of the object...Love becomes the dynamic of God's self-disclosure.[73]

The Biblical command to *"love thy neighbor as thyself"* is actually antithetical to the normal conditions upon which love is *given* and *received*. God desires those being restored or '<u>*conformed*</u>' to the <u>imago Dei</u>—to love as HE loves—altruistically and irrespective of

---

Jan 2010. Parenthesis is mine but the bolded section is the author's.

[72] Anders Nygren, *Agape and Eros* in <u>The Altruism Reader: Selections from Writings on Love Religion and Science</u>, Thomas Oord edt., (West Conshohocken, PA: Templeton Press, 2008), 76.

[73] H. Ray Dunning, 194-195.

mutual reciprocation. Thus, rather than using an anthropocentric model to 'explain' God's love—these passages demonstrate that God's love transcends the natural dynamics of *human relational love*. Indeed, God's love is not based upon the mutual communion of ontological eternal distinctions but on an <u>*altruism* **transcending**</u> relational reciprocation.

Some may object to this by pointing out that altruistic love is *highly relational* and—if God's love is based on altruism—there **must** be an object of God's altruistic love. Furthermore, since love belongs eternally to God—this *object* must also be eternal. The Hebrew construct of God's Love recognizes this truth but does so without introducing ontological distinctions within God's being.

> The LORD hath appeared of old unto me, saying, Yea, I have **loved thee** with **an everlasting love**: therefore with lovingkindness have I drawn thee (Jeremiah 31:3).

This passage is important for two reasons. First, it affirms the *eternality* of God's love—using the word 'everlasting' עוֹלָם (*olam*) which:

> can assume the meaning (unlimited, unforeseeable) duration, eternity, although only in an attributive usage (enduring, eternal...we might therefore best state the basic meaning as a kind of range between the remotest time and perpetuity).[74]

Secondly, the eternal object of Yahweh's love is identified as Israel; in fact, the word '**loved**' is written in the '*perfect tense*' denoting:

> ...in general that which is concluded, completed, and past, that which has happened and has come into effect; but at the same time, also that which is represented as accomplished even though it be continued into the present time or even be actually still future.[75]

This naturally leads to the question "*How can Israel be the eternal object of God's love prior to the substantial existence of Israel?*" There are two primary ways to answer this question theologically, the

---

[74] Ernst Jenni, עוֹלָם.

[75] A. E. Cowely, *The Imperfect and its Inflexion,* in <u>Gesenius' Hebrew Grammar</u>, electronic edition.

first of which is on the basis of God's omnipresence—as defined by Social Trinitarian Stanley Grenz—means:

> ...that all things are present to God in themselves, whether they be events in our past, our present or our future.[76]

In this manner—God could love Israel proleptically before the nation became a visible, substantial reality.

The second way to answer this question is through God's <u>eternal purpose</u>, which is not bound by the strictures of time. Indeed, Jeremiah 31:3 is not the only text revealing God can relationally act <u>upon</u> or <u>toward</u> that which is not yet visibly extant.

> Known unto God are all his works from the beginning of the world (Acts 15:18).

> (As it is written, I have made thee a father of many nations,) before him whom he believed, even God, who quickeneth the dead, and calleth those things which be not as though they were (Romans 4:17).

In the Greek text, Acts 15:18 reads: "Γνωστὰ ἀπ αἰῶνος *(known from eternity)* ἐστιν τῷ θεῷ πάντα τὰ ἔργα αὐτοῦ *(is or exists to the God all the works of him)*. Though some English translations use the phrase *"beginning of the world"* neither 'beginning' nor 'world' is used in the Greek text. Rather, Luke uses the word αἰῶνος, which is *"a long period of time, without reference to beginning or end."*[77] The word '*works*' refers to human <u>and</u> Divine endeavors; thus, refers to *"any product whatever, anything accomplished by hand, art, industry, mind"*[78]

Romans 4:17 declares God καλοῦντος τὰ μὴ ὄντα *(calls by name the not existing)* ὡς ὄντα *(as existing)*. Scripture provides an explicit example of this in Isaiah 44:28-45:3 where God speaks *about* and *even addresses* the Persian leader Cyrus—designating him as <u>His</u>

---

[76] Grenz, *Theology..*, 92. Even if one holds the traditional understanding of omnipresence—this view of love is supported on the basis of God's foreknowledge.

[77] Danker, αἰών.

[78] Joseph Henry Thayer, ἔργον.

'*shepherd*' and <u>His</u> '*anointed*' **prior** to Cyrus' **actual physical birth**! Furthermore, Scripture teaches the church was chosen in Christ **before** the foundation of the world!

> According as he hath chosen us in him before the foundation of the world that we should be holy and without blame before him in love (Ephesians 1:4).

God's altruistic relational love expressed in and through His eternal purpose is further accentuated in the plan of **redemption**.

> According to the **eternal purpose** which he purposed in Christ Jesus our Lord (Ephesians 3:11).
>
> Who hath saved us, and called us with an holy calling, not according to our works, but **according to his own purpose** and grace which was given us in Christ Jesus **before the world began** (2Timothy 1:9).
>
> In hope of eternal life, which God, that cannot lie, promised **before the world began** (Titus 1:2).

The above passages demonstrate the basis of God's 'love' is not ontological distinctions—but is revealed in his eternal plan to redeem fallen <u>humanity</u>—**prior** to the substantial creation of the human family.

The Apostle John teaches redemption was <u>accomplished</u> in the eternal plan and purpose of God when he speaks of "...*the Lamb (the redemptive sacrifice) <u>slain</u>* from <u>the foundation of the world</u>" *(Rev. 13:8).* If God's redemptive act can be spoken of as His eternal plan and purpose then **the basis** of redemption—**God's Love**—is also eternal.

> For God so loved the world, that he gave his only begotten Son, that whosoever believeth in him should not perish, but have everlasting life (John 3:16).
>
> Behold what manner of love the Father hath bestowed upon us, that we should be called the sons of God: therefore the world knoweth us not, because it knew him not (1John 3:1).

The Bible **never** describes God's love as a <u>societal love between multiple hypostases in His being</u> or that the love of God's was a response to the fall of humanity. Rather, Scripture teaches God **loved** the creature *eternally*, before creation became a substantial reality! Indeed, God loved humanity with an everlasting love **before reciprocation** was possible!

Some may reject this Hebraic construct for understanding God's love—on the grounds that it lacks *mutual love;* yet, this is actually the greatest **strength** of this model of God's love.

> For if **ye love** them which **love you**, what reward have ye? Do not even the publicans the same? (Matthew 5:46).

> For if **ye love** them which **love you**, what **thank** have ye? For sinners also **love those** that **love them** (Luke 6:32).

Jesus teaches there is little honor or reward in loving someone who *reciprocates that love*. In fact, he maintains this type of love is exhibited **by sinners**—thus, there is nothing remarkable or divine about it. However, God's love *transcends* normative human relational love—for HE can **not only** love the unlovable—but He can love those He *would create* and those *who would rebel*.

The Apostle Paul confirms this truth in Romans 5:8: *"But God commendeth his love toward us, in that, while we were yet sinners, Christ died for us."* This is difficult to grasp, but God is **not** a man; thus, *his love* is not limited by *time*, *space* or even ***tangible reality***. In short, God's love may be revealed *to* and mirrored *in* humanity, but His love is incomprehensible.[79]

> For my thoughts are not your thoughts, neither are your ways my ways, saith the LORD. For as the heavens are higher than the earth, so are my ways higher than your ways, and my thoughts than your thoughts (Isaiah 55:8-9).

Using the above construct to explain God's *relational love* is more Scripturally consistent than Greek philosophical ideas. Moreover, it effectively debunks the argument that God's relationality is incompatible with strict Hebrew monotheism. Indeed, this view demonstrates the eternality of God's love is ***not dependent*** upon an eternal hypostatic society in God. Most importantly, this model does not sacrifice monotheism at the altar of God's relationality,

---

[79] Millard J. Erickson, Christian Theology (Grand Rapids, MI: Baker, 1998), 292.

which some believe is *"...sacrificed by the social doctrine of the Trinity."*[80]

> ...In order to have love for one another, each Person of the Trinity would have to have their own mind or consciousness. If there are three centers of consciousness, or three minds in the Godhead, we have three Gods, not three distinctions in one God...This is Tritheism, or at least incipient Tritheism.[81]

---

[80] F. D. Macchia, *Pentecostal Theology,* i n <u>The New International Dictionary of Pentecostal and Charismatic Movements</u> (Grand Rapids, MI: Zondervan, 2002), 1128.

[81] Jason Dulle, *'Love in the Godhead?'* <u>www.onenesspentecostal.com</u> internet article.

Hebraic Monotheism—A Deficient Form of Monotheism?

The majority of Christendom acknowledges the Hebraic roots of their faith; yet, many unaware of the extent in which the contours of Hebrew thought permeated the New Testament Church. Some seem to think the church was immediately Hellenized and clearly distinguishable from Judaism; yet, this is not the picture presented in Scripture.[82] Moreover, the Dead Sea Scrolls and Nag Hammadi texts confirm the existence of a Hebrew form of Christianity—so that beneath the *"...hellenic encrustation lay the pristine faith of the original Palestinian believers."*[83] The Apostle Paul boldly proclaimed this Hebraic-Christian faith saying:

> But this I confess unto thee, that after the way which they call heresy, so worship I **the God of my fathers**, believing all things which are written in the law and in the prophets;[84]

Oneness Pentecostals stress the continuity of Hebraic thought in the pristine church, believing *strict monotheism was one of their distinct teachings.* In fact, they argue the controversy between the Oneness and Trinitarian understanding of God hinges on the accuracy or validity of Hebraic Monotheism.[85] Thus, the question must be asked *"Does the New Testament affirm strict Hebrew Monotheism or does it teach a radically different conception of God?"*

Scripture unequivocally demonstrates that the *'church in the wilderness' (Acts 7:38)* did **not** embrace a distorted or deficient view of God for thousands of years. In fact, in his discussion with

---

[82] Acts 18:12-16 reveals the Roman government considered the first-century Apostolic church as a 'sect' or form of Judaism. Hence, the early church enjoyed the same freedom and protection afforded Judaism.

[83] Richard N. Longnecker, *The Christology of Early Jewish Christianity* Studies in Biblical Theology, Second Series 17 (Naperville, IL: Alec R. Allenson, 1970), 5-6.

[84] Acts 24:14. Clearly, the Apostle Paul did not believe he was forsaking the worship of the one God Yahweh. He simply held that Yahweh was visibly manifest in the person and name of Jesus Christ.

[85] There are other issues dividing Trinitarian and Oneness believers; yet, the validity of *strict Hebraic monotheism* is a primary point of contention.

the woman of Samaria—Jesus makes an important statement with respect to the Hebrew perception of God.

> Ye worship ye know not what: we **know** what we worship: for salvation is of **the Jews** (John 4:24).

This passage is critical because Jesus places His **imprimatur** on the Hebraic view of God <u>without qualification</u> and does not intimate there was a forthcoming change or adjustment to their revelatory understanding of monotheism.

This is confirmed by the Greek word οἴδαμεν, meaning to *"know, understand, perceive..."*[86] Yet, even more significant—this word is in the *perfect tense*; thus, expressing the:

> ...idea of 'possessed knowledge' rather than the present aspect of 'acquiring knowledge.'[87]

According to Jesus, the Jewish knowledge of God was not *in the process of **being revealed*** but was currently ***in their possession***. Thus, nothing in Jesus' statement suggests the *'true' or 'complete'* revelation of God's nature had *"...to wait for more than three hundred years for a final synthesis..."*[88]

If—strict Hebraic monotheism is really an *'unintelligible notion,'* as claimed 'Social Trinitarians,'[89] Jesus was <u>completely</u> in **error**, for the Jews did **not** really **know** the God they worshipped. This is an untenable position in light of Jesus' emphatic statement; thus, Oneness theologians argue the early followers of Jesus embraced the same Hebraic comprehension of God sanctioned by the Savior Himself. In fact, the primary distinction between Judaism and the early church was **not** a belief in God's ontological plurality—but

---

[86] Barclay M. Newman Jr., <u>A Concise Greek-English Dictionary of the New Testament</u>, (Stuttgart, Germany: United Bible Societies, 1993), electronic edition prepared by Oak Tree Software Inc.

[87] Denis W. Vinyard, edt., *The New Testament Greek-English Dictionary: Lamda-Omicron* in <u>The Complete Biblical Library</u> 16 vols. (Springfield, MO: World Library Press, 1986), 14:312.

[88] J. N. D. Kelly, <u>Early Christian Doctrines</u> (New York, NY: Harper, 1960), 446.

[89] Boyd., 191.

that Yahweh was visibly personified in the person and name of Jesus.

Admittedly, this study does not cover every aspect of the controversy between Trinitarianism and the Hebrew-Christian or Oneness view of God. However, it is hoped some of the more common objections have been addressed—Biblically, intellectually and most of all without rancor. Moreover, it is the prayer of this author that continuing dialogue on this subject will facilitate a more amiable atmosphere for exchange than previously exhibited.

> The tension between oneness and trinitarian Pentecostal positions may be theologically productive for a Pentecostal intervention and contribution to contemporary ecumenical Christological and trinitarian discussions. The contours of debates between economic and immanent, social-communitarian and modalist models of the trinity...more often than not lay tracks that unwittingly cross the frontier between oneness and trinitarian Pentecostals.[90]

---

[90] Ralph Del Colle, *Oneness and Trinity: A Preliminary Proposal for Dialogue with Oneness Pentecostalism* Journal of Pentecostal Theology 10 (April, 1997): 85-110.

II

Hebraism or Hellenism

New Light or Old Darkness?

An Overview of Pristine Hebraic Christianity and Contributing Factors of Post-Apostolic Transmutation

Introduction

It is said *'one man's heresy is another man's orthodoxy'* and nowhere is more clearly seen than in the criteria used to identify *'heretical cults.'* For example, some define a 'cult' as *"a perversion, a distortion of biblical Christianity and, as such, rejects <u>the historic teachings</u> of the Christian church."*[1] While others maintain a cult is:

> ...a group of people which, claiming to be Christian, embraces a particular doctrinal system taught by an individual leader, group of leaders, or organization, which (system) denies (either explicitly or implicitly) <u>one or more of the central doctrines</u> of the Christian faith <u>as taught in the sixty-six books of the Bible</u>.[2]

Both definitions indicate heretical cults are identified by a denial of Biblical truth; yet, they differ as to *what* constitutes this denial. For Gomes, Scripture is the *litmus test* for assessing orthodoxy, while McDowell and Stewart believe *historical ecclesiastical doctrine* should be included determining heresy. In short, they believe orthodoxy is defined by Scripture—interpreted through the lens of the historic ecumenical councils and creeds of Christendom.

There are serious problems with assessing one's 'orthodoxy' on the basis of creedal compliance—not the least of which is the high degree of subjectivity involved in this approach. This is especially true considering the majority of Evangelicals, *including McDowell and Stewart*—**reject all** but <u>the earliest</u> ecumenical councils!

> Why do evangelicals accept only the creeds from the two centuries when the <u>same church</u> continued to hold ecumenical councils and decide on correct doctrine? Is it because evangelicals do not want to be associated with such doctrines as transubstantiation, papal infallibility...Are not these doctrines...a part of 'historic' Christianity and the 'orthodox historic' faith?[3]

---

[1] Josh McDowell and Don Stewart, *Understanding the Cults* (San Bernardino, CA: Here's Life Pub., 1983), 13, 17. Emphasis mine.

[2] Alan Gomes, *Unmasking the Cults* (Grand Rapids, MI: Zondervan, 1995), 7. Emphasis mine.

[3] J. L. Hall, *Cults, Orthodoxy, and Biblical Christianity*, in <u>Symposium on Oneness Pentecostalism 1988 and 1990</u> (Hazelwood, MO: Word Aflame, 1990), 41.

Most Evangelicals argue the earliest councils *affirm* o r *codify* Biblical teaching—while later councils introduced various extra-biblical doctrines. This *may* be true, but it is highly subjective and ultimately makes personal doctrinal views the supreme authority for determining *which* ecclesiastical council and creed is valid. Of course, this would vary depending on the individual or group making the determination!

If historic ecclesiastical councils are the 'standard' for measuring orthodoxy—consistency demands that one accept **all** the councils, for they were convened by the **same institution.** Anything less than this is an admission that *personal subjectivity* is the standard for measuring one's *orthodoxy*. For this reason, many groups in church history endeavored to abandon their dependency on the historic councils and creedal statements—promulgating the principle of *Sola Scriptura.*

Those familiar with ecclesiastical history recognize *Sola Scriptura* (*Scripture alone*) was the watchword of the Protestant Reformation; yet, it is evident that many of the major reformers did not use this principle to renounce the *historic creeds* of Christendom or abolish the authoritative role of tradition in the development of doctrine.

> ...the reformers did not understand *sola scriptura* to mean that only the Bible was authoritative...the Reformers tried...to interpret the Scriptures in the light of the Church Fathers, putting the Scriptures as the *supreme* rather than the *only* authority.[4]

Flynn is correct—but <u>only</u> in regards to the *magisterial reformers (i.e. Luther, Zwingli).* This is **not** true of the *radical reformers (i.e. Anabaptists)* who refused to make historic creeds or ecclesiastical tradition the authority for determining 'orthodoxy.' In fact, many argue Anabaptists are *"...the only wing of the reformation to apply*

---

[4] David Michael Flynn, *The Oneness-Trinity Debate on the Early Church* in <u>Toward Healing Our Divisions</u> (Springfield, MO: Society of Pentecostal Studies), March 11-13th 1999, 2.

the scriptura sola principle consistently..."[5] Thus, not **all** reformation leaders embraced a high view of historic ecumenical councils and used their creeds as the standard of orthodoxy.[6]

Another problem with using ecclesiastical creeds to '*measure orthodoxy*' is expressed in the adage '*history is written by its victors.*' There is little question this is applicable to doctrinal development in the history of Christianity—for many groups deemed "*heretical*" were anathematized and their writings expunged. In fact, the <u>exact</u> nature of their aberrancy is oftentimes unknown because the sources providing "insight" into their beliefs are hostile witness that knowingly or unknowingly distort their position.

For example, Eusebius claims that Montanus—*the leader of the second-century charismatic group bearing his name*—identified himself as the Paraclete,[7] a charge echoed at the Synod of Laodicea ca. 343-381:

> Thus, Tertullian in quoting expressions of Montanus, actually says: 'the Paraclete speaks'; and therefore Firmillian, Cyril of Jerusalem, Basil the Great, and other Fathers did in fact reproach the Montanists with this identification.[8]

It is unlikely Montanus actually claimed to <u>be</u> the Holy Spirit; in fact, it appears this charge:

> ...may have derived from Montanus' practice of prophesying in the first person...prophesying in the first person was neither blasphemous nor novel during the second century.[9]

---

[5] Alister E. McGrath, *Reformation Thought* (Grand Rapids, MI: Baker, 1993), 144.

[6] One may argue that applying the principle of *Sola Scriptura* is equally subjective. There is some truth in this objection but this is beyond the scope of this study. Suffice to say there may be interpretive 'subjectivity' in applying Sola Scriptura, but there is only one objective standard.

[7] Eusebius Pamphilius, *The False Prophets of the Phrygians* in <u>Nicene and Post-Nicene Fathers</u> vol. 2-01, chapter 14 online edition www.ccel.org.

[8] Phillip Schaff, edt. *The Synod of Laodicea canon 8* in <u>Nicene and Post-Nicene Fathers</u> vol. XIV, online edition www.ccel.org.

[9] William Tabbernee, <u>Fake Prophecy and Polluted Sacraments</u> (Leiden, The Netherlands: Brill, 2007), 120. Other examples can be given such as charging the '*Alogi*' with denying John's Gospel—when it is likely they

Because of the problems associated with using the historic councils and creeds of Christendom to determine one's orthodoxy, many argue that Scripture must be the <u>only</u> arbiter of orthodoxy.

> The Church...must never accept tradition as a rule of faith, and especially not to equate tradition with Scripture...This has proven the great prostitution of Romanism. Holy Scripture is the true Church's only rule of faith, practice, government and discipline.[8]

---

simply rejected the apologists interpretation of the Logos in John 1:1.

[8] Wade H. Phillips, *God the Church and Revelation* (Cleveland, TN: White Wing, 1986), 94.

Ecclesiological Presuppositions

Despite the inconsistency and subjectivity of using ecclesiastical councils and creeds as the standard of orthodoxy—post-modern Christians rarely question the decisions of the historic church councils. In fact, the *process* by which church doctrine was codified seems to pose little difficulty for most professing Christians.

> In short—like the Bible—Christian doctrine is what the church said it was at a given time and place. The creed...is, forever and for all time, **the** standard of Christian belief.[9]

This high view of the historic creeds is based on a belief that the 'faith' or doctrine of the early church was not clearly defined, but *progressively emerged out of specific historical circumstances.*[10]

> ...in the earliest years of it's existence the church did not have much opportunity to study...the process of organizing itself and propagating the faith, and even the struggle for survival in a hostile world **precluded much serious doctrinal reflections.**[11]

This explains why some segments of Christendom hold the writings of the second through fourth century '*Church Fathers*' in such high esteem and readily accept the outcome of historic doctrinal debates articulated through the creeds.

Jean Danielou illustrates the thinking of those embracing the *evolving faith* theory using the concept of '<u>works</u>,' which he argues was a <u>primitive Hebrew theology</u> that was discarded because:

> ...the works in question represented an **incomplete expression of Christian truth**, and gave place to a more **comprehensive understanding.** Secondly, they were the product of a *particular environment*, Christianity *of a Semitic*...structure; and when this environment had completely disappeared, no further interest was taken in the works which had characterized it.[12]

---

[9] Ronald A. Wells, *History Through the Eyes of Faith* (San Francisco, CA: Harper Collins, 1989), 43.

[10] Ibid., 42.

[11] Millard J. Erickson, *Christian Theology* (Grand Rapids, MI: Baker, 1994), 327. Emphasis mine.

[12] Jean Danielou, *The Theology of Jewish Christianity* (Philadelphia, PA: Westminster, 1964), 7. Emphasis mine..

The position of Wells and Erickson, coupled with Danielou's explanation—invariably leads to the conclusion that the outcome of the historical doctrinal struggles—expressed in the creeds—was God's method of bringing the church into the *fullness of truth*. Those who hold this position examine church history **in light of this assumption** and thus, do not question the process or outcome of historic ecclesiastical doctrinal struggles. In fact, challenging either—risks incurring the charge of blasphemy or heresy.[13] Yet, despite wide acceptance the *evolving faith* theory is not without problems.

Any view suggesting the church gradually *evolved* **into** the faith, implies the fourth-century church possessed a more *accurate* and *complete* understanding of truth than those who sat at Jesus' feet. Indeed, supporters of this view argue that doctrinal articulation and comprehension in the early church was *arrested* or *immature;* thus, necessitating a more comprehensive formulation! The arrogance of this position is palpable—causing some to 'soften' their approach by saying the first-century church simply did not ask the same questions as those of later centuries.

> ...it was not necessary in the earlier period to make the proper logical deductions from the axioms provided by Scripture or by Catholic dogma. In other words, controversies had not raised questions to be answered and the implications of the worship and faith of the Church had not been fully recognized.[14]

The above statement may be *'easier on the ears,'* but still leads to the conclusion that the early church lacked *'insight'* into the 'deeper' questions of faith. Those who embrace Sola Scriptura must critically examine this view by asking *"Does Scripture suggest the deeper truths of faith would be revealed after the death of the Apostles?"* Many would answer this with a resounding NO!,

---

[13] This is evident in the anathematizing clause of the 'Athanasian Creed.'

[14] Peter Toon, The Development of Doctrine in the Church, (Grand Rapids, MI: Eerdmans, 1979), xiii.

arguing that the lack of Scriptural support is the primary weakness of the evolutionary model of doctrinal development.

> ...this does not agree with the New Testament writings. We read there was an *established, recognized faith. ...*And this faith... should be sought after. The general idea of an *evolving or formulating faith holds no credence with the New Testament.*[15]

In contrast to the '*evolutionary*' model of church history, many believe Scripture warns of a *deterioration, corruption* and eventual *abandonment* of the faith '*..once delivered unto the saints*' (Jude 3). While not as pervasive in post-modern Christendom—this view enjoys early historical support. In fact, one could argue the basic premise of the Protestant Reformation—in varying degree was:

> ...something went wrong (Anglicans, Lutherans, Calvinists) or **absolutely wrong** (Free Church, Baptists, Mennonites, Quakers) when **the early church abandoned the truth...**[16]

This view of ecclesiastical history maintains the early church of did **not** progressively evolve after the first century, but gradually departed from the faith—resulting in '*an organic apostasy.*' This was the dominate view of historical restorationists; in fact, a cursory reading of early Pentecostal literature confirms that every segment of the movement embraced this view of church history.

Early Pentecostals believed in the reality of an organic apostasy; thus, the church needed to be <u>restored</u>—**not** simply <u>reformed</u>. Moreover, they were convinced the global restoration of Spirit Baptism was a confirmation that Pentecostalism was God's vehicle for restoring the Apostolic faith.

> All along the ages men have been preaching a partial Gospel. A part of the Gospel remained when the world went into the dark ages. God has from time to time raised up men to bring back the truth to the church...Now He is bringing back the Pentecostal Baptism to the church.[17]

---

[15] Thomas Weisser, *Was the Early Church Oneness or Trinitarian?* in <u>Symposium on Oneness Pentecostalism</u> (Hazelwood, MO: Word Aflame, 1986), 59.

[16] Wells, 148.

> ...the reformation under Martin Luther and his constituents was in a measure a success...while they accomplished much in clearing away the rubbish and decay of the 'Dark Ages'...they were never able to unfurl the flag of victory to the breeze at the top of the mast.[18]

> Instead of people full of the Holy Ghost...the professing church became filled with political rulers. It was no longer a persecuted church in a dark and sinful world, but a dark and sinful world came into the visible church; and it sank to the bottom of political corruption, thus descending into the Dark Ages.[19]

A primary difference between these two ecclesiological models is the use of Scripture in substantiating their position. Those who believe the early church apostatized from the faith use four major New Testament passages to support their claim.

> For I know this, that after my departing shall grievous wolves enter in among you, not sparing the flock. Also of your own selves shall men arise, speaking <u>perverse things</u>, to <u>draw away</u> disciples after them (Acts 20:29-30).

> Now the Spirit speaketh expressly, that in the <u>latter times</u> some shall <u>depart from the faith</u>, giving heed to seducing spirits and doctrines of devils...Forbidding to marry, and commanding to abstain from meats...(1Timothy 4:1, 3).

The first passage is a portion of Paul's address to the Ephesian elders prior to his departure. Notice, the Apostle Paul warns them of a coming perversion of the Faith. In fact, the word translated "perverse" is διαστρέφω, which means *"to cause to be distorted...to cause to depart from an accepted standard..."*[20]

The Apostle does not provide explicit details of this perverse speech, but its intent is manifested by disciples who τοῦ ἀποσπᾶν.

[17] W. J. Seymour, edit. *The Pentecostal Baptism Restored*, in <u>The Apostolic Faith</u>, Vol. I Issue 2, pg. 1 (Los Angeles, CA: October 1906).

[18] A. J. Tomlinson, *Fourth Annual Address*, Nov. 4-9 1913 in <u>Historical Annual Addresses</u> Vol. 1 (Cleveland, TN: White Wing, 1970), 27-28.

[19] S.C. McClain, <u>Highlights in Church History</u>, reprint (Hazelwood, MO: Word Aflame, 1990), 30-31.

[20] Fredrick William Danker, **διαστρέφω**, in <u>A Greek-English Lexicon of the New Testament and other Early Christian Literature</u>, (Chicago, IL: University of Chicago, 2000), electronic edition.

This Greek word signifies causing *"...a change of belief so as to correspond more with the beliefs of the person or factor causing the change."*[21] Thus, while the exact nature of this departure from the faith is unknown—by the time John the Apocalypse—the Ephesian church is charged with leaving *"...thy first love"* (Rev. 2:4)

In his first epistle to Timothy—Paul declares by the Holy Ghost ὅτι ἐν ὑστέροις καιροῖς ἀποστήσονταί τινες τῆς πίστεως *(that in subsequent times some will withdraw themselves from the faith).* The word translated "latter times" does **not** pertain to the *end time*, but the *"distant future ...something that is merely second, subsequent."*[22] The warning issued by the Spirit is not merely referring to a waning of faith but an intentional withdrawing from τῆς πίστεως (**the** faith).

The use of the article *(the)* indicates this refers to the body of teaching embraced by the church—and not simply generic 'faith' in the sense of belief. This is confirmed by the fact that Paul specifically identifies two aberrant doctrines that will signify the reality of this departure or withdraw from the **original** apostolic faith.

Neither of the above passages suggest a progressive evolution of 'the faith.' Rather, both warn of a coming withdraw from the established teachings of the church. The Apostle addresses this subject again in his second epistle to the Thessalonians—and Jude's Epistle confirms the departure is beginning to take place.

> That ye be not soon shaken in mind, or be troubled, neither by spirit, nor by word, nor by letter as from us, as that the day of Christ is at hand. Let no man deceive you by any means: for that day shall not come, except there come a **falling away** first...(2 Thessalonians 2:2-3).

[21] Johanes P. Louw and Eugine A. Nida edts., ἀποσπάω, in Greek-English Lexicon of the New Testament Based on Semantic Domains, (New York, NY: United Bible Societies, 1989), electronic edition.

[22] Ceslas Spicq, O. P., ὕστερος, in Theological Lexicon of the New Testament, (Hendrickson Pub, 1994), electronic edition.

...It was <u>needful</u> for me to write unto you, and exhort you that ye should earnestly **contend for the faith** which was <u>once delivered</u> unto the saints (Jude 3).

2 Thessalonians 2:2-3 reveals the *scope and magnitude* of the prophetic departure—that Paul identifies as the "<u>falling away</u>." The Greek word used here is **ἀποστασία**, which means a *rebellion, backsliding, apostasy or departure.*[23]

> ...by this term we understand a dereliction of the essential principles of religious truth—either a total abandonment of Christianity itself, or such a corruption of its doctrines as renders the whole system completely inefficient to salvation...[24]

It is important to note the Apostle uses the Greek article before 'apostasy' **ἡ ἀποστασία** (*literally '**the** apostasy'*). Thus, he is not referring to a generic condition, but a specific event identified as **the rebellion,** which "*...implies that the subject was well known to his readers.*"[25]

> The use of the article here, '*the* apostasy," (Gr.,) Erasmus remarks "signifies the great and before-predicted apostasy." It is evidently emphatic showing that there had been a reference to this before...[26]

> One major event is **the rebellion** (lit., "the falling away," η ἀποστασία...) This is a revolt, a departure, an abandoning of a position once held...Paul referred to a specific distinguishable apostasy that will com in the future...He had already told his readers about it (2Thes.2:5).[27]

Jude 3 is insightful because it reveals that by cira., A.D. 60-80 the church was hastening toward the fulfillment of the Apostle Paul's

---

[23] Denis W. Vinyard, ed., *The New Testament Greek-English Dictionary* 16 vols. in <u>The Complete Biblical Library</u> (Springfield, MO: 1991), 11: 393.

[24] Adam Clark, *Clarke's Commentary The New Testament 1Thess. Through Revelation* Vol. 6b. *electronic edition* (Albany, OR: Sage, 1996), 70.

[25] Ibid, 394. Several New Testament passages refer to this event (i.e. 2Cor. 11:1-4, 13-15; Col. 2:8-10; Rev. 1-3 etc...).

[26] Albert Barnes, '2Th. 2:3,' in <u>Barnes' Notes on the New Testament</u>, electronic edition, Oak Tree Software, Inc.

[27] John F. Walvoord and Roy B. Zuck, "2Th. 2:3" in <u>The Bible Knowledge Commentary</u>, electronic edition, Oak Tree Software, Inc.

early warnings.[28] In fact, according to Jude—conditions were such that his exhortation was ἀνάγκην (*'needful'*), a word expressing the thought of *"a general state of distress and trouble—trouble, distress, troublous times."*[29] This 'distress' compels Jude to 'urge' his readers to struggle for the faith *"once delivered"* to the saints.

Jude's statement regarding 'the Faith' confirms there was a clearly defined, recognizable body of doctrine in the early church. Moreover, the threats against 'the Faith' and the apostolic warning about a departure from 'the Faith' clearly demonstrates the New Testament does not advocate an evolution *into* 'the Faith'. Rather, it teaches a an impending ecclesiastical apostasy—and those who recognize this usually maintain this event culminated with the adoption of the Nicene Creed in A.D. 325.

> The church had already been headed for apostasy for over two centuries before the Council of Nicea convened in A.D. 325... but the council of Nicea provided means whereby the outward institution of the Church was more officially plunged into apostasy...[30]

Supporters of this position argue the New Testament provides evidence of the initial fulfillment of this prophetic apostasy before the close of first-century but *"...in the second-century, this process of doctrinal corruption accelerated."*[31] Thus, in view of the prophetic apostasy, any doctrine boasting of late formulation is viewed with a hermeneutic of suspicion—possibly contributing to the ecclesiastical departure from 'the Faith.' Thus, unlike those who believe in the evolutionary model of church history—those who embrace the apostasy view of church history **do not** hold the historic councils or creeds in high esteem!

---

[28] Richard Heard, *"An Introduction to the New Testament,"* at www.religion-online.org, 2010.

[29] Louw and Nida edts., ἀνάγκη.

[30] Wade H. Phillips, *The Church in History and Prophecy* (Cleveland, TN: White Wing, 1990), 56, 57.

[31] David K. Bernard, *A History of Christian Doctrine* (Hazelwood, MO: Word Aflame, 1995), 1:11.

The competing ideologies of *an evolving of the faith vis-à-vis an abandonment of the faith* have distinct epistemologies. This results in two radically different <u>understandings **of**</u> and <u>approaches **to**</u> examining the historical data related to doctrinal controversy in the post-apostolic church. A primary example of this difference is revealed in the ongoing controversy between those who espouse ecclesiastical Trinitarianism and those embracing a Hebraic or Oneness view of God's nature.

Adherents of both groups are concerned with *truth,* appeal to *Scripture* as their primary foundation and attempt to demonstrate *historicity* for their view in post-apostolic writings. Yet, despite similarities they have very distinct ideas regarding the nature of God, which is due—*in part*—to their belief in an <u>evolutionary model</u> or <u>apostate model</u> of church history. The remainder of this study examines church history through the lens of restorationism, recognizing the Scriptural validity of an ecclesiastical apostasy.

While not exhaustive—this study will analyze the decline of unique features in the early church—that result in a theological shift—ultimately affecting the ecclesiastical view of God's nature. Indeed, it will be demonstrated that:

- The early apostolic Church (ca. 30-70 A.D.) was Hebraic in doctrine and practice; thus, maintaining cultural and doctrinal ties to Judaism. This includes a belief in strict monotheism and a Hebraic understanding of God's name.

- Specific factors contributed to a theological shift in the church by the mid-second century. First, the decline of Hebrew Christianity (*brought about by the <u>death of James</u>, the <u>destruction of the temple</u> and <u>demise of Jerusalem</u>)* exacerbated changes in the church. Second, the influx of educated Gentile believers assuming positions of leadership in the church successfully supplanted the earlier dominant Jewish leadership of the church.

- The Hellenization of the church successfully united Grecian philosophical thought into the Christian faith. This thinking replaced earlier Hebraic contours of thought—ultimately resulting in an altered perception of God's nature.

The Early Hebraic Church (ca. A.D. 30-70)

Those who believe the church *apostatized* from the pristine faith often present an inaccurate picture suggesting the church enjoyed doctrinal harmony until 325 A.D. Yet, the nature of apostasy, *individual* or *collective*—is not instantaneous but is the product of gradualism—*a slow erosion of principles embraced by an individual or collective group.* Even within post-modern Christendom, the reality of gradual doctrinal apostasy is evident as religious movements or organizations forsake the original principles of their forebears.[32]

A mere cursory comparison between the church recorded in the book of Acts and the second-century church reveals a radical transmutation occurred in the visible institution. The first three chapters of Revelation clearly shows the church was facing serious doctrinal challenges by the close of the first-century. Yet, despite the Lord's warning—the church continued to drift from the faith so that by the second-century the church differed *experientially* and *theologically* from the faith of the Apostles.[33]

How did such a radical change take place within these important spheres of Christian faith? The answer to this question is found in the differences existing between *Hebraic* and *Hellenistic* modes of theological thinking. There is strong evidence to support the claim that shifting from a Hebraic to Hellenistic theological mode of thinking was a primary factor in the transmutation of the church—*doctrinally* and *experientially*. This is especially evident when one considers the extent in which the contours of Hebrew doctrine and practice permeated the New Testament church.

---

[32] A good example of this is the Episcopal church's change regarding the right of practicing homosexuals to pastoral ministry. Some view this development as evolutionary growth—while others believe it is an abandonment of the faith.

[33] Experientially this can be seen in the virtual disappearance of Spirit Baptism with the evidence of speaking in tongues as a distinguishable teaching in the second-century church. Ronald A. N. Kydd, *Charismatic Gifts in the Early Church* (Peabody, MA: Hendrickson, 1984), 4.

Some naïvely believe the church was Hellenized from its inception and was clearly and entirely separate from Judaism. However, this is not supported in Scripture (i.e. Acts 15) the Dead Sea Scrolls or Nag Hammadi texts. Indeed, these writings confirm "*...the existence of a Jewish Christian stratum in early Christianity,*"[34] so that beneath the "*...hellenic encrustation lay the pristine faith of the original Palestinian believers.*"[35]

Evidence supporting the continuation of Hebraic theological ideology in the early church is revealed in <u>two doctrines</u> mutually shared by Judaism and pristine Christianity—*<u>exclusive monotheism</u>* and a Hebraic *<u>divine onomatology</u>*. These twin teachings show that the early church embraced a Jewish form of faith that promoted principles and ideas from a Hebrew perspective. Furthermore, they reveal later Hellenistic ideas represented a departure from established norms—ultimately supplanting the original Hebrew-Christian faith.

One of the most distinctive teachings in Judaism is the belief in *strict* or *exclusive* monotheism. This doctrine originated in God's self-disclosure to the Nation of Israel; yet, some argue this view of God was no longer embraced in Second Temple Judaism. Supporters of this school of thought maintain that—rather than *exclusive* monotheism—Judaism of this period embraced an *inclusive* monotheism—allowing for the elevation of secondary '*divine*' beings.

> The deification of intermediaries and mediators—hypostases, principal angels, patriarchs, prophets, kings, high priests ...make us conclude that Jewish monotheism did not exclude the glorification and veneration of other beings than God.[36]

---

[34] Richard N. Longnecker, *The Christology of Early Jewish Christianity* in <u>Studies In Biblical Theology</u>, Second Series 17 (Naperville, IL: Allenson, 1970), 6.

[35] Ibid, 5. An exhaustive examination of this 'original faith' is beyond the scope of this study.

[36] Patrick Chatelion Counet, *The Divine Messiah Early Jewish Monotheism and the New Testament*, in <u>The Boundaries of Monotheism,</u> (Leiden, the

...exclusive monotheism was not clearly the dominant tendency in the Herodian age. Rather, exclusive and inclusive types of monotheism were concurrent, and the inclusive type was also influential.[37]

One of the problems with this view is an over-reliance on Jewish apocryphal works written that—while written during this time period—do not represent normative mainstream Second Temple Judaism. In other words—this view uses Judaic fringe groups as the measure for interpreting the belief system of Judaism during the time of Jesus.

> The most mischievous consequence of basing a representation of Judaism upon the apocalypses is not...in the sphere of eschatology but of theology—the idea of God...writings which Judaism does not recognize over those sources which it has always regarded as authentic.[38]

These sources would be valid **if** the New Testament portrayal of Judaism was in keeping with them; yet this is simply **not the case!**

> The Gospels themselves are the best witness to the religious and moral teaching of the synagogue in the middle forty years of the first-century...The Gospels with the first part of the Acts of the Apostles are thus witnesses to authentic Jewish tradition, while the apocalypses...represent groups, or at least tendencies, outside the main current of thought and life.[39]

Despite the fact the Jewish apocryphal works do not represent normative Second-Temple Judaism—some scholars believe these writings *"...are relevant to the background of the divination of Christ in the New Testament..."*[40]

Netherlands, Brill, 2009), 50.

[37] William Horbury, 'Jewish and Christian Monotheism in the Herodian Age,' in <u>Early Christian and Jewish Monotheism</u>, (New York, NY: T&T Clark, 2004), 43.

[38] George Foot Moore, <u>Judaism</u> Vol. 1 (Peabody, MA: Hendrickson, 1997), 131.

[39] Ibid., 132.

[40] John J. Collins, *"Powers in Heaven: God, Gods, and Angels in the Dead Sea Scrolls,"*i n <u>Studies in the Dead Sea Scrolls and Related Literature</u>, electronic edition (Grand Rapids, MI: Eerdmans, 2005) Oak Tree Software Inc.

The worship of Jesus in the early church is **not** incompatible with Hebraic monotheism. However, this is not because the early church embraced a latter <u>inclusive</u> *(distorted)* view of monotheism taught among fringe groups of Second Temple Judaism!

> ...there has been strong resistance for some time from rabbinic specialists to the line of interpretation presented above; those most familiar with rabbinic Judaism have consistently and firmly denied that rabbinic Judaism ever made room for intermediate beings between God and man...and may by no means be regarded as personal divine beings distinct from God.[41]

Unfortunately, many who support this position believe the early church **denied** the Deity of Jesus and/or radically departed from exclusive Jewish monotheism. Yet, the New Testament teaches the church was birthed out of a <u>*normative Second Temple Jewish milieu,*</u> which espoused an <u>exclusive monotheistic</u> view. Moreover, the pristine apostolic church embraced a high Christology—affirming the absolute deity of Jesus; thus, one is forced to ask:

> Do the New Testament writers presuppose 'monotheism' as the Old Testament and Jewish form of religious faith, not repudiating it but somehow incorporating their innovatory understanding of Jesus into it?[42]

This is a critical question—especially in light of later doctrinal developments concerning God's nature and His identity in Jesus. Is there New Testament evidence to support the claim that the early church embraced a normative Jewish view of monotheism as opposed to that expressed by Second-Temple fringe groups of Judaism? Many believe the answer is 'yes,' considering Jesus' treatment of the 'Shema' in Mark 12:28-32 and his conversation with the woman of Samaria in John 4:20-24[43] where He places His

---

[41] James D. G. Dunn, <u>Christology in the Making,</u> (Grand Rapids, MI: Eerdmans, 1989), 130.

[42] Richard Baukham, <u>Jesus and the God of Israel,</u> (Grand Rapids, MI: Eerdmans, 2008), 60.

[43] Both of these passages were treated in chapter one.

imprimatur on the Jewish conception of God. Yet, several other New Testament passages confirm this truth.

> Seeing it is **one God**, which shall justify the circumcision by faith, and uncircumcision through faith (Romans 3:30).
>
> ...we know that an idol is nothing in the world, and there is **none other God but one**...But to us there is but **one God**, the Father...(1Corinthians 8:4, 6).
>
> Now a mediator is not a mediator of one, but **God is one** (Galatians 3:20).
>
> For there is **one God**, and one mediator between God and men, the man Christ Jesus (1Timothy 2:5).
>
> Thou believest that there is **one God**; thou doest well: the devils also believe, and tremble (James 2:19).

The above passages are given to show that the New Testament affirms normative Hebraic monotheism. It is true that some of these passages present a distinction between God and Jesus Christ (*i.e. 1Cor. 8:4-6; Gal. 3:20; 1Tim. 2:5*) it is beyond the scope of this study to fully address this issue (see. Volume III of this series). Suffice to say—none of these passages support the idea of eternal hypostatic distinctions in God's nature, but emphasize an <u>incarnational</u> distinction between the one true God and the human Messiah—Jesus Christ.

In Romans 3:30, the Apostle begins with the conjunction ἐπείπερ, meaning *"in view of the fact, that, since indeed;"*[44] thus, linking this to the previous verse affirming <u>the God of the Jews</u> (Yahweh) and <u>the God of the Gentiles</u> is **the same**. In the thirtieth verse, Paul uses the words **ἐις ὁ θεός** (*one <u>the God</u>*)–demonstrating he does not have a unique or different apprehension of God, but is referring to THE ONE GOD!

> '...if indeed (as we all agree) God is one' (cf Deut 6:4). It is interesting that as he speaks of the one God Paul goes on to characterize him in terms of his activity of justification...if anyone is justified...it must be by God and there is but one God.[44]

---

[44] Danker, ἐπείπερ.

In 1 Corinthians 8: 4, 6 the Apostle affirms the Hebrew view of monotheism; in fact, most New Testament scholars readily admit *"the confession that God is one is clearly Jewish (cf particularly Deut. 6:4...)."*[45] This is not surprising since Paul's cultural and theological views derived out of a normative Jewish milieu (Phil. 3:3-5) that did not teach the inclusive monotheism of Judaic fringe groups. Furthermore, if Paul wanted to convey the idea of oneness that was not absolute—he would have used the neuter form of εἷς (ἕν) rather than the masculine form.

> {One} (hen). Neuter, not masculine (heis). Not one person (cf. Heis in Ga 3:20), but one essence or nature.[46]

In Galatians 3:20 the Apostle Paul is addressing the subject of mediation in the Godhead—and explicitly declares ὁ δὲ Θεὸς εἷς ἐστίν (*but THE GOD one is*) Like the previous passage, the Apostle uses the masculine form of the numeral 'one;' thus, Paul is not referring to some abstract or compound unity a numerical one. Indeed, his statement is grounded in the Hebrew confession of faith (Deut. 6:4) and the context reveals he is emphasizing:

> ...the promise to Abraham came directly from God, not through angels, nor by means of a merely human mediator such as Moses...In Jesus Christ, God, the one and only God, came himself.[47]

The Apostle Paul again addresses the subject of mediation in 1Timothy 2:5—affirming *'there is one God."* In keeping with the previous passages—Paul supports the Jewish view of God's oneness by using the masculine cardinal numeral one. Some believe this passage is an early Christian hymn and that:

---

[44] Leon Morris, <u>The Epistle to the Romans,</u> (Grand Rapids, MI: Eerdmans, 1994), 180.

[45] Dunn, 180.

[46] A.T. Robertson, <u>Robertson's Word Pictures,</u> in <u>The Online Bible For Windows,</u> (Ontario Canada, The Online Bible Foundation, 2002), electronic edition.

[47] Timothy George, <u>Galatians,</u> in <u>The New American Commentary,</u> vol. 30., (Nashville, TN: Broadman & Holman, 1994), 258.

This hymn affirms the singularity and unity of God as held by Jews, then adds the Christian revelation of Christ as the mediator.[48]

Paul begins with theology to ground God's universal will to same. "There is one God" (v. 5a) is a formulaic abbreviation of the *Shema* (Deut 6:4).[49]

In the final passage—James declares ζὺ Πιστεύεισ ὅτι ὁ θεὸς εἷς ἐστίν (lit. *you believe that the God one is*). The context of this statement is important, for James is addressing the foundation of the Christian faith.

> The content of this faith is also significant, for it is not a clearly Christian confession, but the *Shema* of Judaism, recited twice daily...which was also basic to Christian belief and formed a great distinction between Christians (whether Jewish or not) and pagans...[50]

In short, James 2:19 provides further proof that the early church embraced a normative form of Hebraic monotheism.

If the New Testament teaches the early church embraced an exclusive monotheism—like that of normative Second Temple Judaism—how can this be reconciled with their worship of Jesus In other words, is it possible to hold a high Christology—within the context of strict Hebraic monotheism? Oneness Pentecostals believe the answer is YES and recent scholarship examining the worship of Jesus in the Second Temple period concurs.

> In my view high Christology was possible within a Jewish monotheistic context, not by applying to Jesus a Jewish category of semi-divine intermediary status, but by identifying Jesus directly with the one God of Israel, including Jesus in the unique identity of this one God.[51]

---

[48] Deborah Menken Gill, *The Pastorals*, in Full Life Bible Commentary to the New Testament, (Grand Rapids, MI: Zondervan, 1999), 1231.

[49] Philip H. Towner, The Letters to Timothy and Titus, in The New International Commentary on the New Testament, (Grand Rapids, MI: Eerdmans, 2006), 180.

[50] Peter H. Davids, The Epistle of James in The New International Greek Testament Commentary, (Grand Rapids, MI: Eerdmans, 1982), 125.

[51] Bauckham, 182.

Oneness Pentecostals agree with Bauckham's view; yet, would argue it is more accurate to say the one God of Israel was *identified* or *localized* in the person and **name** of Jesus. This is substantiated in the highly structured *'Divine onomatology'* promulgated in Judaism and *intensified* by the early church. While often neglected, the Hebrew doctrine of God's name and its relationship to monotheism is a *'key'* to grasping the early apostolic view of God and His identity in the person and name of Jesus.

> The name...of God is the key to understanding the Biblical doctrine of God...God's self-revelation in history is accomplished by the giving of his personal name, by which his people may worship and address him as 'Thou.' Thus, God's name signifies the personal relation between God and his people, which is the supreme characteristic of biblical faith.[52]

Ancient Judaism understood that God used His name as a form of progressive self-disclosure beginning in Exodus 3:13-15. It is here that God revealed the <u>one name</u> that would distinguish Him in the Old Testament, יהוה (Yahweh). This name was specifically linked to the Exodus event and bore the designation of God's everlasting memorial; thus, the name 'Yahweh' was understood as the redemptive-covenant and *personal name of God.*

> It was this name which God chose, for it is his only personal Name; the rest are titles. Now, the LORD took this moment to fully reveal the significance of the Name to Moses. In contrast to all the imaginary gods of the heathen, the LORD of Abraham and his seed was Yahweh. This was that very special name of God, which was used by the Hebrews alone...[53]

The significance of *'the name,'* is seen throughout the Old Testament.

---

[52] R. Abba, *Name* in <u>The Interpreter's Dictionary of the Bible</u>, George Buttrick et. al, eds. (Nashville, TN: Abingdon, 1962), 3: 500-501. For a more detailed examination of this subject see <u>A Oneness Pentecostal Christocentric Onomatology</u> James Hogsten, 2012.

[53] Stanley M. Horton, ed. *The Old Testament Study Bible: Exodus*, in <u>The Complete Biblical Library</u> vol. 2 (Springfield, MO: World Library Press, 1996), 35.

...the name (sem) is frequently used of Jahweh's self-manifestation. The term is especially associated with God's revelation of himself (Exodus 23:21), and with his dwelling in the Temple (Deut. 12:11).[54]

The name of God (YHWH) occupies a significant place in Hebrew theology and was never thought of in terms of an identification label or merely an emblematic symbol.[55] Rather, Scripture reveals the salvific import of the memorial name—for wherever God '*placed*' His name—His dynamic presence would dwell.[56]

The early Hebrew-Christian church continued to _develop_ and _intensify_ this highly structured theology of '_the name,_' _in_ and _through_ the name of Jesus. In fact, Scripture reveals the early church understood the name—יהושע Y^ehowshuwa (_Jesus_) as the culminate revelation of God's name. This is not surprising considering the name 'Jesus' is etymologically _linked_ to the Divine name—and carries the meaning *Yahweh-Savior*.[57]

> Since Jesus etymologically embodies the name of Yahweh and the latter theologically anticipates the revealing of a future new name, the name of Jesus is regarded as the proper name of God for this age. It reveals the identity of Jesus and describes his function as Savior of the world.[58]

The importance of Jesus' name in the early church is confirmed in the New Testament—beginning with the Synoptic Gospels, which emphasize the divine origin and salvific meaning of the name Jesus.[59] Likewise, the Gospel of John places stress on the name—by revealing Jesus bears and manifests the Father's name,

[54] Danielou, 147-148. See also Exodus 20:24 and Exodus 33:18-19.

[55] Scripture promises blessings to those who 'know' and 'mediate' on the name (Ps. 91:14-16; Mal. 3:16-18); condemns those who 'forget' the name (Jer. 23:25-27); And forbids taking the name 'in vain' (Ex. 20:7).

[56] Exodus 20:24. Interestingly, Numbers 6:23-27 reveals God's 'name' was liturgically *placed upon* the children of Israel by the priesthood.

[57] Robert Brent Graves, The God of Two Testaments, revised ed. (Hazelwood, MO: Word Aflame, 2000), 27.

[58] David Reed, *Oneness Pentecostalism*, in The Dictionary of Pentecostal Charismatic Movements (Grand Rapids, MI: Zondervan, 1988), 648.

[59] Luke 1:31; 2:21; Matt. 1:21-25.

Yahweh.[60] Moreover, the prominence of the name Jesus continues in the book of the Acts of the Apostles.

> The name of Jesus was used in the same way as **the name of God**...miracles were performed 'in the name of Jesus,' teaching was 'in the name of Jesus,' converts were baptized 'in the name of Jesus.' ...The authority which Jesus claimed and acted out remained centred [sic] in him, and in its exercise in the primitive church was understood as derived immediately from him.[61]

The New Testament church did not abandon the Hebraic view of God's name, but believed the name '**Jesus**' was the apex of His revelatory name. This is especially evident in their treatment of Old Testament passages where "...*the Name can in fact only mean Yahweh,*"[62] yet, they replace the Divine name—יהוה (Yahweh) with that of Jesus.[63] This is important because it demonstrates the early church understood the theological and etymological import of the name Jesus. Furthermore, the New Testament is replete with examples of how the name Jesus functioned theologically and liturgically in the pristine church.[64]

An examination of the New Testament reveals the first-century church—like the Nation of Israel—were a *'people of the name.'* Indeed, they rightly understood the Divine name was personified **in** the person and name of Jesus—which is the comprehensive, culminate name of God.[65] Just as Yahweh was the redemptive

---

[60] John 1:12; 2:23; 20:31; 14:13; 5:43; 17:6.

[61] James D. G. Dunn, *Jesus and the Spirit* (Grand Rapids, MI: Eerdmans, 1997), 194-195.

[62] Danielou., 149.

[63] Philippians 2:9-11—paralleled with Isaiah 45:21-23; Joel 2:32 and Acts 2:21; and Amos 9:11-12 and Acts 15:15-17 etc...

[64] In the book of Acts 'Jesus' is used 67 times—an average of twice per chapter! There are 20 uses of *'the name'* (ref. to Jesus); 5 uses of *'his name;'* and 3 occurrences of *'my name'* for an average of once per chapter.

[65] See Acts 4:24-31(*the name invoked in prayer*); Acts 3:1-6 (*healing with the invocation of this name*); Acts 16:16-18 (*demons expelled by the oral invocation of this name*); Acts 2:38, 8:16; 10:48; 19:5; 22:16.(*baptism occurs with the invocation of the name Jesus*).

name of God under the Old Covenant—the early apostolic church recognized <u>Jesus</u> as the redemptive name of God in the New Covenant.[66]

Continuity of Hebraic monotheism and the revelation of God's name establishes a <u>doctrinal</u> and <u>theological</u> link with Judaism and the first-century church. Yet, the book of Acts also reveals a <u>geographical</u> and <u>ethnic</u> connection—accentuating the dominance of Hebrew culture and thought in the early church. This is especially apparent considering the prominence of the <u>Jerusalem church</u> in establishing ecclesiastical polity—which is manifested in three distinct areas.

First, the Jerusalem church was responsible for the organization of evangelistic outreach (Acts 8:1). Second, the Jerusalem church was the location where doctrinal controversy was addressed, *authoritatively* settled for the entire general church (Acts 15:1-32; 16:4). Third, the local church at Jerusalem was the seat of apostolic authority where ministries were confirmed and given the *'right hand of fellowship'* (Galatians 1:18-2:10). Thus, the book of Acts leaves little doubt that the Jerusalem church was the "mother church" for all the local churches established in the faith.

Perhaps even more important than the prominence of Jerusalem is the fact that the primary ethnicity of the church, both in terms of **leadership** and **laity,** were Jews or Jewish proselytes.[67] In fact, many of these Jewish converts were formerly Judaic priests.

> And the word of God increased; and the number of disciples multiplied in Jerusalem greatly; and a **great company of the priests** were obedient to the faith (Acts 6:7).

---

[66] Acts 4:12 *"Neither is there salvation in any other: for there is none other name under heaven given among men, whereby we must be saved."* This confirms the redemptive significance attached to the name Jesus in the early church.

[67] Luke records the addition of 3,000 Jews on the Day of Pentecost and another 5,000 shortly thereafter; in fact, this number does not include women—thus, the actual number is far greater (Acts 2:41; 4:4).

Luke uses two words that provide insight into the size of this group. The first— πολύς (*great*) denotes *"a relatively large quantity of objects or events—many, a great deal of, a great number of."*[68] The second— ὄχλος (*company*) refers to:

> A relatively large number of people gathered together, crowd...a large mass of people, without reference to status or circumstances leading to its composition.[69]

It is significant Luke records the conversion of a *large number of Jewish priests,* as this would have been unlikely **if** the early church embraced an aberrant form of monotheism that was antithetical to normative Judaism. Luke does not provide any details about the role these priests exercised in the early church but some believe:

> ...it seems plausible to identify these converted priests with the 'Elders' who assisted James and the Apostles in the administration of the church (Acts 15:4, 22-23; 16:4; 20:17-18).[70]

If the former Judaic priests constitute 'body of elders' mentioned later in the book of Acts—it is suggested:

> they probably functioned as a Nazarene Sanhedrin; possibly James the Just was already their president (as in 15:13; 21:18).[71]

This is an interesting hypothesis—but the New Testament does not provide enough evidence to support this claim. However, the influx of Second Temple Jewish into the church—clearly indicates the early church did not embrace a form of monotheism akin to the fringe groups of Second Temple Judaism. Indeed, it shows they espoused the same revelatory understanding of monotheism originally revealed to the Nation of Israel—and taught within normative Judaism of this time period.

---

[68] Louw & Nida, πολύς.

[69] Danker, ὄχλος

[70] Samuel Bacchiocchi, <u>From Sabbath to Sunday</u>, (Rome, Italy: Gregorian University, 1977), 142.

[71] Frederick Fyvie Bruce, <u>The Acts of the Apostles: The Greek Text with Introduction and Commentary</u>, (Grand Rapids, MI: Eerdmans, 1990) 277.

Further evidence that the pristine church enjoyed ties with Judaism is discovered in Acts 18:12-16, which provides insight regarding <u>how</u> the Roman government perceived the church. This passage records an uprising of Jewish leaders against the Apostle Paul who brought him before the Roman proconsul Gallio. These leader charged Paul with promoting a form of worship that was in violation of Roman Law.

> Since they were before a Roman court or tribunal, this would be taken by Gallio to mean contrary to Roman Law. Roman law at that time distinguished between legal and illegal religions. **Judaism under that law was considered a legal religion.**[72]

After hearing the charges—the proconsul responded:

> But if it be a question of words and names, and of **your law**, look ye to it; for I will be no judge of such matters (Acts 18:15).

Gallio's statement confirms that—*during this period of church history*, the Roman government viewed the church as a <u>sect</u> of Judaism and was therefore protected under Roman statute.

> The Jews had obtained from the government a legal license and protection for their religion; and they hoped that on their complaint the preaching of Paul would be suppressed by the magistrate...If it had been any matter of civil right, he would have tried the case...but as it related only to different views of the **Jewish religion**, he declined to interfere.[73]
>
> *Of your law.* a question respecting the proper interpretation of the law, or the rites and ceremonies which it commanded ...Gallio did not regard them as coming under his cognizance as a magistrate.[74]

This is not to suggest the early church was *indistinguishable* from Judaism, but to stress the distinction was **not** the result of a radical departure from the Hebraic monotheism! The New Testament never suggests the early church abandoned the essential

---

[72] Stanley M. Horton, ed., *Acts* in <u>The Complete Biblical Library</u> (Springfield, MO: World Library, 1986), vol. 6, 437. Emphasis mine.

[73] William Arnot, <u>The Church in the House: A Series of Lessons on the Acts of the Apostles,</u> (New York, NY: Robert Carter, 1873), 406-407.

[74] Albert Barnes, *Acts 18.*

principles of Judaic worship but reveals the early church understood themselves as the continuation of God's covenant people (*i.e. Acts 15:16-17; Gal. 6:16*). Moreover, the religious link with Judaism is evident in two specific areas—the first of which is the early church's participation in the synagogue.

> But when they (*Paul and his company*) departed from Perga, they came to Antioch...and went into the synagogue on the sabbath day, and sat down. (Acts 13:13-14).

> And it came to pass in Iconium, that they (*Paul and Barnabas*) went both together into the synagogue of the Jews, and so spake that a great multitude both of the Jews and also of the Greeks believed (Acts 14:1).

The first passage is especially relevant because after reading the Scripture Luke records the rulers of the local synagogue permitted Paul and his company to address the meeting (vrs 15). This shows there was a common form of worship between the early church and Judaism and this would have been **impossible** if the church taught a deviant form of monotheism.

> ...the first Christians were Jews...so did not initially at least see themselves to be a movement separate from Judaism. Christians in Palestine did not cease worshipping in the synagogue and temple until they were barred from synagogues following the destruction of the temple in 70AD.[75]

Second, the Bible reveals the early Christian community continued to participate in the religious life of the temple—at least in the hours of prayer (Acts 3:1-2; 21:26) and the annual Jewish feasts (Acts 18:21; 20:16):

> Luke does nothing to quell this notion, noting how often the early Christians gathered in the temple and its courts (Luke 24:53; Acts 2:46; 3:11; 5:12, 42). More specifically, Luke states that the early followers of Jesus observed the traditional hours of prayer (Acts 3:1; cf. 5:21), which is some cases were also the hours of sacrifice...[76]

---

[75] S. Bracefield, *Worship in the Early Church,* online article www.gtc.ac.nz.

[76] Timothy Scott Wardle, *Continuity and Discontinuity: The Temple and Early Christian Identity,* published doctoral dissertation (Graduate School of Duke University: 2008), 287.

James further substantiates the Jewish identity of the early church—when he said to the Apostle Paul;

> ...thou seest, brother, how **many thousands** of Jews there are which believe; and they are all zealous of the law: (Acts 21:20).

The influence of Hebraic thought was so pervasive in the first-century church that Paul—the 'Apostle to the Gentiles':

> Certainly did not think of himself as leaving Judaism...he reports that after his vision on the Damascus road he 'returned to Jerusalem and was praying in the temple' (Acts 22:17), thus demonstrating his continuing ties with Judaism.[77]

An honest reading of the New Testament leaves little doubt that the link shared between the first-century church and Judaism was both *doctrinal* and *cultural*. Moreover, there is nothing to suggest the leaders of Judaism accused the church of abandoning *strict monotheism* or denying God's *memorial name*. Rather, their primary objection to the church's message was its teaching that the one God of Israel (YHWH) was *localized* in the name and person of Jesus Christ.[78]

Early Christians were firmly committed to the God of Israel and saw no conflict in worshiping Jesus—because they understood He was the God of the Old Testament manifest in flesh. Indeed, the Apostle Paul confirms this truth by equating his worship of Jesus with that of the **God of His Fathers**. This is significant, for the ONLY God his 'fathers' worshipped was—Yahweh!

> But this I confess unto thee, that after the *way they call heresy*, so worship I *the God of my fathers*, believing all things which are written in the law and in the prophets (Acts 24:14).

Clearly, the doctrine and practices of the early church were deeply rooted in Hebraic thought and culture; thus, "...*in the most succinct*

---

[77] J. Julius Scott, *Church of Jerusalem in Acts: The Final Scene,* unpublished paper presented at The National Meeting of Evangelical Theological Society (Philadelphia, PA: 1995), 3.

[78] Certainly there were other issues dividing the two, but the doctrine that God was personified in the name and person of Jesus was central.

terms, to <u>ignore Hebraic ways of thinking is to subvert Christian understanding</u>."[79]

The pristine apostolic church clearly embraced the doctrine of strict monotheism, a Hebrew apprehension of God's name and enjoyed cultural-religious ties with Judaism. These factors provide ample evidence that the original Christian faith (ca. A.D. 30-70) was uniquely Judaic in form. However, the mid second-century reveals a radical theological shift took place in the church that ultimately substitutes Biblical-Hebraic thought with Hellenistic philosophical ideology. There are several explanations one might give for this doctrinal metamorphosis—yet, there are <u>two primary catalysts</u> worthy of mention.

The first catalyst is the 'fallout' that occurs after the death of James, the destruction of the Temple and demise of Jerusalem. These tragic events adversely affected the organizational structure of the church—by effectively diminishing the prominence and authority of the Jerusalem church. The second catalyst is the influx of Gentile believers schooled in Hellenistic philosophy. By the mid second-century some of these educated Gentile believers assumed positions of influence in the church—successfully introducing Greek theological ideas about God—supplanting the original Hebrew-Christian view of the early church.

---

[79] Marvin R. Wilson, *The Contour of Hebrew Thought* in <u>Restore</u> (Atlanta, GA: Restoration Foundation) premiere issue, nd. p. 17.

The Decline of Hebraic Christianity

New Testament scholars generally agree that James, the brother of Jesus and author of the Epistle bearing his name, was a key figure in the Jerusalem church. Scripture does not identify the exact nature of James' position; yet, his prominence is affirmed in several passages.[80] In fact, many scholars consider James as:

> ...the local head of the oldest church and the leader of the most conservative portion of Jewish Christianity...Though not one of the Twelve, he enjoyed...almost apostolic authority, especially in Judaea and among Jewish converts.[81]

According to the non-canonical Recognitions of Clement, James was responsible for governing the church from Jerusalem.

> ...the Church of the Lord which was constituted in Jerusalem was most plentifully multiplied and grew, being governed with the most righteous ordinances by James, who was ordained bishop in it by the Lord.[82]

Church historian Eusebius concurs—claiming James *"...received the episcopate of the church at Jerusalem from the Savior himself..."*[83]

Most agree that James was the bishop of the Jerusalem church; yet, some argue his position of leadership was akin to a chief bishop or general overseer over the entire church. Support for this view is found in the titles lauded on James in early post-apostolic writings such as the Pseudo-Clementine literature.

> ...the Lord, and the bishop of bishops, who rules Jerusalem, the holy church of the Hebrews, and the churches everywhere excellently rounded by the providence of God...[84]

---

[80] For example: Acts 12:17; 15:13; 21:18; 1Cor. 15:7; Gal. 1:19; 2: 9-12.

[81] Phillip Schaff, History of the Christian Church, Vol. 1., Apostolic Christianity A.D. 1-100. online edition, www.ccel.org.

[82] Pseudo-Clementine Literature, *Recognitions of Clement* in Ante-Nicene Fathers vol. 8., Sage Digital Library edition (Albany, OR: Sage Software, 1996), 1:43. *Sage Digital Library Edition is hereafter S. D. L. ed.

[83] Eusebius, *The Church History of Eusebius* in The Nicene and Post-Nicene Fathers of the Christian Church, Phillip Schaff and Henry Wallace ed., S.D.L. ed. (Albany, OR: Sage, 1996), 7:19., p. 448.

[84] Pseudo-Clementine Literature., *The Epistle of Clement to James.*, 1. p 451. Likewise, in the *"Epistle of Peter to James"* one reads *"...to James, the Lord*

One of the most explicit references to James' position is provided by Hegesippus (ca. 170) who says the Pharisees—being disturbed over the number of Jews converting to Christianity—came:

> ...to James, and said:...**restrain the people**: for they are gone astray in their opinions about Jesus, as if he were the Christ. We entreat thee to **persuade all...** For we all listen to thy persuasion...persuade the people not to entertain erroneous opinions concerning Jesus: **for all the people, and we also, listen to thy persuasion**...[85]

The post-apostolic writings of Eusebius, Hegesippus and the Pseudo-Clementine Literature are not inspired but—*like the book of Acts*—they accentuate the dominance of Hebrew leadership in the early church and show:

> ...that although Jewish Christians, either from preference or necessity, observed Jewish religious and cultural life-styles, that there was no compromise in their faith and allegiance to Jesus[86]

This literature also affirms the primacy of the Jerusalem church in terms of doctrine and polity; thus, even if the comments regarding James are exaggerated, it is easy to see how James' death would have an adverse impact on the general church.

The inauspicious effect of James' death was not simply related to his stature or position in the church. Rather, many argue James' death was significant because of the 'type' of Judaic Christianity he represented—namely, a Hebrew-Christian faith that:

> ...recognized the difference between Judaism and the new faith, accepted the gospel of salvation by grace through faith and did not seek to impose Jewish Law and customs upon Gentile believers.[87]

---

and bishop of the holy Church," 1. p. 446.

[85] Hegesippus, *Concerning the Martyrdom of James, the Brother of the Lord*, in The Ante-Nicene Fathers vol. 8., Phillip Schaff and Henry Wace ed., S.D.L. ed. (Albany, OR: Sage, 1996), 8:1530.

[86] Bacchiocchi., 153.

[87] Scott., 3.

This is in contrast to the more radical Hebrew factions, such as the 'circumcision party' (Acts 11:2; 15:5) who may *"...have been responsible for the various groups with which Saint Paul clashed in Corinth, Colossae and Galatia."*[88]

It is necessary to distinguish between these two Jewish parties in the church, for the *"...Judaizing tendency is the heretical counterpart of Jewish Christianity."*[89] Internal evidence suggests that, under the watchful eye of James, the radical strain of Hebrew Christianity was kept *'in check'* and the more moderate position represented standard first-century Hebrew-Christianity.[90]

Hegesippus confirms this view—stating, *prior* to James' death, the church was untainted by doctrinal division; yet, *after* his death— there was an internal 'power struggle' involving one named 'Thebulis', which resulted in several heretical Jewish factions.

> Therefore was the Church called a virgin, for she was not as yet corrupted by worthless teaching. Thebulis...displeased because he was not made bishop, first began to corrupt her by stealth. He too was connected with the seven sects which existed among the people...From these have come false Christs, false prophets, false apostles—men who have split up the one Church into parts through their corrupting doctrines, uttered in disparagement of God and of His Christ....[91]

Even if only partially accurate—there is little question that the loss of James exacerbated the decline of the Jerusalem church and the church as a whole. Yet, on the heels of this tragedy—Hebrew Christianity was subjected to further trauma through Vespaisan's siege of Jerusalem in A.D. 63. Both Hegesippus and Eusebius specifically link this event to the martyrdom of James.

---

[88] Daneilou., 7-8.

[89] Philip Schaff., *History of the Christian Church*, electronic edition., in The Online Bible for Windows, (Winterbourne, OT: 1997), 1708.

[90] The Apostle Paul describes 'Judaizers' who *'...came from James,'* causing problems in Galatia (Galatians 2:12). Yet, it appears they only *used* his name to gain credibility, for James disavows their claims in Acts 15:24.

[91] Hegesippus., 1534.

...the more sensible even of the Jews were of the opinion that this was the cause of the siege of Jerusalem, which happened to them immediately after his martyrdom.[92]

The siege of Jerusalem eventually lead to the destruction of the temple in A.D. 70—the focal point of Judaism. However, Eusebius maintains neither of these events resulted in the *total demise* of the Jerusalem church because:

...the people of the church in Jerusalem had been commanded by a revelation, vouchsafed to approved men there before the war, to leave the city and to dwell in a certain town of Perea called Pella.[93]

Some believe Clement's "*Recognitions*" corroborates Eusebius' statement—and regard it as "*...the oldest reference to the flight from Jerusalem by Christians at the time of the first century war with Rome.*"[94] Objections to this view usually center on the uncertain date of Clement's work and whether this is truly a reference to the flight from Jerusalem.[95] Yet, even if Clement is not referring to this event—the passage in question is significant in that it contains evidence that the name of Jesus continued to be used in the rite of water baptism within Hebrew-Christianity.

He instituted baptism by water amongst them, in which they might be absolved from all their sins on **the invocation of His name**...Subsequently also an evident proof of this great mystery is supplied in the fact, that every one who, believing in this Prophet who had been foretold by Moses, is **baptized in His name,** shall be kept unhurt from the destruction of war which impends over the unbelieving nation, and the place itself...[96]

---

[92] Eusebius., 2:5, pp. 224. See also Hegesippus "*Fragments from his Five Books of Commentaries on the Acts of the Church,*" book V., in Ante Nicene Fathers volume 8.

[93] Ibid., 3:5, pp. 236.

[94] Julius Scott, "*Did Jerusalem Christians Flee to Pella? Evidence from Biblical, Historical, Archaeological and Critical Studies,*" unpublished paper read at Wheaton College Archaeology Conference, (Wheaton, IL: November 1998).

[95] Ibid.

[96] Pseudo-Clementine Literature, *Recognitions.*, 1:39., pp. 140.

Scholars recognize that Jewish forms of Christianity continued to exist after the <u>death</u> of James, the <u>destruction</u> of the Temple and <u>demise</u> of Jerusalem in A.D. 135.[97] Yet, these events severely weakened Jewish leadership in the church—leading to the rise of aberrant Jewish-Christian schisms. In fact, ecclesiastical history reveals the Jewish wing of the church never again exercised the degree of influence they enjoyed in the first-century.

---

[97] Patristic evidence (*i.e. Eusebius and Epiphanius*) substantiate this claim. In fact, Epiphanius' work against heresies specifically identifies Hebraic-Christian sects such as the Nazarenes and Ebionites—claiming they originated in Pella (Haer 29:7; 30:2, 18).

Hellenization: A Theological Metamorphosis

The decline of Hebrew leadership in the church coupled with its expansion throughout the known world—resulted in two major changes. First, there was a demographic shift in the constituency of the church—replacing a Jewish majority with that of Gentile. In the late first and early second century this posed no threat to church doctrine or polity—as most Gentiles espoused a Hebrew-Christian view of monotheism that located Yahweh in the person of Jesus—in accordance with the pristine faith.

> Gentile Christians of the unphilosophical type...thought of Jesus as the only divine being they needed. They had found salvation through Him. He had first filled life with meaning for them, and they simply took Him as Lord of their lives. If it had not been for...the philosophers with their intellectual views... this early, simple, Christian idea would long have prevailed, and would have satisfied the minds of the rank and file.[98]

Second, the mid second-century witnessed the influx of a *'higher class'* of Gentiles—schooled in Greek philosophy. Initially, these individuals represented only a minor segment of the church and exercised no significant positions of leadership. However, by the close of the second-century, this educated minority, *personified in the apologists*, made an impact on the development of ecclesiastical doctrine by fusing Greek philosophy into the Christian faith— further exacerbating the church's break with Hebrew Christianity.

In all probability, the 'apologists' motivation was simply to make the Christian faith intelligible to the Greek audience they were trying to convert. Hence, they incorporated scholastic Greek concepts into their *'explanation'* of the faith and unfortunately, *"... in doing so, they introduced several innovations...*[99] The changes

---

[98] Rufus M. Jones, <u>The Church's Debt to Heretics</u>, (New York, NY: George H. Doran, 1924), 62. Scripture confirms early Gentile converts were mostly composed of Jewish proselytes (*Acts 6:5; 13:43*) or 'God fearers' who embraced Hebrew monotheism but were not in full fellowship with Judaism (Acts 10:22, 35; 13:16, 26; 17:4, 17).

[99] David K. Bernard, <u>Oneness and Trinity A.D. 100-300</u>, (Hazelwood, MO: Word Aflame, 1991), 63.

introduced by the apologists were not immediate but gradual and subtle. Moreover, since the apologists claimed to be 'defenders' of original faith—it was difficult for many to see the <u>genuine danger their ideas posed to the coporeal church</u>.

> Greek thought was a threat to the early church precisely because it was not an organized counterforce but rather a way of **thinking within the faith**.[100]

The apologists syncretism of Greek philosophy into the doctrine of the church has been rightly described as:

> ...the weak point of the Christian theologians who flourished in Alexandria during the second and third centuries.[101]

One of the greatest examples of this weakness is the apologists understanding of the 'Logos' as a distinct *hypostasis in God*. The Greek word λόγος expresses the idea of:

> a communication whereby the mind finds expression, word of utterance, chiefly oral.[102]

> ...those things which are put together in thought, as of those which having been thought i.e. Gathered together in the mind, are expressed in words...yet not in the grammatical sense...but language, vox, i.e. a word which, uttered by the living voice, embodies a conception or idea.[103]

The first chapter of John's Gospel uses 'logos' in reference to the eternality of God's redemptive purpose actualized in the person and name of Jesus—the λόγος <u>*made flesh*</u> (John 1:14). John's use of λόγος is <u>intentional</u>—but his view of this word is informed by Hebraism **not** *second-century Hellenistic philosophy*. In fact, the Semitic nature of John's work is revealed in his knowledge of the Hebrew language, ideas, traditions and mode of thought:

> He was not only a Jew, but a Palestinian Jew; not a Hellenist, but a Hebrew....this is shown indirectly by his own Greek style; directly, by his interpretation of Hebrew words and his

---

[100] Wells., 39.

[101] Justo L. Gonzalez, <u>A History of Christian Thought</u>, vol. 1 (Nashville, TN: Abingdon 1987), 46.

[102] Danker, λόγος.

[103] Joseph Thayer, λόγος.

quotations of from Hebrew Scriptures...John was not a man of the lowest class socially...He would be able to understand and speak Greek from his boyhood, possibly even to write it. But he would think in Aramaic. Aramaic would mould the form of his thoughts.[104]

It is impossible to extensively examine the Hebraic foundation of John's use of λόγος; yet:

> In recent years the attention of scholars has turned from Greek to Jewish sources as the background for John in general and the logos concept in particular...the divinely spoken "word" (*dabar*) of God in the OT communicates the creative power of God...God's *dabar*, in its creative faculty, possesses the power of self-realization (Isa 55:10, 11)...Not found in the OT is the idea of God's word as a distinctive "entity" existing alongside God...one does not find a hypostasis.[105]

Even if one rejects the idea that John's use of the 'logos' is grounded in Hebraic thought—one must remember that Classical or Hellenic understanding of the logos does not support the idea of hypostatic distinctions.

> ...*Logos* stood for reason...the Stoics saw *Logos* as both divine reason and reason distributed in the world (and therefore the mind). It is a creative force, the rational principle of order.[106]

Regardless of whether one appeals to the Hebrew or Hellenic understanding of the λόγος, one must interpret this word in light of its meaning in these languages. This is important for, when one's hermeneutic is in keeping with the definition of this word *in these languages*, John's use of 'logos' can be properly ascertained.

εν ἀρχῇ ἦν ὁ λόγος καὶ ὁ λόγος ἦν πρὸς τὸν θεόν καὶ θεὸς ἦν ὁ λόγος (lit. in beginning was the word and the word was toward the God and the word was God) (John 1:1).

John 1:1 affirms the eternality of the 'word;' yet, the Apostle does not envision the 'word' as a distinct hypostasis in this verse. Even

---

[104] J.B. Lightfoot, <u>Biblical Essays,</u> (London, England: Macmillan, 1904), 125, 127.

[105] James Parker, *The Incarnational Christology of John,* i n <u>Criswell Theological Review</u> 3:1 (Criswell Colloge, 1998), 34-35.

[106] Daniel L Akin, edt., <u>A Theology for the Church,</u> (Nashville, TN: B&H, 2007), 493.

the phrase πρὸς τὸν θεόν, rendered *'with God,'* (KJV) does **not** mean *'with'* in the sense of *alongside of God*. In fact, this *phrase* is used twenty-one times in the New Testament and is only rendered "with God" twice but **NEVER** with the idea of *"alongside"* of God.[107] Likewise, the Septuagint employs *this phrase* over **69** times but **never** renders this *'with God.'*[108] In fact the in the Septuagint and in the New Testament— πρὸς τὸν θεόν is translated as *'to'* or *'unto'* God—expressing the thought of something *'pertaining'* or *'with reference'* to God.

Interestingly, the KJV translates πρὸς τὸν θεόν *'pertains to'* or *'pertaining to'* God in three other passages:

> I have therefore whereof I may glory through Jesus Christ in those things which **pertain to God** πρὸς τὸν θεόν (Romans 15:17).

> Wherefore in all things it behoved him to be made like unto his brethren, that he might be a merciful and faithful high priest in things **pertaining to God** πρὸς τὸν θεόν, to make reconciliation for the sins of the people (Hebrews 2:17).

> For every high priest taken from among men is ordained for men in things **pertaining to God** πρὸς τὸν θεόν, that he may offer both gifts and sacrifices for sins: (Hebrews 5:1).

In other cases the King James translators render this phrase "to God" (i.e. John 13:3; Acts 4:24) or *"toward God"* (i.e. Acts 24:26; 1John 3:21). Thus, based on how Scripture uses this word and they way it is translated—there is no justification for interpreting logos in John 1:1 as a hypostasis that is "alongside" of God. In fact, according to John—the logos that *'pertains to'* or is *'with reference to'* God is identified as the **same God!** In short, God's utterance— His reason, His thought, His expression was *'in the beginning'* and

---

[107] Maurice A. Robinson and William G. Pierpont, <u>The New Testament in the Original Greek: Byzantine Textform</u>, electronic edition with morphological tagging, 2005. Romans 5:1 is rendered 'with' "...*peace with God*" **not** in the sense of 'alongside of' but <u>toward</u> or <u>unto</u> God.

[108] Alfred Rahlfs, edt., <u>Septuaginta: Greek Septuagint</u>, (Stuttgart, Germany: Deutsche Bibelgesellschaft, 2006), electronic edition, 2012.

this 'word' became *personal, visible and substantial in the person and name of Jesus Christ (John 1:14)*. James Dunn rightly notes that:

> ...if we translated *logos* as 'God's utterance' instead, it would become clearer that the poem did not necessarily intend the Logos in vv. 1-13 to be thought of as a personal divine being. In other words, the revolutionary significance of v. 14 may well be that it marks....*the transition from impersonal personification to actual person.*[109]

Perhaps the translators of John 1:1 intended to convey the idea of '*with reference to'* when they rendered πρὸς τὸν θεόν as 'with' God. However, it seems most comprehend 'with' as 'along side of' and interpret this verse in a way that makes the logos something **other than** God. Of course, this view of the text is directly linked to the innovative teachings of the Greek apologists. In fact, Justin Martyr appears to be the first to introduce this idea to the church but Origen of Alexandria would expand and systematize his teaching in the mid second-century.

Justin Martyr and Origen ignored the Hebraic and Hellenic basis for John's use of λόγος—and introduced a Christological teaching that united middle-platonic philosophy with the sacred text. In fact, their model of the logos was not derived from Scripture—but is from the writings of Philo, the Alexandrian Jew best known for his allegorical method of interpretation and his fusion of *Platonic philosophy into Jewish monotheistic belief.*[110]

It may seem shocking that a _non-Christian_ could exercise such powerful influence over the theological orientation of the church; yet, Philo's works *"...contain the seeds of nearly all that afterwards grew up on Christian soil."*[111] Moreover, Eusebius confirms the significant influence Philo exercised in the mid to late second-century church—describing him as *"...sublime and **elevated in his**

---

[109] Dunn, *Christology*, 243.

[110] Everett Ferguson, Backgrounds of Early Christianity, (Grand Rapids, MI: Eerdmans, 1993), 450-451.

[111] Edwin Hatch, The Influence of Greek Ideas on Christianity, (Gloucester, MS: Peter Smith, 1970), 182.

views of Divine Scripture."[112] One of Philo's "elevated views" *embraced* <u>by</u> and *elaborated* <u>on</u> by the apologists—was Philo's teaching on the λόγος. Philo abandoned the Hebraic view of λόγος and went beyond the early Hellenic understanding of this word and maintained the λόγος was:

> ...the instrument of creation and the intermediary between God and humanity, and he called <u>the Logos</u> the <u>Son of God</u>, first-begotten of God, and **Second God**. He did not attribute distinct personality to the Logos however.[113]

Philo was Jewish—but did not embrace a normative Jewish view of God. Rather, his concept of God was more akin to the Second Temple fringe groups responsible for the apocryphal works. Moreover, like the Greek philosophers of his day, Philo believed God was transcendent and unapproachable; thus, necessitating an intermediary being capable of revealing God to humanity. Philo identified this "being" or "entity" as the λόγος and even used Genesis 1:26 to support his position.

> ...It is on this account that Moses says, at the creation of man alone God said, "Let us make man," which expression shows an assumption of <u>other beings</u> to himself as assistants...[114]

> Why is it that he speaks as if of some other god...for no mortal thing could have been formed on the similitude of the supreme Father of the universe, but only after the pattern of ***the second deity***, who is the Word of the supreme Being...But he who is superior to the Word holds his rank in a better and most singular pre-eminence.[115]

Although the apologists drew from Philo's works—he is not the first to view the logos as a secondary deity. In fact, Philo's doctrine of the logos is rooted in the philosophical thought of Plato—who

---

[112] Eusebius., 8:18.

[113] J.R. Ensey ed., <u>New Cyclopedic Theological Dictionary</u>, (Willis, TX: Advance Ministries, 1999), 339.

[114] Philo., *"On Creation,"* in <u>The Works of Philo</u>, trans. By C.D. Yonge (Peabody MS: Hendrickson, 1993).

[115] Ibid., *Questions and Answers on Genesis II*. Interestingly, Eusebius' "Preparation of the Gospel" Book VIII Chapter 13 quotes this passage of Philo.

first postulated the idea of an *intermediary* or *secondary* <u>god</u> in his metaphysical work entitled *Timaeus*.

> ...of the divine he (the supreme being) undertook to be the maker: the task of making the generation of mortals he laid **upon his own offspring**.[116]

Philo's contribution to this Platonic idea was to link Plato's divine *"offspring"* to the 'logos.' While some suggest Philo's '*intermediary language'* was metaphoric—this is irrelevant in terms of his influence on ecclesiastical doctrine. Indeed, there is **no question** the Greek Apologists understood Philo's concept of the 'logos' to be *literal* and *applicable* to the Christian faith; hence:

> ...Philo's philosophy of religion became operative among Christian teachers from the beginning of the second century, and at a later period actually obtained the significance of a **standard of Christian theology**.[117]

Justin Martyr is credited with being the first to pick up the mantle of Philo's 'logos' theory—linking the 'logos' to Jesus Christ. Yet, the systemization of this teaching would be accomplished by Origen who integrated "the logos" doctrine into Christology via the theory of *'eternal Sonship.'* Origen's doctrinal understanding of the logos and eternal Sonship represents an explicit and radical departure from the Hebraic-Christian monotheism embraced by the early church. Indeed, Origen taught:

> God the Father is absolutely transcendent One above the Logos and the world. The Logos-Son is transcendent but a Unity, an idea of ideas, a form of forms. He is eternally generated by his Father, thus his is of the same substance. Since he is generated he exists differently than the Father who created him.[118]

---

[116] Plato., <u>Timaeus</u>, trans. By Francis M. Cornford (Indianapolis, IN: Bobbs-Merrill, 1959), 83. Plato's *'eternal offspring'* would eventually make its way into Christianity through the *'eternal Sonship'* doctrine!

[117] Adolf Harnack., <u>History of Dogma</u>, (Gloucester, MS: Peter Smith, 1976), 1:113-114.

[118] Robert M. Berchman, <u>From Philo to Origen Middle Platonism in Transition</u>, (Chico, CA: Scholars Press, 1984), 140.

Origen's systemization of 'logos Christology' successfully united Christian doctrine and Greek philosophy, insomuch that:

> ...the future of Hellenism was certain. The Logos doctrine started a crystallizing process which resulted in further deposits.[119]

The effect of the logos theory on the church is evident in three ways. First, it relegated Jesus to the position of Philo's *deuteros theos* (*the second god*) resulting in a <u>fundamental shift</u> from Biblical monotheism. In fact, this is confirmed by Origen Himself!

> ...and that we do not hesitate to speak in one sense of <u>two Gods,</u> and in another sense of one God...
> Origen said <u>we profess to Gods</u>?
> Heraclides said <u>yes,</u> [but the power is one]
> Origen said: But *since our brothers are shocked* at the statement <u>that there are two Gods,</u> we must <u>treat this matter carefully.</u>[120]

Secondly, the logos theory diluted the *significance* of the name Jesus, so that, *by the close of the third-century,* there was very little emphasis placed upon the fact that 'Jesus' is the comprehensive, culminate name of God. Thirdly, Origen's doctrine of the 'logos' and <u>eternal sonship</u> planted the seeds—ultimately germinating in the doctrine of the Trinity;[121] and thus, fulfilling Paul's warning to the Colossians.

> Beware lest any man spoil you through **philosophy** and vain deceit, after the **tradition** of men, after the **rudiments of the world** and not after Christ. For **in Him** dwelleth all the **fullness of the Godhead bodily** (Col. 2:8,9).

---

[119] Harnack., 2-3:13.

[120] Origen <u>Treatise on the Passover and Dialogue of Origen with Heraclides and His Fellow Bishops on the Father, The Son and the Soul,</u> in <u>Ancient Christian Writers</u> translated by Robert J. Daly (Mahwah, NJ: Paulist Press, 1992). Emphasis Mine.

[121] Gonzalez., 292. Gonzalez admits that Origen's teaching influenced Athanasius' view of the Godhead.

Conclusion

Most scholars admit the church experienced a radical change in its theological orientation in the late second through fourth centuries. This study has endeavored to show the primary cause of this transmutation was adopting a Greek philosophical view of God at the expense of Biblically revealed monotheism. Some Christians view this post-apostolic development as *progressive and positive.* Yet, this writer holds the historic restorationist view embraced by early Pentecostals—believing the church gradually departed from the truth—culminating in an organic apostasy.

The preceding pages are only a cursory overview of events, teachings and individuals contributing to theological changes within the church. Hopefully, there has been enough evidence presented to demonstrate why some deny the evolutionary model of church history in favor of the apostasy and restorationist view. At the very least—this study has endeavored to show how one's understanding of ecclesiastical history informs their interpretation of historical doctrinal changes in the church.

A correct perception of this *rationale* may assist in the current debate between Oneness and Trinitarian Pentecostals. Indeed, it is helpful to realize the differences between the two are not based on a deliberate twisting of truth. Rather, it is the result of *interpreting historical data in light of their ecclesiological perspective.* While the information in this small examination my not alter the position of either camp—it does provide an explanation regarding how the historical ecclesiastical sources are understood. It is hoped this will facilitate a more amiable atmosphere for dialogue between the two parties.

James D. Hogsten

III

A "Pretender of Yesterday?"

Elements of Monarchism and Patripassianist Theological Thought in the Post-apostolic writings of Ignatius of Antioch.

Introduction

1. We believe in one God the Father Almighty, Maker of heaven and earth, And of all things visible and invisible.

2. And in one Lord Jesus Christ, the only-begotten Son of God, Begotten of the Father before all worlds; [God of God], Light of Light. Very God of very God, Begotten, not made, Being of one substance with the Father; By whom all things were made;

3. Who, for us men, and for our salvation, came down from heaven, And was incarnate by the Holy Ghost of the Virgin Mary, And was made man.

4. He was crucified for us under Pontius Pilate; And suffered and was buried;

5. And the third day he rose again, according to the Scriptures;

6. And ascended into heaven, And sitteth on the right hand of the Father;

7. And he shall come again, with glory, to judge the quick and the dead; Whose kingdom shall have no end.

8. And [I believe] in the Holy Ghost, the Lord, and Giver of life; Who proceedeth from the Father [and the Son]; Who with the Father and the Son together is worshiped and glorified; Who spake by the Prophets.

9. And [I believe] in one holy catholic and apostolic Church

10. We acknowledge one baptism for the remission of sins;

11. And we look for the resurrection of the dead;

12. And the life of the world to come.[1]

****

The above view of God has been the touchstone of faith for most of Christendom for over fifteen-hundred years. Yet, this *well-defined* creedal articulation did not emerge in a vacuum or without controversy. Unfortunately, it is often assumed:

---

[1] Phillip Schaff, *The Nicene Creed (expanded A.D. 381)* in <u>Creeds of Christendom, with a History and Critical Notes</u>. Volume 1 internet resource Christian Classics Ethereal Library, <u>www.ccel.org</u>.

...during the patristic period the church was relatively homogenous in nature and that it developed in a uniform fashion.[2]

Ecclesiastical history reveals the fallacy of such thinking, for several groups in the mid second to late third century retained a more Hebraic understanding of God's nature and opposed the doctrinal formulation articulated in the ecumenical creeds.

Patripassianists, Modalistic Monarchians and Sabellians refer to one of these opposing groups whose *raison d'être* was to preserve God's monarchy—which they defined as:

...the doctrine that there is in the Godhead only one principle (ἀρχή), cause (αἰτία), source or fountain (πηγή) of deity...[3]

The above groups opposed *Logos Christology* and the development of Trinitarianism. Regrettably, there is no extant literature penned by adherents of such groups to explain their precise teaching. Yet, contemporary *'hostile'* witnesses give insight into their beliefs and confirm they were a threat to the apologists doctrine of God.

Hippolytus identifies early Bishops of Rome who supported or were sympathetic to the teachings of the Monarchians.[4] In fact, the apologist Tertullian claims the majority of believers in his region espoused a view of God like the Monarchians—rejecting the *proto-*

---

[2] Ronald A.N. Kydd, *Jesus, Saints and Relics: Approaching the Early Church Through Healing,* Journal of Pentecostal Theology 2 (April, 1993): 91-104.

[3] Century Dictionary and Cyclopedia, *'Monarchy,'* internet resource at www.finedictionary.com. In Trinitarianism the same definition applies but continues after the word deity, *"...namely God the Father, from whom the Son and Holy Ghost derive their divinity."* In short, Trinitarianism uses this word to show the hypostasis of the Father is the principle source of deity.

[4] Hippolytus, Philosophumena, in Ante-Nicene Fathers (Hereafter A. N. F), ed. Alexander Roberts and James Donaldson. (Grand Rapids, MI: Eerdmans, 1993), Vol. 5: 130. Hippolytus identifies two early Bishops of Rome, considered "Ante-Popes," as Sabellian—Zephrinus (198-217 A.D.) and Callistus (c. 160-222 A.D.) In this study 'Monarchian' denotes Patripassianists, Sabellians and Modalistic Monarchians.

Trinitarianism of the apologists.[5] Interestingly, the apologists provide a partial picture of the Monarchian or Patripassianists comprehension of God's nature and His revelation in the person and name of Jesus Christ.

Although there were a variety of Monarchian groups separated by time and geographical location, they apparently share two fundamental characteristics. First, they espoused a strict form of monotheism—affirming God is numerically one with no eternal distinctions in His nature. Second, they embraced the absolute deity of Jesus Christ—*without* introducing the concept of distinct hypostases or espousing the doctrine of '*eternal sonship.*' According to Hippolytus, they believed:

> ...the Spirit, which became incarnate in the virgin, is not different from the Father, but one and the same. And he adds, that this is what has been declared by the Saviour: Believest thou not that I am in the Father, and the Father in me? For that which is seen, **which is man**, he considers to be the Son; whereas the Spirit, which was contained **in the Son**, to be the Father.[6]

Hippolytus' description of Patripassianism reveals they did **not** believe Jesus was the incarnation of only *one hypostasis* in God but:

> ...they taught that Christ was God himself incarnate, the Father who had assumed flesh...If Christ is God, he must certainly be the Father; for, if he is not the Father, he is not God.[7]

This explanation indicates Monarchians could also be classified as 'Alogians,' (*against Logos*) because they did **not** support the Greek apologists doctrine of God and the Logos—who taught that:

> God the Father is the absolutely transcendent One above the Logos and the world. The Logos-Son is transcendent but a

---

[5] Tertullian, *Against Praxeas,* A. N. F., 3: 598. The word *'proto'* is used because Tertullian cannot rightly be called an orthodox Trinitarian—as this view was not fully developed until 100 years after his death.

[6] Hippolytus, 130. Emphasis mine.

[7] Philip Schaff, edt. *Monarchianism,* i n Religious Encyclopedia or Dictionary of Biblical, Historical, Doctrinal and Practical Theology, Vol. II., (New York, NY: Funk & Wagnalls, 1883), 1555.

Unity, an idea of ideas, a form of forms. He is eternally generated by his Father, thus he is of the same substance. Since he is generated he exists differently than the Father who created him.[8]

Monarchian rejection of *Logos Christology* is one of the primary reasons their view engendered hostility from the apologists.

The real peril to the Logos Christology between 180 and 240 was not the dynamistic Monarchianism...but the view which regarded Christ as God in person and as the Father incarnate.[9]

...modalism in fact was offensive only to the theologians, particularly to those who felt the influence of the Plantonic philosophy.[10]

The truth of McGiffert's statement is important considering the origin of 'Logos Christology' is grounded in the work of Philo, the Alexandrian Jew, who postulated that:

...it was impossible that anything mortal should be made in the likeness of the most high God the Father of the universe; but it could only be made in the likeness of the *second God*, who is the Word of the other.[11]

Philo's 'logos' teaching built upon Plato's work;[12] yet, unlike Plato:

...Philo's exegesis is soteriological. His concern is with the question, 'How can man know God?' ...the logos with many names is, in Philo, a mediating figure which comes forth from

---

[8] Robert M Berchman, From Philo to Origen- Middle Platonism in Transition (Chico, CA: Scholars Press, 1984), 140.

[9] Johann Jakob Herzog, Phillip Schaff, *Monarchianism,* i n The New Schaff-Herzog Encyclopedia of Religious Knowledge, Vol. VII (New York, NY: Funk and Wagnalls, 1910), 458.

[10] Arthur C. McGiffert, A History of Christian Thought (New York, NY: Charles Scribner & Sons, 1954), 1: 240.

[11] Philo, *'On Providence'* i n The Works of Philo, electronic edition, TheWord 2003-2010. This is quoted twice by Eusebius (i.e. Ecclesiastical History and Preparation for the Gospel). The significance of Philo in the development of ecclesiastical doctrine was discussed in chapter two of this work.

[12] Plato, *Timaeus,* translated by Francis M. Cornford (Indianapolis IN: Bobbs-Merrill, 1959), 83. *"of the divine, he (the supreme being) undertook to be the maker: the task of making the generation of mortals he laid **upon his own offspring"** (emphasis mine).*

God and establishes a link between the remotely transcendent God and the world or man...[13]

Philo's uniqueness is in merging Plato's 'logos' with Scripture, identifying the 'logos' as an impersonal personification of God.[14] The apologist Justin Martyr to this one step further by specifically linking the <u>logos</u> to <u>Christ</u>.

> In his account of doctrine, the Logos is God's preexistent Spirit —a second God—who became incarnate in Jesus Christ...Justin identified Jesus Christ with the 'cosmic Logos,' who is God's offshoot and agent in creation...this Logos (Christ) was in the world before Jesus Christ.[15]

Origen of Alexandria further developed and systematized this teaching—through the doctrine of *eternal sonship*—postulating that the λόγος (Logos) is *eternally begotten* by the Father.

> The Logos became united with a human soul and the two grew together in the preexistent state...the 'intermediate instrument' that became incarnate, then was the composite reality of the divine Logos (something or someone eternal but somehow less than God the Father) and the preexistent rational soul of Jesus.[16]

Admittedly, the above is somewhat difficult to understand; in fact, most post-modern supporters of eternal sonship—do not realize what this doctrine actually teaches.

> The Logos is a mediator between God the Father...and creation...Does this mean that the Logos is a second God besides the Father? Justin and several other early theologians did not shrink form speaking about the Word in this way, as 'another God' or 'a second God.' Provided that the priority of the Father as the source of all divine being and power was preserved...[17]

---

[13] Charles H. Talbert, <u>The Development of Christology during the First Hundred Years</u>, in <u>Supplements to Novum Testamentum 140</u>, (Leiden, The Netherlands: Brill, 2011), 96.

[14] Ibid.

[15] Roger E. Olson, <u>The Story of Christian Theology</u>, (Downers Grove, IL: InterVarsity, 1999), 60-61.

[16] Ibid, 110-111.

[17] Richard A. Burridge and Graham Gould, <u>Jesus Now and Then</u>, (Grand Rapids, MI: Eerdmans, 2004), 161. Such language would be appalling to

In contrast, those embracing Monarchianism rejected the notion that the 'logos' is a hypostasis in God. Rather, they espoused an earlier—more Hebraic—understanding of the logos as rationality, intelligence, purpose and speech.[18] Of course, this does not mean they denied the eternality of the logos or failed to acknowledge Jesus as the logos. Rather, they believed the eternal logos refers to Jesus in a *proleptic sense*—in the Old Testament and was *tangibly expressed* through the incarnation in the New Testament.

The apologists reveal the Monarchian comprehension of God was widespread and—*in many regions*-**the dominate position**. If correct—the historicity of the Patripassian or Monarchian view of God and His relationship to Jesus must be closely examined. In fact, its dominance forces one to ask: *"Is Monarchianism or Patripassianism an earlier view of God or a new second-century innovation that swept through the ranks of the church—encompassing the majority of non-philosophical members?"*

Evidently, the Monarchians argued their position accurately reflected the early church's understanding of God's revelation in the person and name of Jesus. This is confirmed in Tertullian's polemic against Praxeas—whom he accuses of being a *'pretender of yesterday.'*[19] Tertullian denies the veracity of this claim and insists that **his** view of God represents the teaching of the early church. Yet, strangely—at the same time—Tertullian declares his understanding is the result of being *"...better instructed by the Paraclete, who leads men indeed into all truth."*[20]

---

most post-modern Christians; yet, this is the historical view of eternal sonship.

[18] Rufus M. Jones, The Church's Debt to Heretics (New York, NY: George H. Doran, 1924), 65.

[19] Tertullian, 598. The precise identity of the Patripassianist 'Praxeas' is unknown because Praxeas means 'busybody;' thus, most believe this is a term of derision.

[20] Ibid.

The above statement is *inconsistent* with Tertullian's insistence that his view of God enjoys historicity. In fact, if Tertullian's teaching is the result of being <u>better instructed by the Spirit</u>—this strongly suggests his doctrine is a latter innovation that was progressively revealed by the Spirit! Evidently, the *"majority of believers"* in his region believed this to be the case for Tertullian maintains this was their primary reason for rejecting his view of God!

> The simple, indeed, (I will not call them unwise and unlearned,) who always *constitute **the majority of believers,*** **are startled** at the dispensation (of the Three in One), on the ground that **their very rule of faith** withdraws them from the world's plurality of gods to the **one only true God**...[21]

This statement raises serious doubts concerning Tertullian's claim of representing the historic faith; in fact, it actually counters his accusation that Praxeas is a 'pretender of yesterday' for three reasons. First, it is unreasonable to believe an *'aberrant'* concept of God could have *"recently"* been introduced and—*without modern means of communication*—enveloped the "<u>majority of believers.</u>" Second, if this **was** the case—it is strange that Tertullian describes these believers as *'startled'* (terrified) by his teaching of *'three in one.'*[22] Of course, such a reaction is nonsensical if his doctrine was the historical position of the church!

The '<u>terrified</u>' reaction of the "<u>majority</u>" indicates they were *unfamiliar* with Tertullian's teaching—**not** simply rejecting his view of God. Moreover, when coupling their reaction with Tertullian's claim of progressive revelation—this strongly suggests his doctrinal understanding of God is actually the more recent position. Third, Tertullian's claims are even less credible considering the rejection of *the majority* is grounded in an appeal to the historic *"rule of faith"* that *"withdraws them from the worlds*

---

[21] Ibid. Emphasis mine.

[22] The Latin word Tertullian uses in this passage is *"expavescunt,"* which means *"to be terrified, fear greatly or dread"*.

plurality of gods to the one only true God." In other words, they cite historic Hebrew-Christian monotheism as their **reason** for not embracing Tertullians doctrine that God is three in one!

In other words, it seems the majority of believers were *'terrified'* by Tertullian's doctrine because they believed his "revelation" was a departure from Biblically revealed monotheism and was tantamount to *ditheism* or *tritheism.* This is confirmed by Tertullian who says "the majority:"

> ...are constantly throwing out against us that we are preachers of two gods and three gods, while they take to themselves pre-eminently the credit of being worshippers of the One God...[23]

The remainder of this study seeks to demonstrate *how* or on *what basis* the Monarchians could have appealed to the historic *'rule of faith'* when defending their understanding of God—using the Patrisitc writings of Igantius of Antioch.

---

[23] Tertullian, 598.

Patristic Considerations

Ecclesiastical historians acknowledge the existence of a variety of Jewish-Christian groups in the late first to mid second-century. Like the Monarchians, the precise teachings of such groups is largely unknown; thus, it is impossible to establish a definitive historical connection to any one group. Moreover, it appears that many of theses Jewish-Christian groups were minor sects and often relegated to the fringes of the mainline church or confined to a specific geographical location.

In contrast to these 'fringe' groups—the apologists acknowledge that the Monarchian teaching was widespread and influential. Hippolytus maintains this view is *"casting the greatest confusion among all the faithful throughout the world"*[24] and laments that *"the school of these successive [teachers] continued to grow stronger and increased..."*[25] If Monarchian belief was as prevalent as the apologists indicate—this points to a significant degree of doctrinal transmission. Thus, one should expect to find evidence supporting the ecclesiastical historicity of Monarchian tradition.

One such link may be found in the post-apostolic writings of Ignatius of Antioch. Ignatius is widely recognized as a legitimate representative of the early post-apostolic church and not a part of one of the Jewish-Christian groups on the fringes of the church. Interestingly, his articulation of the Godhead and his views on the incarnation offers some support for the historicity of Monarchian tradition.

Most scholars agree Ignatius was the Bishop of Antioch in Syria and what is known of his life and theological teachings is almost exclusively derived from his seven letters, written in route to Rome where he faced martyrdom ca. 98-117a.d.[26] Because the writings of Ignatius are situated **after** the death of the Apostles

---

[24] Hippolytus, Philosophumena, IX., F. Legge, trans., (New York, NY, Macmillan, 1921), 117.

[25] Ibid, 118.

and **before** the rise of the apologists—they serve as a *'conceptual bridge'* between the Apostolic comprehension of God and that which was embraced by the second-century church.

Before examining Ignatius' epistles—there are four important facts one should consider to facilitate a better understanding of the material. First, none of the Epistles are exclusively devoted to an explication of God's nature; yet, there is enough information in Ignatius' letters to ascertain the *predominant* understanding of God in this time period. Secondly, it is inaccurate to label Ignatius as an *'anti-Trinitarian'* or a *'pre-Trinitarian'* because the groundwork of this doctrine was yet to be formed.

Third, these epistles make no claim of inspiration—thus, they cannot be used to <u>establish doctrine.</u> Moreover, an examination of the *'long recension'* of these Epistles demonstrates later copyists felt it necessary to freely *"correct"* what they deemed doctrinal errors. This clearly indicates later copyists did not believe the Epistles of Ignatius always reflected or conformed to *"established orthodoxy."*

Finally, it is important to allow Ignatius' understanding of God and His relationship to Jesus to inform the post-modern reader, rather than interpolating later doctrinal views into his works. Utilizing this approach, it is evident that Ignatius' view of God and the logos bears a greater likeness to the Monarchian position that that which was advanced by the apologists. In fact, these Epistles confirm that neither Praxeas or "the majority" are 'pretenders of yesterday,' but actually embraced an early Hebrew-Christian understanding of God and His identity in Jesus Christ.

---

[26] Daniel Hoffman, *"The Authority of Scripture and Apostolic Doctrine in Ignatius of Antioch"*, in <u>The Journal of Evangelical Theological Society</u> 28 (March, 1985): 71.

<u>Ignatius and Divine Passibility</u>

A cursory examination of the epistles of Ignatius reveal a highly developed Christology—which some believe was a response to the *Docetic heresy* that denied the substantial reality of Jesus Christ.[27] This may be partially true; yet, the Epistles of Ignatius express ideas about Jesus transcending a refutation of Doceticism. For example:

> Being the followers of God, and stirring up yourselves by the **blood of God**.[28]
>
> ....and I desire the **<u>drink of God</u>**, namely **His blood**, which is incorruptible love and eternal life.[29]

The above statements are Anti-Docetic, but go beyond a simple response to this heresy in their reference to God's "blood!" Such an assertion would have been repugnant to the apologists; yet, Patripassianists would have no issue with such language. In fact, they could use such verses to show their view of God's suffering in the person of Jesus was **not** a recent innovation and, in fact, echoes the words of Luke in Acts 20:28.[30]

Neither Luke or Ignatius suggests the nature of God is composed of blood, but they maintain the one undifferentiated Spirit of God <u>obtained</u> blood *in* the person of Jesus. This statement is important—especially considering a primary bulwark of the apologists view of God rests on the Greek doctrine of Divine Impassibility, which teaches:

> ...nothing external can affect God—that nothing external can cause God to be in any state, and in particular can cause him to feel negative emotions like grief...[31]

---

[27] Ibid., 77.

[28] Ignatius, *"Letter to the Ephesians,"* A. N. F., 1: 49.

[29] Ibid, *"Letter to the Romans,"* A.N.F. 7:77.

[30] *"Take heed therefore unto yourselves, and to all the flock, over the which the Holy Ghost hath made you overseers, to feed the church of **God**, which **he** hath purchased with **his own blood**."*

[31] Brian Leftow, *"Immutability"*, <u>The Stanford Encyclopedia of Philosophy</u>, (Winter 2012 edition), online <u>http://plato.standord.edu</u>.

> Despite the emphasis on divine passion in the Bible, early Christian theologians gradually agreed on divine impassibility as the orthodox position...the apologists frequently agreed with the Greeks that emotions are not fitting for deity. Immutability and impassability were increasingly linked together.[32]

A belief that God is incapable of suffering was a corollary to the apologists view of the Logos as the mediatory agent between God and humanity. Indeed, this concept was a primary source of contention between the apologists and the Monarchian view of God—a fact confirmed by both Tertullian and Hippolytus.

> Nay, but you <u>do blaspheme;</u> because you allege not only that <u>the Father died,</u> but that He died the death of the cross...the Spirit of God, whatever suffering it might be capable of in the Son, yet, inasmuch as <u>it could not suffer in the Father,</u> *the fountain of the Godhead,* but only in the Son, it evidently could **not have suffered, as the Father**.[33]

> For there is one God in whom we must believe, but unoriginated, **impassible**, immortal, doing all things as He wills, in the way He wills, and when He wills...[34]

The doctrine of Divine impassibility is a *distinctly* Hellenistic philosophical mode of thought rejected by the Monarchians. Instead, they embraced a Biblical Hebraic view of God that affirms his ability to suffer—a belief that was shared and taught by Ignatius of Antioch.

> For these men are not the planting of the Father. For if they were, they would appear as branches of the cross and their fruit would be incorruptible. By it He calls you through **his passion**...God, who is the Saviour Himself.[35]

The Greek word used by Ignatius in this passage is παθει, which is the neuter singular Dative form of πάσχω, meaning "*to suffer*

---

[32] Warren McWilliams, <u>The Passion of God,</u> (Macon, GA: Mercer, 1985), 10-11.

[33] Tertullian, 3.0162. Emphasis mine.

[34] Hippolytus, "*Against the Heresy of One Noetus,*" A.N.F Vol. 5 <u>Extant Works and Fragments of Hippolytus Part II Dogmatical and Historical,</u> 226.

[35] Ignatius, "*Letter to the Trallians,*" A.N.F. electronic edition 1:XI.

pain — pain, suffering, to suffer, to be in pain."[36] This is an important passage—not simply because it affirms Divine possibility—but because "his passion" is specifically linked to 'the Father.' This explicitly shows that Ignatius embraced a concept of God that acknowledged 'the Father' is the Savior and *in some sense suffered on the cross in this person of Jesus!* This idea is echoed again in Ignatius Epistle to the Romans.

> Permit me to be an imitator of the **passion of my God**.[37]

In the Greek text the words *"passion of my God"* (**του παθους του θεου μου**) literally translate *"the suffering of the God of me."* This leaves little doubt that Ignatius believed in a passible God who suffered *in* and *through* the person of Jesus Christ. Moreover, because Ignatius specifically links suffering to "the Father" it is obvious he did **not** believe the *deity resident in Jesus* was *a singular 'hypostasis'* **of God**—but the one God and Father Himself. In fact, the Epistle to Polycarp provides additional evidence that Ignatius believed God's passibility was *acquired* through the incarnation.

> ...Weigh carefully the times. Look for Him who is above all time, eternal and invisible, yet *who became* visible for our sakes; impalpable and *impassible,* yet *who became* *passible* on our account; and who in every kind of way suffered for our sakes.[38]

This passage uses contrasting words to highlight the fact that God's ability to enter into human suffering is directly linked to His incarnation in the person of Jesus. For example, **αορατον** (*unseen, invisible*) is contrasted with **ορατον** (*visible, seen*) and **απαθη** (*impassible*) is contrasted with **παθητον** (*passible*).[39] Thus, while

---

[36] Johannes P. Louw and Eugene A. Nida, **πάσχω**, in <u>Greek-English Lexicon of the New Testament Based on Semantic Domains</u>, (New York, NY: United Bible Societies, 1989), electronic edition.

[37] Ignatius, *"Letter to the Romans,"* A.N.F., 1:6, 77.

[38] Ignatius, *"Epistle to Polycarp,"* A.N.F., electronic edition, 1.04.08: III.

[39] Ibid., Greek Text online edition, <u>www.textexcavation.com</u>.

ascribing an impassible quality to God's nature—Ignatius teaches that God _became_ passible for 'our account', or 'for our sake.'

This clearly shows Ignatius believed God suffered in and through Jesus Christ—which is consistent with the teaching of the New Testament (*i.e. Acts 20:28; 2Cor. 5:19; Heb. 9:14*). Of course, this early Hebrew-Christian idea was at **variance** with the philosophical teaching of Divine impassability taught by the apologists!

> On this principle, too, the Father **was not** associated *in suffering* with the Son. The heretics, indeed, fearing to incur direct blasphemy against the Father, hope to diminish it by this expedient: they grant us so far that the Father and the Son are Two; adding that, since it is the Son indeed who suffers, the Father is only His fellow-sufferer. **But how absurd are they** even in this conceit![40]

It is obvious from reading Tertullian's remarks to Praxeas that he would have considered Ignatius' statements on 'the passion of the Father' to be absurd and tantamount to blasphemy—because Ignatius—like the Monarchians taught the Father suffered in and _through_ Jesus Christ! This idea was simply unacceptable to the apologists who could not fathom the thought of the Father suffering at all.

> But this view after all implies suffering on the Father's part, and the principle must be laid down that the Father is impassible. ...Even if the divinity in the Son had suffered, this suffering could not have flowed back to the Father. But there is no need to dwell on this supposition, for the divine spirit as such did not suffer.[41]

---

[40] Tertullian, Chapter 29, 626. see also Hippolytus 5.01.16-V. *"...and in this way Callistus contends that the Father suffered along with the Son..."*

[41] Alexander Souter, trans., Tertullian Against Praxeas in Translations of Christian Literature Series II Latin Texts, (New York, NY: Macmillan, 1920), xxii-xxiii.

Ignatius: The Passible God and the Logos

An honest comparison between the apologists view of God's impassibility and the teaching of Ignatius reveals they are in direct conflict with each other. Thus, even if Praxeas or his peers did not appeal to these writings—Ignatius affirms the historicity of the belief that God **is** passible. Of course, this is not the only doctrine of the Monarchians that engendered hostility from the apologists. Indeed, the apologists strongly objected to the idea that the Deity resident in Christ was the one undifferentiated Spirit of the Father.

> For that <u>which is seen</u>, which <u>is man</u>, *he considers* to be the Son; whereas the Spirit, which was contained **in** the Son, **to be the Father**. "For," says (Callistus), "I will not profess belief in two Gods, Father and Son, but in one...[42]

In this passage, Hippolytus reveals the Monarchians recognized a distinction between the Father and Son; yet, did **not** believe this to be an eternal distinction of divine "<u>persons</u>." Rather, the Father-Son distinction was understood as a *consequence* of the incarnation. In other words, they believed God was localized in the person of Jesus—yet, simultaneously continued to exist as transcendent Spirit. Thus, the Divinity 'resident' in Jesus was **not** a *distinct eternal hypostasis (person)* **within** God—but the **one** indivisible God.

In contrast, the apologists understood the Father-Son distinction to be an ontological *eternal distinction* and that the Deity '*in*' Christ was **one hypostasis** of God—the eternal *'person' of the λόγος Logos*.

> ...the **very Word Himself**... **He** became also the Son of God, and was begotten when He proceeded forth from Him...But you will not allow Him to be **really a substantive being**...(*as being constituted <u>second to</u> God the Father*,) to make <u>two</u>, the Father and the Son, God and the Word. For you will say, *what is a word*, but *a voice* and *sound of the mouth*, and (as the grammarians teach) *air when struck against*, intelligible to the ear, but for the rest a sort of void, empty, and incorporeal thing.[43]

---

[42] Hippolytus, *"The Refutation of All Heresies"* A.N.F. electronic edition, 5.01.16-V. Emphasis mine.

[43] Tertullian, 626. Emphasis mine.

Tertullian's comments reveal how differently supporters of Logos Christology viewed the incarnation—and identified the Deity resident in the man, Christ Jesus. Clearly, the apologists espoused a view of the Logos similar to Philo's δευτερον θεον *(second god)* for according to the above text—an entity '*second to God*' was incarnate in the person of Jesus. It is also important to note that Tertullian's statement clearly reveals the Monarchians did **not** deny the eternality of the 'Logos,' but simply rejected the idea that the 'Word' was an eternally distinct '*substantive being.*'

Ignatius does not explicate the doctrine of the incarnation; yet, he provides insight into how he understood this subject.

> There is one Physician who is possessed both of flesh and spirit; both made and not made; *God existing in flesh*; true life in death; both of Mary and of God; first possible and then impossible,—even Jesus Christ our Lord.[44]

The phrase '*God existing in flesh*' is a translation of εν ανθρωπω θεος *(lit. "in man God")*.[45] This indicates Ignatius believed Jesus was simply the one true God incarnate—not—a *distinct person* **of** or **within** the Godhead. It is obvious later copyists understood this to be the meaning of Ignatius' words, for they intentionally replaced θεος with λόγος *(lit. "in man Word")*.[46] Apparently the copyists felt the need to soften Ignatius' language—so as to conform to logos Christology and avoid any intimation of Monarchianism.

Ignatius' comments regarding '*God's blood,*' '*God's passion*' and '*God's existence*' in human form—suggests he is totally unaware of the idea that Jesus is the incarnation of a *substantial entity*, second to God the Father. In fact, there is strong evidence to suggest that Ignatius believed the distinction between the Father and the Son has its origin in time—specifically <u>in</u> and <u>through</u> the incarnation.

---

[44] Ignatius, *"Letter to the Ephesians,"* A.N.F., 1:52. (emphasis mine).

[45] Ibid, online Greek Text, www.textexcavation.com.

[46] Ignatius, *"Letter to the Ephesians" (Long Recension)*, in <u>The Apostolic Fathers</u>, trans. J. B. Lightfoot (Grand Rapids, MI: Baker, 1981), 3: 255.

...God Himself being manifested in human form for the renewal of eternal life. And now **that took a beginning** which **had been prepared** by God. Henceforth all things were in a state of tumult, because **He meditated** the abolition of death.[47]

This passage explicitly teaches God's assumption of humanity is the _point of origin_ or _'beginning'_ of what God eternally prepared. Of course, this would be offensive to those who identified the Logos as a distinct entity who assumed human flesh.[48] Yet, this language is perfectly acceptable to those who understand the Greek word λόγος as a reference to God's redemptive _purpose_ and _expression_ that becomes tangible and substantial in the person of Jesus—which is apparently what the Monarchians taught!

For Spirit, as the Deity, is, he says, not any _being_ different from the Logos, or the Logos from the Deity; therefore this one person...is divided nominally, but substantially not so. He supposes this one Logos to be God, and affirms that there was _in the case of the_ Word an incarnation.[49]

Evidently the Monarchians—embraced the same idea as set forth in Ignatius' letter to the Ephesians—identifying the one who takes on _"a beginning"_ as the visible expression or localization of God's Word. The Monarchians recognized the eternality of God's word—identifying Jesus as the _"word made flesh;"_ yet, like Ignatius, they did not believe the λόγος is something _other than the one God._

...there is one God, who has manifested Himself by Jesus Christ His Son, who is _His eternal_ **Word,** not proceeding forth from silence, and who in all things pleased Him that sent Him.[50]

Several features of this passage deserve attention. First, Ignatius maintains the <u>one God</u> is manifest "<u>by</u>" Jesus Christ His Son. The word rendered 'by' is the preposition δια—used with the Genitive, which is defined as "_of the means or instrument by which anything is_

---

[47] Ignatius, _"Letter to the Ephesians,"_ A.N.F., 1:19, pg., 57.

[48] This idea is continues to be rejected by most post-modern Christians!

[49] Hippolytus, _Noetus and Callistus,_ A.N.F. Vol. 5, Book X chap XXIII, 148.

[50] Ignatius, _"Letter to the Magnesians,"_ A.N.F. 1:8, pg. 62.

effected."[51] Thus, Ignatius is expressing the idea that God has made himself visible *in* and *through* Jesus Christ. Further support for this interpretation is his use of the word φανερωσας (*manifested*)—the same word used by the Apostle Paul in 1Timothy 3:16 *"...God was manifest in flesh..."*

Second, the Magnesian passage identifies the 'Son,' as the tangible manifestation of the λόγος without intimating this word refers to an eternal hypostasis in the Godhead. In fact, Ignatius appears to believe the distinction between θεος (God) and αυτου λογος (His word) is *a consequence* of God's incarnation in the person of Jesus Christ—**not** an ontological part of His being. Thus, when comparing Ignatius' understanding and use of λόγος with the apologists—their comprehension is obviously very different.

Thirdly, in some manuscripts the phrase *"not proceeding forth from silence"* actually reads: *"proceeding from silence."*[52] The Greek word translated '*silence*' is σιγης, which:

> ...as a noun generally meant 'silence.' As an adverb it could mean 'silently' or 'quietly, 'secretly.'[53]

The word rendered '*proceeding forth*' is the participle προελθων, meaning *"...to proceed so as to be ahead, to continue to advance, to come to the fore."*[54] Therefore, depending on the text used—this passage

---

[51] Joseph Henry Thayer, διά, in Thayer's Greek-English Lexicon of the New Testament, electronic edition.

[52] The translations of J.B. Lightfoot and C.H. Hoole prefer '*proceeding forth from silence."* Whereas Roberts and Donaldson prefer *"not proceeding forth from silence."* Lightfoot claims there is strong evidence to support the omission of '*not*' and claims the fourth-century *"Marcellus of Ancyra expressed his Sabellianism in almost identical language; he spoke of Christ as the Logos issuing from Silence..."* In his view, 'orthodox' scribes altered the text to *"...save the reputation of St Ignatius from complicity in heretical opinions."* (J.B. Lightfoot *"Essays on Supernatural Religion,"* internet resource www.anglicanlibrary.org.

[53] Thoralf Gilbrant, edt. The New Testament Greek-English Dictionary Sigma-Omega, Vol. 16., in The Complete Biblical Library, (Springfield MO: World Library Press, 1991), 48.

says God's word _did_ or _did not_ come to the fore or proceed from silence or secrecy.

If one interprets this to mean the word did **not** come from silence—Ignatius may be simply reminding his audience that the visible manifestation of God's λόγος was not shrouded in secrecy but revealed (_i.e. in Scripture_). However, if understood as the word **did** come from silence—this could mean that God's _hidden purpose_ is manifest _in_ and _through_ the incarnation. In either case, this text confirms that the incarnation is the _visible expression of God's eternal word_.

It is important to point out that the apologists major objection to the Monarchian understanding of 'the Word' was their refusal to recognize the λόγος as a substantially distinct _being in the Godhead_.

> for you do not want it [the word] to be regarded as in itself material through the independence of its matter, lest it might appear as a sort of object and person and, being **second to God**, might thus be able to make two...For what, you say is word, but voice and a sound of the mouth and as the school teachers teach, a striking against air intelligible to the hearing...For whatsoever the being of the Word was, I call it **a person**...I claim **he is second to the Father**.[55]

Ignatius' comprehension of the λόγος may not be identical to the Monarchian position, but it bears a greater resemblance to the teaching of Praxeas than that of the apologists!

Two additional passages confirm that Ignatius understood the λόγος as God's eternal redemptive purpose that is actualized in His assumption of humanity in the person of Jesus Christ. Indeed, for Ignatius—the incarnation is the pivotal moment in time when God takes on human existence—while retaining His existence as transcendent Spirit. Thus, as a consequence of God's localization

---

[54] Fredrick William Danker, A Greek-English Lexicon of the New Testament and other Early Christian Literature, third edition, (Chicago IL: University of Chicago Press, 2000) electronic edition Oak Tree Software Inc.

[55] Souter, 40-41.

in the person of Jesus Christ—the λόγος becomes visibly manifest and *substantially distinguished* from God who <u>simultaneously</u> exists <u>in</u> the λόγος and <u>as</u> transcendent Spirit.

> For <u>**our God**</u>, Jesus Christ, was, according to the appointment of God, conceived in the womb by Mary, of the seed of David, but by the Holy Ghost...[56]

The Greek text begins: **ο γαρ θεος ημων Ιησους ο Χριστος** (lit. *for* <u>*the God*</u> *of ours Jesus the Christ*). Ignatius' use of the article (the) before 'God' demonstrates he is not merely asserting that Jesus is *divine,* but is identifying Him as '**the God**.' In addition, this passage teaches the visible manifestation of <u>the Christ</u> occurs by God's appointment. Thus, Ignatius understands the incarnation as *the <u>causal agent</u> of '<u>The</u>' God's visible personification in human flesh.* This is further supported by the word **οικονομιαν** (appointment) which signifies an *'arrangement, order, plan.'*[57]

> Oikonomia is the activity of the oikonomos (Luke 16:2-4), in the form of the dispensation of salvation, its actualization for each one, thanks to the minister of God.[58]

This passage does <u>**not**</u> teach there is an **ontological** distinction between *two eternal substantive beings* in the Godhead. Rather, it is a confirmation that the Deity resident in the man, Christ Jesus is the <u>**selfsame one**</u> who 'appointed' his conception. This means the distinction between God and Jesus is a consequence of God's simultaneous existence <u>***in***</u> human flesh and <u>***beyond***</u> the incarnate as transcendent Spirit. In other words, God's localization in Jesus <u>*creates the condition*</u> wherein a tangible distinction between God and His word, Father-Son is evident.

The '<u>long recension</u>' of this passage strengthens the accuracy of the above interpretation—as later supporters of Logos Christology

---

[56] Ignatius, *"Letter to the Ephesians,"* in A.N.F. Vol. 1:18, pg. 57.

[57] Danker, *"οικονομια"*

[58] Ceslas Spicq, *"οικονομια"* in <u>Theological Lexicon of the New Testament</u>, edit., James D. Ernest, (Hendrickson Publisher: 1994), electronic text, Oak Tree Software Inc.

felt it necessary to alter this passage in order to avoid such an understanding of the text.

> For the Son of God, who was begotten before time began, and established all things according to the will of the Father, He was conceived in the womb of Mary, according to the appointment of God.[59]

Notice, instead of describing Jesus as the incarnation of "the God," the copyists intentionally changed the wording so that Jesus is the embodiment of the *eternal Son* — a singular hypostasis of God.

Unlike the supporters of Logos Christology—the Monarchians would have accepted Ignatius' claim that the visible actualization of God's eternal word was dependent on the incarnation. In fact, they opposed the apologists idea that the Father-Son relationship was an ontological eternal intra-relationship in God's nature.

> ...Father and Son, so called, are one and the same (substance), not one individual produced from a different one, but Himself from Himself; and that He is styled by name Father and Son, according to *vicissitude of times.*[60]

This is an important statement—for it shows the Patripassionists believed the Father-Son distinction was linked to the "*vicissitude* of times.*" Interestingly, the word *vicissitude* is defined as:

> the quality or state of being changeable: mutability, natural change or mutation visible in nature or in human affairs.[61]

A close reading of the Monarchian teaching reveals the *vicissitude* referred to by Hippolytus was the incarnation. In other words, they believed the incarnation—an event in historical time **not** eternity—marks the beginning of the Father-Son distinction.

The second passage addressing Ignatius' comprehension of the incarnation is discovered in his Epistle to the Romans.

> I desire the bread of God, the heavenly bread, the bread of life, which is the flesh of Jesus Christ, the Son of God, who became

---

[59] Ignatius, *Letter to the Ephesians*, (long recension) 1:18, 57.

[60] Hippolytus, *'Refutation,'* Book 9: Chapter 5.

[61] Merriam-Webster Online Dictionary, *vicissitude*, internet resource at www.Merriam-Webster.com.

> afterwards of the seed of David and Abraham; and I desire the drink of God, namely His blood, which is incorruptible love and eternal life.[62]

The ideas set forth in this passage demonstrate Ignatius' view of Jesus is quite different from the apologists. He begins by identifying Jesus as the *'heavenly bread;'* yet this terminology does not denote an eternal hypostasis—but refers to *"...the 'flesh' of Jesus Christ, **the Son of God**..."*

According to the text—the title 'heavenly bread' is a reference to 'the flesh' or humanity of Jesus. Yet, interestingly the same is true of the title Son of God, for Ignatius identifies 'the Son' as του εκ σπερματος Δαυειδ (*the one out of the seed of David"*). This is significant for—*unlike the apologists*—Ignatius does not use 'Son of God' as a title of *Deity alone* or in reference to *a distinct eternal hypostasis* of God. Rather, Ignatius understands *'Son of God'* in the context of the incarnation—thus, affirming Jesus is **fully** but not **exclusively** human, for he is also the visible manifestation of the one true God!

It is also important to note that by describing the Son of God as του εκ σπερματος Δαυειδ (*the one out of the seed of David"*), Ignatius affirms the 'Son' was *begotten in* and *through* the incarnation. This is evident through his use of σπέρματος (spermatos) which is defined primarily as *"the source from which someth. Is propagated, seed...male seed..."*[63] Of course, this idea is totally at variance with the teaching of the apologists who argued the Logos was literally and substantially *'the Son'* **prior** to the incarnation.

> ...there was nothing contemporaneous with God...And as the Author...He begat the Word...I shall not speak of two Gods, but of one; of two persons...for the Father indeed is one, but there are two persons, because there is also the Son.[64]
>
> From that moment God willed creation to be effected in the Word, Christ being present and ministering unto Him: and *so*

[62] Ignatius, *"Letter to the Romans,"* A.N.F. 1:7, pg. 77.

[63] Danker, σπέρμα.

[64] Hippolytus, "Against the Heresy" A.N.F. 5, pg. 227.

God created...Now if He too is God, according to John, (who says.) "The Word was God," (Joh 1:1) **then you have two**.[65]

Although Ignatius subscribes to the eternality of God's Logos, his understanding of *what this means* is different from the apologists. In fact, the typical second-century 'Logos' language is noticeably absent in his epistles. Moreover, he does **not** appear to believe the "Son" is an *eternally begotten hypostasis within God's being*. Rather, Ignatius teaches the manifestation of the Son of God is brought about *through* the incarnation—God's assumption of humanity in the person of Jesus Christ.

> ...and in Jesus Christ, who was of the seed of David according to the flesh, being both the Son of man and the Son of God.[66]

Ignatius' Epistles identify Jesus as *'the God,' 'Son of God,' 'Son of man'* and stress He is the *visible actualization* of God's eternal λόγος. Yet, Ignatius **never** uses this terminology to indicate Jesus is an ontological eternal distinction in the Godhead!

> I glorify God, <u>even Jesus Christ</u> who has given you such wisdom...being fully persuaded with respect to our Lord, that he was truly <u>of the seed of David</u> according to the flesh, (Rom1:3) and <u>the Son of God</u> according to the will and power of God; that he was truly born of a virgin...[67]

This passage does not suggest Jesus is a 'person' of God nor does it teaches Jesus is merely Divine. Rather, Ignatius declares Jesus is <u>THE God</u> by using the Greek article "THE" before the word God (τον θεον). This did not go unnoticed by latter copyists who felt it necessary to change his words to bring them into conformity with so-called "orthodoxy." Indeed, the opening phrase of the 'long recension' completely obscures Ignatius' message saying: *"I glorify the God and Father of our Lord Jesus Christ, who by Him as given you such wisdom."*[68]

---

[65] Tertullian A.N.F., 3:12.

[66] Ignatius, *"Letter to the Ephesians,"* A.N.F. 1:20, pg 58.

[67] Ignatius, *"Letter to the Smyrnaeans,"* A.N.F 1, pg 86.

[68] Ibid, (Long recension). The so-called 'corrections' made by the copyists are given to show that they obviously interpreted the text like that of

Interestingly, the Smyrnaean verse teaches the incarnation is a visible manifestation of God's *will and power* and <u>the basis</u> upon which Jesus is called '*the Son of God.*' This is especially evident in the words γεγεννημενον αληθως εκ παρθενου (*the one truly/really 'produced' out of a virgin*). The Greek word γεγεννημενον means "*to cause something to come into existence primarily through procreation or parturition.*"[69] This word is used in the *perfect tense*—thus,

> ...the focus is on the continuing effects of a completed action...the perfective aspect emphasizes **the consequences** of the action.[70]

In short, Ignatius teaches Jesus' *Sonship* is a consequence of the incarnation; thus, he uses "*Son of God*" in reference to the human Messiah—the one who is <u>*simultaneously*</u> God and man.

---

this author; thus his interpretation is not innovative.

[69] Danker, γεννάω.

[70] Gerald L. Stevens, *Perfect Tense*, <u>New Testament Greek</u>, second edition (University Press of America), electronic format, 1997. Emphasis mine.

The Divinity Resident in the Son

According to the apologists—Monarchians linked the 'Sonship' of Jesus to the *'vicissitude of times.'* Thus, they did not use the title 'Son of God' to denote Deity alone but in reference to the Messiah who is **both** God and man in human flesh. This may explain why Tertullian charges Praxeas with *denying* the Father and the Son; yet, also accuses him of believing the Father *is* the Son.

> Away, then, with those "Antichrists who <u>deny</u> the Father and the Son." For they <u>deny</u> the Father, when they say that He is the <u>same as</u> the Son; and they <u>deny</u> the Son, when they suppose Him to be the <u>same as</u> the Father...[71]

Tertullian's statement is either a genuine misunderstanding of Monarchian teaching or a *deliberate hyperbolic distortion.* In truth, Praxeas and the majority of believers affirmed the eternality of the λόγος, the absolute deity of Jesus—and acknowledged Jesus as the 'Son of God.' However, they **denied** that Jesus was the incarnation of an *eternally distinct entity* who substantially existed in a *Father-Son* relationship *prior* to the incarnation.

This is confirmed by Hippolytus—who quotes one of the leading proponents of Monarchianism as saying:

> I will not profess belief in two Gods, Father and Son, but in one. For the Father, **who subsisted in** *the Son* Himself, after He had taken unto Himself our flesh, raised it to the nature of Deity, by bringing it into union with Himself, and made it one; so that Father and Son must be styled one God, and that this Person being one, cannot be two.[72]

If quoted accurately—it is clear that Monarchian believers did **not** deny the Father or the Son! Rather, they embraced an *incarnational view* of the 'Son of God,' emphasizing the Deity **resident in** Jesus is the **one indivisible** Spirit of God. Hence, regardless of Tertullian's intent—his accusation is without merit.

---

[71] Tertullian, A.N.F. 3:31.

[72] Hippolytus, *'Refutation,'* 9:7. Interestingly, this is reportedly a quote from Callistus—recognized by Roman Catholicism as one of the popes (see www.newadvent.org).

Hippolytus' quotation also reveals Patripassianists maintained the Father-Son distinction is *integrally* linked to God's *concurrent* existence *within* and *beyond* His incarnation. Thus, they did **not** "*deny*" the Father—but *localized* the Father **in** the *person* of the Son.

> And so, Father and Son are one God because **the single divine spirit called the Father** united himself to the human flesh, and this compound is called the Son. The Father is **in** the Son. The names "Father" and "Son" have neither the same sense nor the same reference: "Father" refers to the divine spirit **in** the Son, whereas "**Son**" refers to the human flesh **united** to the Father.[73]

This description suggests a view that is closely akin to Ignatius' position with respect to Jesus being the incarnation of THE GOD rather than a hypostasis OF God. Indeed, Ignatius plainly teaches that Jesus is God in flesh and the 'Son of God' by **virtue of** the incarnation and not substantive being *prior to the incarnation*. Furthermore, evidence strongly suggests Ignatius believed the Deity resident in Jesus is the **one God and Father**!

While the epistles of Ignatius do not expressly address the *inner composition* of God nor do they describe the incarnation as '*the Father subsisting in the Son.*' Yet, **they do** affirm that the distinction between the Father and Son is not an eternal ontological intra-relationship in God's nature. Moreover, when speaking of Jesus as God incarnate—Ignatius consistently uses the article with θεος to accentuate He is the incarnation of '**The God**!' In fact, he **never** intimates the Divinity resident in Jesus is a one hypostasis of other hypostases in God. Even when using the term λόγος in reference to Jesus—his emphasis is the visible expression of the 'Word,' which is actualized *in* and *through* the incarnation.

In addition, the epistles of Ignatius teach the one God incarnate concurrently exists in transcendency *beyond His incarnation*. Unlike the apologists, who taught a distinct entity of God resides in Jesus,

---

[73] Mark DelCogliano, *The Interpretation of John 10:30 in the Third Century: Anti-Monarchian Polemics and the Rise of Grammatical Reading Techniques*, i n Journal of Theological Interpretation, 6:1 (Winona Lake, IN: Eisenbrauns, 2012), 124.

Ignatius used no such terminology. Rather, these epistles employ language supporting the idea that the Father *subsists* or is *localized* in the Son!

> Christ will reveal these things to you, [so that ye shall know] that I speak truly. He is the mouth altogether free from falsehood, <u>by which</u> the **Father** has truly spoken.[74]

The relevancy of this passage in relation to the Father <u>subsisting</u> <u>in</u> 'the Son' is evident in the Greek text, which identifies Jesus as the mouth εν ω ο πατηρ ελαλησεν αληθως (*in whom* the Father has *truly spoken*). The inclusion of the preposition εν (in) is significant, because it "...*denotes being or remaining within, with the primary idea of rest and continuance.*"[75] This preposition:

> ...expresses the idea of 'within,' whether of rest or of motion depending on the context. Compare vernacular English, "Come in the house..." The preposition in itself merely states that the location is **within** the bounds marked by the word with which it occurs. It does not mean 'near,' but '**in,' that is 'inside**.'[76]

The Greek text confirms that Ignatius is **not** simply saying Jesus is the spokesman **of** the Father—but his use of the preposition εν indicates the Father spoke *within* the person of Jesus. Thus, unlike a prophet who is a 'mouthpiece' *for* God—Jesus is described as the one *within whom the Father has spoke*. Indeed, the primary force of this preposition is **locative**; thus, showing Ignatius believed the Deity <u>resident</u> **in** the Son is *<u>the Father!</u>* Further support for this view is found in the Epistle to the Trallians:

> But **the Father** is faithful <u>in</u> Jesus Christ to fulfill both mine and your petitions:...[77]

---

[74] Ignatius, *"Letter to the Romans,"* A.N.F. 1:8, pg., 77.

[75] E.W. Bullinger, *"Notes and Appendixes"* in <u>The Companion Bible</u>, (Grand Rapids MI: Kregel, 1999).

[76] A.T. Robertson, <u>A Grammar of the Greek New Testament in the Light of Historical Research</u>, (Nashville, TN: Broadman, 1934), 585-586. Emphasis mine.

[77] Ignatius, *"Letter to the Trallians,"* A.N.F. 1:13, pg 72.

The Greek text reads αλλα πιστοσ ο πατηρ εν Ιησου χριστω (*but faithful [is] the father __in__ Jesus Christ*). Notice that, like the previous passage—the preposition εν is used—showing the Father indwells the person of Jesus Christ. This is totally at variance with Logos Christology and the apologists would have condemned such a view. Moreover, lest someone accuse this writer is *'reading into'* the text—it appears later copyists interpreted it similarly, for they altered the wording to expunge any trace of Monarchianism.

> But the Father of Jesus Christ is faithful to fulfill both mine and your petitions.[78]

The Greek apologists rejected any doctrine suggesting the Father was localized in the Son. In truth, their perception of the λόγος as a distinct hypostasis precluded such a view and helps explain why they vehemently opposed the Monarchian belief that:

> The Logos Himself is Son, and that Himself is Father, and that though denominated by a *different* title, yet that in reality He is one indivisible spirit.[79]

According to Hippolytus—a primary error of Monarchianism was the belief that *the one God and Father was resident in the Son*. This being the case—they would have rebuked Ignatius because he taught **the same thing**!

Two additional passages confirm Ignatius' belief that the Father was localized in the person of Jesus.

> ...our Saviour Jesus Christ, which suffered for our sins, and which *the Father*, of his goodness, *raised up* again.[80]

> Now, He suffered all these things for our sakes, that we might be saved. And He suffered truly, even as also *He truly raised up Himself*...[81]

In the seventh chapter of Smyrnaean letter—Ignatius clearly says the 'Father' was responsible for the resurrection of Jesus; yet, in

---

[78] Ibid. long recension.

[79] Hippolytus, *"Refutation,"* A.N.F. 9:7.

[80] Ignatius, *"Letter to the Smyrnaeans,"* A.N.F. 1:7, pg. 89.

[81] Ibid., 1:2, pg. 87.

the second chapter he credits Jesus with **his own resurrection**! This teaching would be contradictory if one understands the Father and Son as two substantive entities—like the apologists. However, Ignatius correctly recognized the Divinity in Jesus is the one undifferentiated Spirit of God—thus both statements are true.

As in other passages, later copyists recognized the implication of Ignatius' statement in the second chapter; thus, they 'corrected' his terminology in accordance with Logos Christology.

> <u>The Word</u> raised up again His own temple on the third day, when it had been destroyed by the Jews fighting against Christ.[82]

Some may be inclined to believe the copyists are expressing the same truth as Ignatius—but this is not the case. Rather, they are crediting the eternally distinct hypostasis residing in Jesus (*i.e. the eternal Logos*) for the resurrection!

Interestingly, Hippolytus sarcastically attacks the Monarchians for emphasizing the **<u>same truth</u>** expressed by Ignatius.

> That this person suffered by being fastened to the tree, and that He commended His spirit unto Himself, having died *to appearance,* and not being (in reality) dead. And He raised Himself up the third day.[83]

> See, brethren, what a rash and audacious dogma they have introduced, when they say without shame, the Father is Himself Christ, Himself the Son, Himself was born, Himself suffered, Himself raised Himself. But it is not so.[84]

In truth, the Monarchian teaching was not as naïve as portrayed by Hippolytus. Like like Ignatius, they credited the Deity resident in the Son with the resurrection—and they identified this Deity the one God and Father. Of course, the basis for understanding Jesus resurrecting Himself is revealed in the Gospel of John.

> Jesus answered...destroy this temple, and in three days **<u>I will raise it up</u>**...he spake of the temple of his body (John 2:19, 21).

---

[82] Ibid., long recension.

[83] Hippolytus, *'Refutation'* Book IX, 128.

[84] Ibid, 224.

Actually, Hippolytus knew *exactly* what the Monarchians taught on this subject, for in his next chapter he gives a more accurate explanation of their teaching.

> And he is disposed (to maintain) that He who was <u>seen in the flesh</u> and <u>was crucified</u> <u>**is Son**</u>, but that <u>the Father it is</u> who <u>dwells **in him**</u>.[85]

One final passage identifying the Divinity of Jesus as the one selfsame Spirit of God is in the Epistle to the Magnesians.

> Fare ye well in the harmony of God, ye who have obtained the inseparable Spirit, <u>who is Jesus Christ</u>.[86]

This passage is important because there is no suggestion that the Spirit inhabiting believers is another eternally <u>distinct hypostasis</u> in the Godhead. Rather, Ignatius explicitly identifies the Spirit as the post-resurrected glorified Jesus—spiritually manifest in the life of believers. This is at variance with the apologists who taught the Spirit of God is, *in some respect,* a <u>distinct entity</u> in God.

> ...we who are followers of the Paraclete, not of human *teachers,* do indeed definitively declare that ***Two* Beings** are God, the Father and the Son, and with the addition of the Holy Spirit, **even *Three*,** according to the principle of the *divine* economy, which introduces *number*...[87]

> For the Father indeed is One, but there are <u>two Persons</u>, because there is also the Son; and then there is the third, the Holy Spirit.[88]

This writer is not suggesting Ignatius is a Monarchian whose beliefs are identical to Praxeas, Noetus or Sabellius. Moreover, there is no evidence that the Monarchians appealed to Ignatius' Epistles to support the historicity of their doctrine. Yet, an honest reading of these epistles demonstrate that Ignatius' early <u>post-apostolic</u> view of God bears a closer resemblance to Monarchian teaching that that of the apologists.

---

[85] Ibid., book X, pg 148.

[86] Ignatius, *"Letter to the Magnesians,"* A.N.F. 1:15 pg. 65.

[87] Tertullian, A.N.F. Vol. 3 chap XIII.

[88] Hippolytus, *Refutation*, 228.

Ignatius and Alleged Pre-Trinitarian Ideas

The epistles of Ignatius clearly reflect ideas about God's nature and His assumption of humanity in the person of Jesus that are antithetical to Logos Christology. Yet, some maintain his epistles contain some *pre-trinitarian* ideas. Before delving into these—it is important to remember the major points about the nature of God discussed in this Epistles as this will allow for a more consistent and accurate interpretation of the alleged *pre-trinitarian* passages.[89]

> 1. The epistles of Ignatius expressly deny the Greek doctrine of impassability—a major bulwark of Logos Christology. Indeed, Ignatius consistently refers to God's blood and the Father's passion when discussing the price paid at Calvary.
>
> 2. The epistles of Ignatius never describe Jesus as the incarnation of a substantive being in the Godhead. Rather, they teach the one God was localized in Jesus while simultaneously existing as transcendent Spirit.
>
> 3. Ignatius explicitly supports the eternality of God's λόγος; yet, does <u>not</u> suggest the λόγος is an eternally distinct being apart from God. Rather, Jesus is the visible expression of God's λόγος, which is God's eternal purpose, plan and expression.
>
> 4. Ignatius affirms a distinction between the Father and the Son but **not** an *eternal distinction* of two tangible beings. Instead, these epistles confirm the dissimilarity is a consequence of the incarnation—showing the Father-Son relationship is assumed *in time* through the historic incarnation.
>
> 5. Ignatius never uses the title '*Son of God*' in reference to Divinity **alone** or a singular hypostasis in God. Rather, his use of this title is **always** linked to the incarnation; thus, referring to *humanity* or *humanity united with Deity*.
>
> 6. Ignatius appears unaware of any teaching that asserts the Deity resident **in** Jesus is a distinct entity *of* or *within* God. In fact, he explicitly maintains the Father is localized in the person of Jesus Christ—the Son of God.
>
> 7. Ignatius does not teach the Holy Spirit is an eternally distinct hypostasis of God—but identifies the Spirit as the glorified Christ.

---

[89] Strictly speaking, Ignatius is neither *anti-Trinitarian, Trinitarian or pre-trinitarian* because this doctrine was not yet developed. Thus, the term pre-trinitarian is used loosely in reference to ideas that might have been used by latter Trinitarians to support their teaching.

Despite these clear affirmations, some believe Ignatius' epistles contain early expressions of Trinitarian thought. Three passages are cited to substantiate this view—the first of which is in the Epistle to the Magnesians.

> ...who are most dear to me, and are entrusted with the ministry of Jesus Christ, <u>who was with</u> the Father before the beginning of time, and in the end was revealed.[90]

Although interpreting this text in reference to Jesus' pre-existence as a distinct hypostasis would be in conflict with other statements in Ignatius' Epistles—the English translation can lend itself to such a view.[91] Yet, the Greek text of this passage is more ambiguous.

In the Greek text—the preposition παρα (*'with'*) is joined to πατρὶ (*Father*) which is in the *dative case*. This is significant because when παρα is used with the dative it often:

> ...indicates that something is or is done either in the immediate vicinity of someone, or (*metaphorically*) <u>*in his mind*</u>...[92]
>
> from (generally of origin causality)...from (generally of procedence).[93]

Understood in this manner—Ignatius is not describing Jesus in a pre-existent tangible state of being, but a prolepsis in the eternal plan and purpose of God that would be substantially revealed in the incarnation.

This view is strengthened by Ignatius' use of χριστος (Christ) which is **always** used in reference to the human Messiah and **never** as a title of Divinity. In short, when used of Jesus—this title

---

[90] Ignatius, *"Letter to the Magnesians,"* A.N.F. 1:61.

91 This author realizes it is not essential to harmonize conflicting ideas in these epistles because they are not inspired. Yet, in light of the many statements by Ignatius that link the origin of Jesus to the incarnation—it is prudent to examine this passage.

[92] Joseph Thayer, <u>A Greek-English Lexicon of the New Testament</u> (Grand Rapids, MI: Zondervan, 1889), 477. Louw & Nida concur that when used with the dative—this word is a *"marker of potential agent."*

[93] J. Lust, E. Eynikel and K. Hauspie, <u>A Greek-English Lexicon of the Septuagint</u>, (Stuttgart, Germany: Deutsche Bibelgesellschaft, 2003) electronic edition.

is **<u>exclusively</u>** linked with the incarnation. Moreover, it is obvious that later copyists did not believe this verse clearly affirmed Jesus' pre-existence as an eternal hypostasis for they altered the text to read:

> ...He being begotten by the Father before the beginning of time, was God the Word (λόγος)...[94]

It is interesting to note that Archbishop Wake's translation of Vossius' 1646 Greek Text renders this verse:

> ...the ministry of Jesus Christ, who *was the Father* before all ages, and appeared in the end to us.[95]

This writer is uncertain why Archbishop Wake's translation is different from other English translations. Perhaps the answer to this question can be discovered by examining Vossius' manuscript or the twelfth-century manuscript that forms the basis of Vossius' work. The following page contains a facsimile of a 1711 Greek text of Magnesians that may provide some insight.[96] The underlined words may be the issue with Wake's translation as it is difficult to make out the word πρὸ and παρα with certainty.

Even if this does not account for Wake's translation, the long recension demonstrates later copyists did not believe this verse was a clear statement regarding the *'orthodox'* view of the λόγος or Trinitarianism. Moreover, when employed with other passages of Ignatius' epistles—this text could actually be used to support a Monarchian view of God.

---

[94] Ignatius, *"Letter to the Magnesians,"* A.N.F. 1:61 (Long Recension).

[95] William Wake, *"Magnesians 1:5"* i n <u>The Forbidden Books of the Original New Testament</u>, (London, England: E. Hancock, 1863), 136.

[96] William Whiston, *Ignatius' Epistle to the Magnesians,* in <u>Primitive Christianity Revived In Four Volumes</u>, (London, England: 1711), 176. Vossius' manuscripts of the epistles of Ignatius continues to find scholarly support; however, I have been unable to find a facsimile of the 12th century manuscript forming the basis of the above text.

The Larger and Smaller

Smaller.

Ἐπεὶ ἓν ἐν τοῖς προ-
γεγραμμένοις προσώποις
τὸ πᾶν πλῆθΘ ἐθεώρησα
ἐν πίστει καὶ ἠγάπησα, παραινῶ ἐν ὁμονοίᾳ θεῦ
σπουδάζετε πάντα πράσ-
σειν, προκαθημένου τῶ ἐπισκόπου εἰς τόπον θεῦ, καὶ
τῶν πρεσβυτέρων εἰς τό-
πον συνεδρίου τῶν ἀποστό-
λων, καὶ τῶν διακόνων,
τῶν ἐμοὶ γλυκυτάτων,
πεπιστευμένων διακονίαν
Ἰησῦ Χριστῦ, ὃς πρὸ αἰώ-
νων παρὰ πατρὶ ἦν, καὶ
ἐν τέλει ἐφάνη. Πάντες
ἕν, ὁμοήθειαι θεῦ λα-
βόντες, ἐντρέπεσθε ἀλλή-
λοις, καὶ μηδεὶς κατὰ σάρκα βλεπέτω τὸν πλησίον,
ἀλλ' ἐν Ἰησῦ Χριστῷ ἀλ-
λήλους διαπαντὸς ἀγαπᾶ-
τε. Μηδὲν ἔστω ἐν ὑμῖν
ὃ δυνήσεται ὑμᾶς μερί-
σαι, ἀλλ' ἑνώθητε τῷ ἐπι-
σκόπῳ, καὶ τοῖς προκαθη-
μένοις, εἰς τύπον καὶ δι-
δαχὴν ἀφθαρσίας.

Larger.

Ἐπεὶ ἓν ἐν τοῖς προγεγραμμέ-
νοις προσώποις, τὸ πᾶν πλῆθΘ
ἐθεώρησα ἐν πίστει, καὶ (*) ἀγάπῃ
παραινῶ, ἐν ὁμονοίᾳ θεῦ σπουδά-
σατε πάντα πράττειν, προκαθημένου
τῶ ἐπισκόπου εἰς τόπον θεῦ· καὶ τῶν
πρεσβυτέρων, εἰς τόπον συνεδρίου
τῶν ἀποστόλων· καὶ τῶν διακόνων τῶν
ἐμοὶ γλυκυτάτων, πεπιστευμένων
διακονίαν Ἰησῦ Χριστῦ, ὃς πρὸ αἰώνων παρὰ τῷ πατρὶ γεννηθείς, Λύ
λόγΘ θεός, μονογενὴς υἱός· καὶ
ἐπὶ συντελείᾳ τῶν αἰώνων ὁ αὐτὸς
διαμένει· ἦ γὰρ βασιλεία αὐτῦ οὐκ
ἔσται τέλΘ, φησὶ Δανιὴλ ὁ προ-
φήτης. πάντες ἓν ἐν ὁμονοίᾳ ἀλ-
λήλους (†) ἀγαπήσωμεν· καὶ μηδεὶς κατὰ σάρκα βλεπέτω τὸν πλησίον, ἀλλ' ἐν Χριστῷ Ἰησῦ. μηδὲν
ἔστω ἐν ὑμῖν, ὃ δυνήσεται ὑμᾶς
μερίσαι· ἀλλ' ἑνώθητε τῷ ἐπισκό-
πῳ, ὑποτασσόμενοι τῷ θεῷ δι'
αὐτῦ ἐν Χριστῷ.

The second passage some believe teaches an incipient form of Trinitarianism is in the epistle to the Ephesians.

> ...as being stones of the temple of the Father, prepared for the building of <u>God the Father</u>, and drawn up on high by the <u>instrument of Jesus Christ,</u> which is the cross, making use of the <u>Holy Spirit as a rope</u>, while your faith was the means by which you ascended, and your love the way which led up to God.[97]

This passage affirms a belief in the Father, the Son and the Holy Ghost; yet, use of these Scriptural terms does not mean Ignatius

---

[97] Ignatius, *"Letter to the Ephesians,"* A.N.F. 1:9, pg 53.

subscribed to the idea of eternal hypostatic distinctions in God. In fact, Monarchians used these terms <u>without</u> reference to distinct *persons in the Godhead.*

It is problematic to use the above passage as an implication of <u>pre-trinitarian</u> thought for two primary reasons. <u>First,</u> the Epistle to the Ephesians contains explicit statements regarding God's localization in Jesus and clearly teaches the Father-Son distinction is a consequence of the incarnation. Therefore, it seems unlikely that the ninth chapter of Ephesians is an example of incipient Trinitarianism.

Ephesians 1
"stirring up yourselves by the blood of God"
Ephesians 7
"There is one Physician who is possessed both of flesh and spirit, both <u>made and not made</u>; God existing in flesh...both of Mary and of God..."
Ephesians 18
"For <u>our God</u>, Jesus Christ, was <u>according to the appointment of God</u>, <u>conceived</u> in the womb by Mary, of the seed of David, but by the Holy Ghost."
Ephesians 19
*"<u>God Himself</u> being manifested in human form for the renewal of eternal life. And <u>**now**</u> that **took a beginning** which had been prepared by God."*

<u>Second,</u> the context of this passage <u>argues against</u> an *ontological interpretation*—because Ignatius is addressing God's role in the redemption process. In fact, the distinctions—Father, Jesus Christ, and Holy Ghost—are used in relation to the personal and experiential aspects of salvation—thus demanding a <u>soteriological</u> interpretation. Understood in a salvific context, the <u>Father</u> is the *preparer or originator* of the redemptive 'building' that is tangibly activated through "the instrument" *(the cross)* by human Messiah <u>Jesus Christ</u> and applied to the believer by the <u>Holy Spirit</u> who is identified by Ignatius as the glorified man, Christ Jesus.[98]

---

[98] See Magnesians 1:15 "the inseparable Spirit, who is Jesus Christ."

The ninth chapter of Ephesians sets forth a distinction between the Father, Jesus Christ and the Holy Spirit, but **not** an *ontological eternal* distinction. In fact, Ignatius' reference to *the cross* as the instrument '*of Jesus Christ*'—places this squarely in the context of the <u>historical incarnation</u>. Therefore, at best, the distinction in this passage is between Deity and humanity—<u>both of which</u> Ignatius localizes in Jesus Christ!

One final passage used to show pre-trinitarian ideas in the Epistles of Ignatius is also in the letter to the Magnesians.

> Be ye subject to the bishop, and to one another, as Jesus Christ to the Father, according to the flesh, and the apostles to Christ, and to the Father, and to the Spirit.[99]

Like Ephesians nine—this passage contains the Biblical terms of Father, Jesus Christ and Spirit. As hitherto stated—this Scriptural language was used by the apologists <u>and</u> Monarchians; thus, does not necessarily mean three *co-equal, co-eternal and consubstantial* persons in God's nature. This is evident in Hippolytus' description of the Monarchian view—wherein he states:

> And he maintains that the Father is not one person and the Son another, but that they are one and the same; and that all things are full of the Divine Spirit, both those above and those below. *And he affirms* that the Spirit, which became incarnate in the virgin, is not different from the Father, but one and the same.[100]

There is also strong contextual evidence the Magnesians passage is also linked to the incarnation. First, Ignatius refers to the subjection of Jesus Christ, "*according to the flesh;*" thus, he is explicitly speaking of the **human Messiah**. Second, Ignatius uses the title '*Christ*' *(anointed)* — which is a messianic designator that is specifically linked to the human being in whom God is incarnate.

Finally, a contextual reading of the text reveals Ignatius is not making an ontological statement but an ***ethical directive*** to his readers. Ignatius is not asking his readers to emulate the behavior

---

[99] Ignatius, *"Letter to the Magnesians,"* A.N.F. 1:13, 64-65.

[100] Hippolytus, *Refutation*, Book IX, 130.

of an *eternal hypostasis in God* but is using the historical Christ as a model of submission. In other words, Ignatius is teaching a Christocentric ethic of submission—**not**—a pre-trinitarian concept of theology! Thus, based upon the contextual evidence—the Monarchians of Tertullian's day could have easily affirmed the content of this passage without compromising their belief in strict monotheism and the absolute Deity of Jesus Christ.

<u>Conclusion</u>

The Epistles of Ignatius are not doctrinal explications of God's nature or His incarnation in the person and name of Jesus. However, they provide valuable insight into the manner in which an early patristic writer understood aspects of Christology and the doctrine of God. Given the content of these epistles, it is little wonder that:

> ...the epistles ascribed to Ignatius have given rise to more controversy than any other documents connected with the primitive church.[101]

Ignatius' comprehension of God may not be the <u>primary</u> source of this contention; yet, there is little argument his perception of God is at variance with the teaching of the apologists. In fact, Ignatius' understanding of God resembles aspects of Monarchian teaching, which has caused some scholars to conclude that:

> If we limit our view of the teaching of the Fathers by what they expressly state, St. Ignatius may be considered *as a* <u>*Patripassian*</u>...[102]

In truth, such a definitive conclusion may be '*over-reaching.*' Yet, this sentiment accentuates the truth that the Epistles of Ignatius set forth a more Hebraic concept of God that is more akin to Monarchianism than the doctrine of the apologists. This should not seem surprising considering that early non-philosophical Gentiles:

> ...thought of Jesus Christ as the only divine being they needed. ...If it had not been for...the philosophers with their intellectual views of an eternal spiritual principle, this early, simple, Christian idea would long have prevailed, and would have satisfied the minds of the rank and file.[103]

---

[101] A. Cleveland Coxe, Introductory Note Ephesians, A. N. F., 1:46.

[102] John Henry Cardinal Newman *"An Essay on the Development of Christian Doctrine,"* sixth edition, reprint 1878 project Gutenburg www.gutenburg.org, January, 2011.

[103] Rufus M. Jones, <u>The Church's Debt to Heretics</u> (New York, NY: George H. Doran, 1924), 62.

The reason for this is because many first and second-century Gentile converts came from the ranks of 'God Fearers.'

> The God-fearers...frequent the services of the synagogue, they are monotheists in the biblical sense, they participate in come of the ceremonial requirements of the Law...it was from the ranks of the God-fearers that Christianity supposedly had recruited a great number of its first members.[104]

> The two monumental inscriptions found on a marble block in Aphrodisias records the names of 68 Jews, 3 proselytes, and 54 gentile God-fearers (*theosebeis*) ...Thus, we have conclusive proof of a group of gentile God-fearers, of high rank and significant number, who were publicly and actively associated with the local Jewish community.[105]

This early Gentile link to Judaism is important when examining Monarchian belief—especially considering one of the objections Tertullian levels against Praxeas is that Monarchian belief 'bears a likeness' to Hebraic teaching!

> But, (this doctrine of yours bears a likeness) to the Jewish faith, of which this is the substance—so to believe in One God as to refuse to reckon the Son besides Him, and after the Son the Spirit. Now, what difference would there be between us and them, if **there were not this distinction** *which you are for breaking down?*[106]

This statement is amazing considering the church *should* bear a "*likeness*" to the Jewish faith—since it emerged from a Hebraic theological milieu. Yet, perhaps more stunning is Tertullian's claim that the *primary distinction* between Judaism and the church is the belief that God's nature is composed of multiple hypostases! Clearly, Monarchianism acknowledged there was a distinction between Judaism and the church—yet, they would have objected to the notion this differentiation was rooted in the concept of eternally distinct hypostases in God!

---

[104] A. T. Kraabel, *'The Disapperance of the 'God-Fearers'* in Numen vol. 28, (December, 1981: Brill), 113-114.

[105] Lee I. Levine, The Ancient Synagogue: The First Thousand Years, (New Haven, Connecticut: Yale University, 2005), 293-294.

[106] Tertullian, *'Against Praxeas,'* A.N.F vol 4: 31.

Indeed, it appears Monarchians believed the primary difference between Judaism and Christianity centered on the *incarnation*. In short, they believed the pivotal doctrine separating these schools of thought was the belief that Yahweh took on an *additional* form of existence in Jesus—without compromising His transcendent existence as omnipresent Spirit. Thus, the difference between the two streams of thought is **not** *ontological but incarnational*—God's simultaneous existence within and beyond His incarnation!

Tertullian accused Praxeas of being a *'pretender of yesterday,'* suggesting his view of God enjoyed no apostolic historicity; yet, the Epistles of Ignatius reveal this is a false accusation. Indeed, these writings are a witness to an earlier, more simplistic view of God's identity in Jesus Christ that avoids the complexity and 'pitfalls' of the Greek philosophical ideology.

> Patripassianism, owing to the decision of the Roman bishops, was for a time admitted within the Church. This was only possible because it was thought to be a more precise expression of an older teaching. The heresy came from Asia Minor, and we find there a theology of which Patripassianism was a natural growth—the theology of Ignatius.[107]

Despite the apologists claim—Monarchianism was not a *new innovation;* in fact, Justin Martyr (ca. A.D. 155-57) declares:

> For they who affirm that the Son is the Father, are proved neither to have become acquainted with the Father nor to know that the Father of the universe has a Son...[108]

Because the context of this passage addresses the Jews and their belief the Father appeared to Moses—some believe this is **not** a reference to Monarchianism. Yet, in his dialogue with Trypho, Justin Martyr re-addresses this subject—specifically incorporating some group of Christians into his charge.

---

[107] E.J. Thomas, *Tertullian: Adversus Praxean,* in Review of Theology and Philosophy, Allan Menzies, edt., Vol. III (Edinburgh, Scotland, Otto Shulze, 1908), 152.

[108] Justin Martyr, *The First Apology of Justin,* A.N.F. Vol. 1, 184.

When describing this group's belief system—Justin Martyr uses the same language later used by Monarchians when explaining their understanding of God's nature.

> ...I know that some wish...to say that the power sent from the Father of all which appeared to Moses...is called an Angel because He came to men...and they call Him the Word because He carries tidings from the Father to men: but maintain that this power is indivisible and inseparable from the Father, just as they say that the light of the sun on earth is indivisible and inseparable from the sun in the heavens...so the Father, when He chooses, say they, causes His power to spring forth, and when He chooses He makes it return to Himself...[109]

As hitherto stated—there is nothing to prove Ignatius embraced the teachings of second century Monarchianism. Yet, his epistles, coupled with the statements of Justin Martyr—clearly reveal that Monarchian ideas were present **prior** to the theological construct of God developed by the apologists. Hence, one must honestly ask *"who is **really** the pretender of yesterday?"* The answer to this query presents a challenge—*especially to those who embrace the principle of primitivism*—to lay aside *'creedal spectacles'* of the fourth and fifth centuries and re-examine the Hebraic perception of God's identity in Christ in early patristic thought.

---

[109] Justin Martyr, *Dialogue with Trypho*, A.N.F. Vol.1, 264.

James D. Hogsten

IV

Oneness Pentecostalism

Heretical Cult or Christian Heterodoxy?

Introduction

Perhaps no greater charge within the Evangelical community can be leveled against a group or individual, than the charge of heresy or the label of a 'cult.' While many groups claiming to be Christian, may deserve such a designation—this is not true in every case. Moreover, as previously discussed in the second study of this volume, the criterion for determining *heresy* is often replete with subjectivity. Consequently, there is no *standardized formula* or *'litmus'* test to determine what is *'heretical.'* Yet, there appears to b e *two predominant views* regarding *how* one can discern heresy from orthodoxy. The first uses Scripture in conjunction with the ecumenical creeds—while the second advocates using Scripture alone.

Interestingly, those who believe Scripture <u>and</u> the creeds are *the standard* for measuring orthodoxy usually accept **only** the creeds of the third and fourth century. This is inconsistent considering *the same institution* is responsible for the early and latter creeds. While the rationale for rejecting subsequent creeds and dogma is based upon their alleged departure from Scripture—this is a subjective argument. In fact, this reasoning fails to consider the <u>authoritative loci</u> for *every creed* is the church that created them. Thus, if one accepts the authority of *some* of the creeds, subsequent creeds should be vested with the <u>same authority</u>.

This problem has caused many evangelical groups in history to eliminate ecclesiastical creeds as a measure of orthodoxy, opting instead for Scripture alone. In fact, many early restorationist groups advocated for a complete break from all 'man-made creeds.' In the Reformation period this *creedal* aversion was most pronounced among the Anabaptist *"...the most Protestant and yet the furthest removed from Protestantism."*[1] Yet, this attitude is also a hallmark of early Pentecostalism.

---

[1] William R Estep, <u>The Anabaptist Story: An Introduction to Sixteenth-Century Anabaptism</u>, (Grand Rapids, MI: Eerdmans, 1996), 196.

...But we know that no uninspired man or men can make an infallible creed. We admit some truth in all, but will some truth justify the false? ...If one is excusable for false doctrine, all are, and if one is rejected, then all are unless their creed is infallible. So on goes all the creed systems, the blind leading the blind and falling into the ditch of the apostasy.[2]

Despite the anti-creedal motif in evangelical history—fidelity to ecclesiastical creeds is still the most common method used to determine 'orthodoxy' within post-modern Christendom. This is unfortunate because it disenfranchises groups that would not otherwise be rejected if Scripture alone was the litmus test for judging orthodoxy. Hence, many argue the restoration mantra *sola Scriptura* should be restored to its proper place as the **supreme and only test** of orthodoxy.

The Church...must never accept tradition as a rule of faith, and especially not to equate tradition with Scripture...This has proven the great prostitution of Romanism. Holy Scripture is the true Church's only rule of faith, practice, government and discipline.[3]

Employing this principle would facilitate unity and afford liberty to those who are *heterodox* with regard to creedal adherence; yet, embrace Scripture as their rule of faith and practice.

One group that would benefit from this approach are Oneness Pentecostals.[4] This branch of Pentecostalism claims approximately 30 million adherents worldwide; yet, continues to be the most despised, ridiculed, persecuted and misunderstood segment of the movement.[5] Consequently, the Oneness movement has gravitated towards isolationism. This posture has allowed the movement to

---

[2] R. G. Spurling, The Lost Link, (Turtletown, TN, 1920), 19, 26.

[3] Wade H. Phillips, God the Church and Revelation, (Cleveland, TN: White Wing, 1986), 94.

[4] Oneness Pentecostals are sometimes referred to as "Modalists," "Jesus Name," "Apostolic" "Hebrew Christian Monotheists" and in disdain "Jesus Only."

[5] Talmadge L. French, Early Interracial Oneness Pentecostalsim, (Eugene, Oregon; Pickwick, 2014), 6. This misunderstanding is evident in the larger segment of Pentecostalism and outside of the Movement.

retain much of its original restorationist impulse; yet, it has also contributed to the perception it is a heretical cult—not a legitimate form of Christianity.[6]

Interestingly, if Scripture alone is the standard used to measure 'orthodoxy' Oneness Pentecostalism presents a challenge to those who would classify the movement as heretical. While there may be segments of the Oneness Movement that are heretical—the same can be said of Trinitarian Pentecostalism.[7] Thus, in order to gain an accurate perception of Oneness Pentecostal beliefs—it is necessary to hear from the mainline voices of the movement and not those of a more radical nature.

Perhaps the most effective way to begin this process is to examine some of the doctrines and practices that are mutually shared by Oneness Pentecostals, Trinitarian Pentecostals and the larger Evangelical Movement. Subsequently, one can investigate those areas wherein Oneness Pentecostals are considered heretical by the majority of Christendom.

---

[6] This tendency is changing as more Oneness Pentecostals seek higher education and theological training. For example, the United Pentecostal Church launched "Urshan Graduate School of Theology," in 2001, receiving full accreditation from the 'Association of Theological Schools' in 2010.

[7] Examples of such segments include the '*Branhamites*' or '*Divine Flesh*' among the Oneness branch of Pentecostalism and *Serpent handling* churches in both camps of the movement.

The Authority of Scripture

Like Evangelicals and Trinitarian Pentecostals—those embracing Oneness Pentecostalism share a deep commitment to the authority of Scripture. Indeed, they firmly espouse the Bible as their only rule of faith—and affirm the doctrine of verbal plenary inspiration of Scripture.

> Since the Bible is God's Word, all parts of it are inspired. Moreover, every word of the Bible is inspired...The Scripture is both inerrant and infallible in its original writings.[8]

In light of this commitment—many Oneness Pentecostals believe Scripture **alone** must be the foundation for determining heresy and orthodoxy.

> The only logical course is for Christians to accept biblical Christianity as the only measurement of orthodoxy, for no other gospel or doctrine is valid...If all Christians would submit to the authority of the Scriptures...a true ecumenical climate could emerge in the Christian community.[9]

Some argue this does not apply to Oneness Pentecostalism because the main tenets of this movement are rooted in subjective 'latter-day' revelation—not Scripture.[10]

To bolster the charge of 'subjective revelation,' critics often point to the *revelatory language* frequently found in Oneness literature and used in oral testimonies. However, a cursory reading of early Pentecostal literature (*Trinitarian **and** Oneness*) demonstrates that all Pentecostals believed in immediate revelation. Indeed, the forbears of Pentecostalism espoused a strong restorationist motif reminiscent of early Anabaptists—and believed God was using this Movement to restore Biblical truth that was abandoned in the

---

[8] Marvin D. Treece, *"The Bible,"* in <u>Doctrines of the Bible</u>, (Hazelwood, MO: Word Aflame, 1993), 48, 50.

[9] J. L. Hall, *"Cults,"* in <u>Doctrines of the Bible</u>...pg., 42.

[10] This charge is frequently used in oral and written debates concerning the doctrine of the Oneness Movement. This accusation is designed to dismiss their claims of legitimacy and relegate the movement to the status of a 'cult' akin to Jehovah Witnesses or the Latter-day Saints.

corporeal apostasy that culminated in A.D. 325 with the adoption of the Nicene Creed.[11]

Closely connected with their restorationist motif—Pentecostal forbears were firmly committed to the principle of primitivism, *the desire to emulate the original doctrine and practice of the pristine apostolic church.*

> Ever since the days of Martin Luther and his fellow reformers men have been searching for the old paths...do not expect to rest until the very deepest mystery is solved and the Church of God is revealed in her completeness as she appeared in the days of the apostles...she will be rediscovered only by climbing back to apostolic order...[12]

Restorationism gave early Pentecostals their *raison d'être* and helps explain why they anticipated revelatory disclosure. Yet, neither Trinitarian **nor** Oneness Pentecostals used the term 'revelation' to convey the idea of something extra-Biblical. Rather, their use of such terminology was always understood in the context of a Scriptural illumination by and through God's Spirit wherein the truths of Scripture opened up to God's people (i.e. 1Corinthians 2:9-13). In fact, history has proven that the Pentecostal Movement will not tolerate those who claim an immediate subjective revelation that is contrary to the objective revelatory word of God.

> Many church groups, including Oneness Pentecostals, have used the word *revelation* to mean that the Spirit helps them to understand a doctrine or Bible passage. But care should be taken in the use of this term since the Bible is God's full revelation, and any "revelation" a person may receive that does not harmonize with the Bible must be rejected.[13]

---

[11] The entire early Pentecostal Movement viewed ecclesiastical history through the lens of an organic apostasy and did not accept the idea that the early church 'evolved' in the faith. The two ecclesiastical views were previously discussed in chapter two.

[12] A. J. Tomlinson, *"Fifth Annual Address 1914,"* in Historical Annual Addresses, (Cleveland, TN: White Wing, 1970), vol. 1, pg., 37-39. Tomlinson was not a Oneness Pentecostal, but his comments confirm the restorationist motif was common throughout the Movement.

[13] Hall, *"Cults,"* 50.

Salvation by Grace Through Faith

Another teaching Oneness Pentecostals share with Evangelicals and Trinitarian Pentecostals is salvation based upon the atoning death of Jesus Christ and obtained by grace through faith. Yet, in keeping with other mainline Holiness-Pentecostal groups—they maintain:

> ...saving faith expresses itself in our obedience to Christ's gospel and by our identification with Him. It is a living faith that works.[14]

Oneness Pentecostals stress the necessity of full salvation—which is an appropriation of *the blood, the water* and *the Spirit*; thus,

> ...they maintain that the same instructions Peter gave on the Day of Pentecost are the proper instructions that the church should give to those wanting to be saved.[15]

Other teachings commonly held by Oneness Pentecostals, Evangelicals and Trinitarian Pentecostals include the depravity of man; the universality of sin; the necessity of repentance; eternal life for the righteous, eternal punishment for the wicked and the belief in bodily resurrection. They also share a common view of eschatology—to include *the same disputes regarding pre-tribulation, mid-tribulation and post-tribulation* views of the rapture. Moreover, they embrace a similar view of ecclesiology—including those who support dispensationalism and covenant theology.[16]

In spite of their agreement on several *essential Biblical doctrines*, many continue to regard the Oneness Movement as heretical for

---

[14] David K. Bernard, The New Birth, (Hazelwood, MO: Word Aflame, 1990), 61. This understanding of 'saving faith' has been the historical position of both the Holiness and Pentecostal Movements.

[15] J. L. Hall, The United Pentecostal Church and the Evangelical Movement, (Hazelwood, MO: Word Aflame, 1990), 32. The 'instructions' Hall is referring to are those found in Acts 2:38.

[16] Other commonly held beliefs include the belief that God is an invisible Spirit; Jesus is the only way to salvation; the belief in a personal Devil and in keeping with their Holiness roots—they deny the doctrine of eternal security etc...

two primary reasons—both of which are based on a <u>creedal interpretation</u> of Scripture.

> 1. Oneness Pentecostals embrace a heterodox view of God's nature, rejecting *ecclesiastical Trinitarianism* and the *doctrine of eternal sonship*.
>
> 2. Oneness Pentecostals deny the validity of the triadic formula of water baptism—believing baptism is valid <u>only</u> when the name of Jesus is orally invoked over the baptismal candidate. Hence, they baptize new converts and *'re-baptize'* those previously baptized using the triadic formula.

The remainder of this study examines these unique and often controversial aspects of the Oneness Movement. The intent is to provide the reader with the Scriptural rationale used by Oneness Pentecostals in defense of their teachings and practices. Moreover, this study demonstrates that Oneness interpretation of Scripture is based on *accepted* principles of hermeneutics and in keeping with early restorationism and the quest for Apostolic primitivism.

Oneness Pentecostals and the Trinity

The Oneness rejection of Trinitarianism is well known; however, few understand *the rationale* behind the rejection of this dogma. First, they maintain there is continuity or harmony between the Old and New Testament **not** discontinuity or contradiction. Thus, God's revelatory disclosure in the Old Testament is still valid unless the New Testament specifically abrogates a premise taught therein. This principle of interpretation is coupled with the idea that 'Scripture interprets Scripture' and no where is the principle applied more explicitly than in the Oneness view of strict Hebrew Monotheism.[17]

The '*Shema*' is the classic expression of Biblical monotheism and the *touchstone* of both Judaism and Christianity.[18] Oneness scholars insist the Jewish and early Christian view of the Shema, precludes the idea of eternally distinct hypostases in God's nature. In fact, they maintain that Second-Temple Judaism **and** the first-century church understood Deuteronomy 6:4 to teach:

> God is absolutely and indivisibly one. There are no essential distinctions in His eternal nature...any plurality associated with God merely relates to attributes, titles, roles, manifestations, modes of activity, relationships to humanity, or aspects of God's self-revelation.[19]

Most importantly, it is believed the nation of Israel—the original recipients of Monotheism correctly and accurately grasped God's revelatory disclosure set forth in the Shema. Furthermore, it is

---

[17] That idea that Scripture interprets Scripture simply sets forth the idea that the Bible is to be viewed holistically and one verse is not pitted against another or several clear verses made subservient to one obscure text (see David K. Bernard, Understanding God's Word; Kenneth J. Archer Forging a New Path).

[18] Deuteronomy 6:4 *"Hear O Israel, the LORD our God is one LORD."* The word *Shema* is the Hebrew word for "Hear," the first word in this verse.

[19] David K. Bernard, *"The Oneness View of Jesus Christ,"* paper presented at the 19th Annual Meeting of the Society for Pentecostal Studies, (Fresno, CA: 16-18 November, 1989), 2.

argued that the New Testament does not intimate a forthcoming change in the Jewish perception of this truth; in fact:

> Jesus put an imprimatur on the Jewish belief in God when he said to the woman at the well of Samaria, '...We know what we worship: for salvation is of the Jews' (John 4:22). Instead of condemning the Jewish perspective of God, Jesus put a stamp of approval on their strict monotheistic view.[20]

<u>Second</u>, Oneness Pentecostals maintain that Trinitarianism lends itself to <u>tritheism</u>. Although, 'orthodox' Trinitarians would reject this charge, historical and modern 'Christian Art' repeatedly demonstrates the truth of this allegation (*i.e. Alacario Otero's "Trinity" painted in 2001*).

Tritheistic tendencies are even more pronounced in Trinitarian Pentecostalism, for example: This tritheistic tendency is even more pronounced in Trinitarian Pentecostalism, which may be the result of a over reaction to the Oneness branch of the movement.

> You can think of God the Father, God the Son, and God the Holy Ghost as three different persons exactly as you would think of any three other people--their 'oneness' pertaining strictly to their being <u>one</u> in purpose, design, and desire.[21]

> ...See, God the Father is a person, God the Son is a person, God the Holy Ghost is a person. But each one of them is a triune being by Himself. If I can shock you—maybe I should—there's nine of them...[22]

Some may object to these quotes because neither Swaggart nor Hinn are preeminent spokesmen for Trinitarian Pentecostals. Yet,

---

[20] Robert A. Sabin, *"Must God be Triune to Love?"* in <u>Oneness News & Journal</u> 4 (Winter-Spring 1994): 1. For a more complete discussion on this subject see chapters one and two.

[21] Jimmy Swaggart, *"Brother Swaggart, Here's My Question,"* <u>The Evangelist</u>, (July, 1983), 15.

[22] Benny Hinn, "A New Spirit" a sermon delivered at Orlando Christian Center and aired on TBN broadcast "Praise the Lord" October 13, 1990. In an interview with Charisma magazine Hinn admitted this was "dumb," and suggested he was joking; however, the video gives no indication this was a joke!

it should be noted that their perception of the Godhead *mirrors* the teaching of Dake's Annotated Reference Bible which continues to be popular among Pentecostal laypersons. According to Dake:

> What we mean by Divine Trinity is that there are three separate and distinct persons in the Godhead, each one having His own personal spirit body, personal soul, and personal spirit in the sense that each human being, angel, or any other being has his own body, soul and spirit.[23]

> He (God) has a personal spirit body...bodily parts such as, back parts, heart, hands, and fingers, mouth, lips and tongue, feet, eyes, hair...He wears clothes, eats, dwells in a mansion and inn a city located on a material planet called heaven.[24]

The propensity toward tritheism among Trinitarian Pentecostals has also made inroads in Pentecostal scholastic circles through the doctrine of '*Social Trinitarianism*.'[25] This teaching addresses the so-called '*intra-trinitarian*' relations—maintaining that:

> ...within the inner divine being there is relationship; God is not alone...He is threefold—Father, Son and Holy Spirit, mutually related, loving one another eternally...Hence an understanding of the Trinity must begin with the fellowship of a plurality of persons, understood as three centers of conscious activity...[26]

Social Trinitarianism is bolstered through the Eastern Church's idea of *perichoresis* (περιχώρησις) a word used to:

> indicate the intimate union, mutual indwelling or mutual interpenetration of the three members of the Trinity with each other.[27]

---

[23] Finis Jennings Dake, *"Trinity"* in Dake's Annotated Reference Bible, (Lawrenceville, GA: Dake Ministries, 2013), 834. I am unaware of any Pentecostal denomination that officially adopts this view, but I have spoken with many Pentecostal pastors share this position.

[24] Finis Jennings Dake, God's Plan For Man, (Lawrenceville, GA: Dake Ministries, 1977), 57.

[25] This writer attended the 'Church of God Theological Seminary' from 2000 to 2006—where 'Social Trinitarianism' was eagerly embraced and taught by most of the staff.

[26] Norman Metzler, *"The Trinity in Contemporary Theology: Questioning the Social Trinity,"* Concordia Theological Quarterly, Vol., 67:3/4 (Fort Wayne, IN: Concordia, July/October 2003), 273, 276-277. Emphasis mine.

Perichoresis is formed from the Greek words περὶ (*peri*-around) and χορεύω (*choreau*-dance). This theological (<u>not Biblical</u>) term describes the 'mutual relationship' enjoyed in the Godhead, which is often referred to as '<u>*the divine dance*</u>'[28]

> The concept of *perichoresis*—envisioned through the metaphor of dance—holds possibilities for praising the triune unity. The concept of dancing together provides a way of portraying the distinctiveness and unity of the persons of the Trinity...[29]

Oneness Pentecostals argue Social Trinitarianism is—at best, incipient tritheism. Indeed, they would contend Metzler's '<u>*three centers of conscious activity*</u>' demand <u>three distinct consciousnesses,</u> which necessitates **three distinct entities!** Thus, they argue that, despite protests to the contrary—the Social Trinity doctrine ultimately results in three gods.[30] Moreover, it is believed this is proven by the corollary teaching of *perichoresis*, which is deemed a *philosophical* attempt to rescue Social Trinitarianism from overt tritheism.

In truth, most Oneness believers would consider terminology used by supporters of the Social Trinity (*i.e.'divine dance'*) as blasphemous and some scholars recognize:

> ...those holding to the social doctrine of the Trinity will find it more difficult to dialogue with Oneness pentecostals and will be more easily stereotyped as tritheists...Indeed, the important monotheistic roots of Christianity seem to be sacrificed by the social doctrine of the Trinity.[28]

---

[27] Donald K. McKim, *"Perichoresis,"* i n <u>Westminster Dictionary of Theological Terms</u>, (Louisville, KY: John Knox, 1996), 207.

[28] This phrase was used repeatedly by the staff at the Church of God Theological Seminary from 2000-2006.

[29] Ruth C. Duck, <u>Praising God: The Trinity in Christian Worship</u>, (Louisville, KY: John Knox Press, 1999), 36.

[30] This writer recognizes Social Trinitarianism is more complex than presented here. Furthermore, this writer recognizes that many of the most renown Trinitarians the concept of <u>three centers of consciousness</u> in God (*i.e. Karl Barth and Karl Rahner*).

[28] F. D. Macchia, *"Theology, Pentecostal,"* i n <u>International Dictionary of Pentecostal Charismatic Movements</u>, (Grand Rapids, MI: Zondervan,

Third, it is believed that any discussion about *intra-personal* relations within God is a *philosophical* and **not** a *Biblical* approach to discovering God's identity. This is important, in that, Jesus name Pentecostals contend that all streams of Trinitarian theology *flow from the river of Hellenism* **not** Biblical Hebraism. Moreover, they believe support for this charge is revealed in the twin pillars undergirding Trinitarian thought—namely, incomprehensibility and impassability. Indeed, the idea God:

> ...is incomprehensible was passed from Grecian philosophy into the creedal Christian faith almost without change. The very word incomprehensible was used several times in the Athanasian creed and the idea of incomprehensibility in regard to what the Greeks thought of as the 'One' was applied...not only to the Godhead...but also to the separate persons of the trinity.[29]

Though often accused of denying 'God's mystery,' this is not an accurate perception. Oneness theologians agree that God cannot be understood through intellect alone and affirm His mystery in accordance with Scripture (*i.e. 1Timothy 3:16*). However, they reject the notion that God is an unknowable mystery—in fact, Scripture teaches the church is to be the repository and steward of the mysteries of God.[30] Thus, while the *fullness* of God's revelation awaits the coming eschaton—Oneness theology recognizes the church can experience a revelatory understanding of the mighty God in Christ through the illumination of the Spirit!

In truth, the doctrine of God's incomprehensibility is viewed as a central weakness of Trinitarianism, not because it is *contrary to reason,* but because *reason cannot judge it at all!* Furthermore, it is

---

2002), 1127-1128.

[29] Robert A. Sabin, *"The Incomprehensible Trinity,"* Special Oneness News and Journal, (St. Paul, MN: Oneness Ministries International, n.d.), 41.

[30] 1Corinthians 4:1 *"Let a man so account of us, as ministers of Christ, and stewards of the mysteries of God."* (Luke 8:10; Ephesians 3:1-10; 1Timothy 3:16). Oneness Pentecostals also point out that Scripture demonstrates that God desires to reveal Himself to His people.

argued this philosophical idea is antithetical to the basic meaning of *revelation* —which signifies the uncovering of something hidden.

> What is the Trinity? It may be said, It is the doctrine of the Three in One...but when we come to remember, this is a mere speech, this is a mere exsiccated shell...till we say what sense is. Reason is no judge of that sense after it is once announced ...therefore, in the court of intellect must be held by hypocrites; or else some conception must be given, in what sense God can be Three, and yet the most simple of all possible existence.[31]

Equally objectionable is the doctrine of Divine <u>impassability</u>, which asserts that God is incapable of suffering. Although this *rampart* of historical Trinitarianism is designed to protect God's "otherness," Oneness scholars maintain it is contrary to Scripture. In fact, they contend this teaching actually denies the <u>reality of the incarnation</u>, for if God **cannot** suffer—He *did not* literally assume humanity in the person of Christ and the <u>Deity resident in Christ</u> must be something **other than God**!

In other words, the idea of Divine impassability abnegates the the atonement because God could not be localized in Christ;[32] thus, the one who was crucified **can not be the Fulness of God**!

> The horror aroused among the orthodox by the thought that God the Father had been nailed to a tree approached hysteria: and this...resulted from the fact that no one ever quite accepted the doctrine that Jesus was truly God. For were He actually so, why was it less horrible for him to suffer crucifixion?[33]

<u>Finally</u>, the doctrine of the Trinity is rejected based upon a restorationist view of ecclesiology—commonly found in early

---

[31] John Miller, <u>Is God A Trinity?</u>, reprint., (Hazelwood, MO: Word Aflame, 1975), 28-29. Miller was a Presbyterian minister and penned this work in the late 1800's.

[32] Scripture reveals God was localized in the person of Jesus. In Christ, God became something he was not—a human being and—**as a human**, He experienced conception, birth, suffering, death, burial, resurrection, glorification and ascension (2Cor. 5:19; 1Timothy 3:16; Colossians 1:15; 2:9 etc...).

[33] Martin A. Larson, <u>The Story of Christian Origins</u>, (Washington, D.C: New Republic, 1977), 541.

Oneness and Trinitarian Pentecostalism.[34] This position asserts the visible church gradually departed from the faith—culminating in a corporeal apostasy with the adoption of the Nicene Creed in 325 AD.[35]

> The Church had already been headed for apostasy for over two centuries before the Council of Nicaea...the council of Nicaea provided means whereby the outward institution...was more officially plunged into apostasy...Christ was dethroned as the head of the Church...the Church subtly lost its identity as the Church of God. It became the Church of Rome...[36]

If one embraces the principle of *Sola Scriptura* **and** espouses a restorationist view of church history—it is only logical to view the doctrine of the Trinity with a hermeneutic of suspicion. This is especially true when supporters of this teaching admit *"No such doctrine as that of the Trinity can be adequately proven by any citation of Scriptural passages."*[37] While many scholars would argue this is an exaggerated opinion—most Trinitarians would concur:

> There is no formal doctrine of the Trinity in the New Testament writings, if this means an explicit teaching that in one God there are three co-equal divine persons.[38]

It is true the **absence** of a *formal or explicit* Trinitarian doctrine in the New Testament does not necessarily invalidate this teaching. However, Oneness Pentecostals argue that Scripture formally and explicitly affirms Hebrew Monotheism—*which precludes eternal*

---

[34] Restorationist ecclesiology dominated Pentecostalism for the first 50 years through the writings of such leaders as Charles Parham, William Seymour (Trinitarian); Frank Ewart and G.T. Haywood (Oneness) etc...

[35] Acts 20:28-30; 2Thessalonians 2:1-3; Jude 3, 19. See Chapter II of this work for a more detailed analysis of this view.

[36] Wade H. Phillips, The Church in History and Prophecy, (Cleveland, TN: White Wing, 1990), 56-57. Supporters of this view recognize that God's people enjoyed experiential during the "dark ages." Yet, they argue the *original apostolic 'faith'* was *'buried'* by man-made creeds—thus, necessitating a *restoration* and not simply a *reformation*.

[37] Charles Hodge, Systematic Theology, (New York, NY: Charles Scribner & Sons, 1883), Vol 1, 446.

[38] E. J. Fortman, The Triune God, (Philadelphia, PA: Westminster, 1972), 32.

distinctions in God—thus, invalidating Trinitarianism. This means the rationale behind their rejection of the Trinity is in keeping with the original impetus of *Sola Scriptura, restorationism* and *primitivism*—the original hallmarks of Pentecostalism.

The Oneness contribution to Christianity is their desire to restore the pristine Hebraic-Christian understanding of God's identity in the name and person of Jesus Christ. Simplistic explanations of Oneness teaching such as *"they believe Jesus is his own father"* or they *"...contend that Jesus is all. According to them, He is the Father; He is the Son; and He is the Holy Ghost"*[39] fail to do justice to a theology that is deeply rooted in Hebraic thought and expression.

---

[39] Wade H. Horton, Fifty Undeniable Facts that Prove the Trinitarian Concept of God, (Cleveland, TN: Pathway Press, 1964), 6. Simple and trite explanations of Oneness belief are common in Trinitarian Pentecostalism. Unfortunately *many* Oneness believers are guilty using the same type of explanations with respect to Trinitarianism.

The Mighty God In Christ

Oneness theology begins with an understanding that God is one, incorporeal and invisible Spirit, with no eternal distinctions in His nature. The <u>Father, Son,</u> and <u>Holy Ghost</u> are not perceived as <u>eternally distinct hypostases</u> in God—but descriptive appellations that emphasize:

> God's redemptive roles or revelations...Father refers to God in family relationship to humanity; Son refers to God in flesh; and the Spirit refers to God in spiritual activity.[40]

God is Father by virtue of creation (Mal. 2:10), and through the begetting of *'the Son'* (Heb. 1:5); howbeit, unlike Trinitarians, they do not subscribe to the idea that the "Son of God" is a distinct hypostasis in God's being. Rather, when used of Jesus, "Son of God" is an <u>incarnational title</u> that denotes Jesus' *full humanity* **or** the **union** of <u>humanity</u> and <u>Deity</u> resulting from God's visible manifestation in flesh.[41]

Likewise, instead of viewing the Holy Spirit as an ontological eternal distinction in God—Oneness theology retains a more Hebraic conception—simply identifying the Spirit in terms of the one true God in transcendence and spiritual activity. Therefore, it is believed Jesus Christ is **not** the incarnation of one hypostasis of God—the one indivisible Spirit of the Father—thus, he is **all** the fullness of the Godhead bodily.

> It is not the Second Person of the Trinity but the Spirit, the full undifferentiated Deity, who becomes incarnate in the human person, Jesus...In Father-Son terms, the Father is the divine Spirit who indwells the human Son...Yet the Father continues in transcendence after the Incarnation in the same manner as does the divine Logos in Trinitarian theology.[42]

In light of the above explanation—it seems strange that Oneness believers are often accused of *denying* the Father. In fact, it seems

---

[40] David K. Bernard, *"The Oneness View of Jesus Christ,"* 8.

[41] This is examined more extensively in the next section.

[42] David Reed, *"Oneness Pentecostalism,"* in <u>Dictionary of Pentecostal Charismatic Movements,</u> (Grand Rapids, MI: Zondervan, 1988), 650-651.

they actually *locate* the Father **in** the *person* and *name* of Jesus Christ. In short, Oneness theology teaches that in the incarnation God came to exist in a new way—as a human being—without compromising His simultaneous existence as transcendent Spirit. Thus, they neither *deny* the Father **nor** do they teach Jesus *is* the Father. Rather, they believe the Father is **fully**, *but not exclusively,* **localized** in Jesus Christ.[43]

> ...our knowledge and experience of God is a radically Christocentric one: only in the human face of the Son and His name can one see the Father. Not that the Father and the Holy Spirit are absorbed in the Son, but He who was in the human Son is the one divine Person who is elsewhere called Father and Holy Spirit...all that God is, is seen in Jesus Christ.[44]

Oneness Pentecostals affirm the full Deity and humanity of Jesus Christ—believing that He is the visible incarnation of Yahweh, the one true God and Father. Thus, they accept Jesus' declaration *"...and he that seeth me seeth Him that sent me" (John 12:45).* Jesus is **both** the me and Him—because He is the visible embodiment of the one God and Father—not merely the incarnation of a singular hypostasis in God!

> To wit, that **God** was **in** Christ reconciling the world unto himself...(2Corinthians 5:19).

> ...great is the mystery of godliness: **God** was manifest in the flesh, [who? God] justified in the Spirit, [who? God] seen of angels, [who? God] preached unto the Gentiles, [who? God] believed on in the world, [who? God] received up into glory, [who? God] (1Timothy 3:16).

> Who is the **image** of the **invisible God**, the firstborn of every creature: (Colossians 1:15).

> For **in** **him** dwelleth all the **fulness** of the Godhead bodily (Colossians 2:9).

---

[43] This raises questions concerning the accuracy of the common term "Jesus Only." In the earliest years of the Movement—this label was at times used as a self-designator. However, in recent years it is most often used as a term of derision; thus, most Oneness believers have abandoned this label due to the inaccurate perception it conveys.

[44] David Reed, *"Aspects of the Origins of Oneness Pentecostalism,"* Aspects of Pentecostal-Charismatic Origins, (Plainfield, NJ: Logos, 1975), 150.

One of the primary differences between Oneness and Trinitarian views of God is their understanding of the Deity resident in the person and name of Jesus. The doctrine of the Trinity precisely identifies the Deity of Jesus as the eternal hypostasis referred to as "God the Son."

> The incarnation was the act of <u>God the Son</u> whereby <u>he</u> took to himself a human nature...the <u>eternal Son of God</u> took to himself a truly human nature.[45]

Oneness scholars point out this perception of the incarnation is based on a second-century view of the Godhead and is radically different from the first-century Hebrew-Christian understanding of God. Indeed, they maintain that the Bible never teaches that "God the Son" or a singular "hypostasis of God" was incarnate in the person of Jesus Christ!

Interestingly, the above author also argues it would have been impossible for the Father to be incarnate!

> Could God the Father have come instead of God the Son to die for our sins? Could the Holy Spirit have sent God the Father to die for our sins, and then sent God the Son to apply redemption to us? **No**, it does not seem that these things could have happened...[46]

Oneness Pentecostals object to Grudem's position on the grounds that Scripture explicitly teaches the Deity localized in the person and name of Jesus—is the <u>Spirit of the Father</u>.

> If ye had known me, ye should have known **my Father** also: and <u>from henceforth</u> ye <u>know him</u> and have **seen him**. Philip saith unto him..He that hath <u>seen me</u> hath <u>seen the Father</u>...the words that I speak unto you I speak not of myself: but the **Father that dwelleth in me**, he doeth the works (John 14:7-10).

John 14:7-10 is unique for three primary reasons. First, Jesus plainly tells his disciples "ἀπό ἄρτι γινώσκω αὐτός καί ὁράω αὐτός" (*...from henceforth ye know him, and have seen him*) with reference to the Father. The word translated "henceforth" is the

---

[45] Wayne Grudem, <u>Systematic Theology</u>, (Grand Rapids, MI: Zondervan, 1994), 543, 557. Emphasis mine.

[46] Ibid, 249-250. Emphasis mine.

Greek word ἄρτι, which refers to *"a point of time simultaneous with the event of the discourse itself—'now.'*[47] Thus, Jesus claims <u>right now</u> the disciples can ὁράω (see)—*"to perceive by the eye"*[48] the Father. Interestingly, John specifically uses the perfect tense form of "see;" thus, emphasizing *"the continuing effects of a completed action..."*[49] In other words, the Father is <u>now seen</u> because He made himself visible at a specific point in time.

Second, when Philip questions Jesus about these words—asking him to "shew" the Father—Jesus responds by asking Philip why he does not recognize or 'know' him. The Greek word translated 'know' is ἔγνωκάς, which means:

> to learn to know a person <u>through direct personal experience</u>, implying <u>a continuity of relationship</u>--'to know, to become acquainted with, to be familiar.[50]

After his question Jesus explicitly states, *"he that hath seen me hath seen the Father."* As previously stated, the primary definition of the word translated "seen" (ὁράω) is *"to see with the eyes."*[51] Oneness scholars maintain this statement can <u>only</u> be true **IF** Jesus is the visible incarnation of the Father!

Third, John 14:10 affirms Jesus is the incarnation of the Father and **not** an eternal hypostasis <u>in</u> God—through Jesus' unequivocal declaration that the one doing the works in his ministry is ὁ δὲ πατὴρ ὁ ἐν ἐμοὶ μένων (*lit. but the Father the (one) in me dwelling*).

---

[47] Louw & Nida, νῦν, in <u>Greek-English Lexicon of the New Testament Based on Semantic Domains</u>, (New York: NY, United Bible Societies, 1989), eletronic edition Oak Tree Software, Inc.

[48] Fredrick William Danker, ὁράω, in <u>A Greek-English Lexicon of the New Testament and other Early Christian Literature</u>, (Chicago, IL: University of Chicago, 2000), electronic edition.

[49] Gerald L. Stevens, "Perfect Active and Future Perfect" in <u>Stevens' NT Greek Grammar</u>, Second Edition, (University Press of America, 1997) Electronic Edition, Oak Tree Software, Inc.

[50] Louw & Nida, γινώσκω. Emphasis mine.

[51] Joseph Henry Thayer, D.D., ὁράω in <u>Thayer's Greek-English Lexicon of the New Testament</u>, electronic edition, Oak Tree Software, Inc.

Oneness theologians argue that John 14:10 expressly identifies the Deity resident in Jesus—as the FATHER by using the preposition *'in' (ἐν)* which:

> ...expresses the idea of 'within,' whether of rest or of motion depending on the context...The preposition merely states that the location is within the bounds marked by the word with which it occurs. It does not mean 'near,' but 'in,' that is 'inside.'[52]

John couples ἐν with the word **μένων** *'dwelleth'* meaning:

> remain, stay...a person or thing remains where she, or it is. Of a location stay, often in the special sense live, dwell, lodge...[53]

> a primary verb; to stay (in a given place, state, relation...abide, continue, dwell...[54]

John 14:7-10 clearly teaches the Deity residing or abiding **within** the man, Christ Jesus is that of the Father. Oneness Pentecostals point out that this is contrary to the teaching of Trinitarianism. Moreover, they argue there is **no Scripture** intimating Jesus is the incarnation of one hypostasis in the Godhead. Rather, they insist the Bible repeatedly affirms Jesus is the visible personification of Yahweh, the one true God who is designated as **FATHER** (Isa. 63:16; 64:8; Malachi 2:10; Isaiah 7:14; 9:6; Matthew 1:23; 1Timothy 3:16; 2Corinthians 5:19 etc...).

---

[52] A. T. Robertson, *Proper Prepositions in the N.T.*, in Grammar of the Greek New Testament in the Light of Historical Research, electronic edition, 2006.

[53] Fredrick William Danker, μένω.

[54] James Strong, μένω, in Strong's Greek Dictionary of the New Testament, electronic edition.

The 'Sonship' of Jesus Christ

Oneness Pentecostals fully embrace the <u>absolute Deity</u> and <u>genuine humanity</u> of Jesus Christ and affirm He is the *"Son of God."* However, their understanding of "Sonship" is different from Trinitarianism, for they believe Jesus is *"...the Son of God since God's Spirit literally caused His conception."*[55] Thus, the title '<u>Son of God</u>' and the redemptive-mediatoral work of '*Sonship*' is integrally linked to the incarnation. In contrast, Trinitarians espouse an ontological model of Sonship—grounded in eternal <u>intra-personal relationships</u> within God.

Oneness scholars reject the Trinitarian model of Sonship because it is contrary to Biblically revealed Monotheism.[56] Moreover, this view places Jesus **in** the Godhead—which is impossible given that θεοτης (Godhead) is a **singular** *"...abstract noun for theos."*[57] In other words, there is nothing inherently unique in this word to support the idea of eternal hypostatic distinctions in God—rather, θεοτης argues against such a notion for it is defined as:

> the state of being god, divine character/nature, deity divinity, used as an abstract noun for θεός.[58]

> ...θεότης is abstract of θεός...the former means Godhead, that which makes God, God; the latter means divinity, that which renders divine.[59]

The Bible does not teach that Jesus is a distinction **in** the Godhead—but declares that *"...**in him** dwelleth all the fulness of the*

---

[55] David K. Bernard, *"Oneness Christology,"* <u>Symposium on Oneness Pentecostalism,</u> (Hazelwood, MO: Word Aflame, 1988), 128.

[56] The First and Second study of this volume clearly demonstrated the revelation of Monotheism bequeathed to the nation of Israel, sanctioned by Jesus and embraced by the early Hebrew-Christian church precluded the idea of distinct hypostases in God's being.

[57] Denis W. Vinyard, ed., <u>The New Testament Greek-English Dictionary: Zeta-Kappa,</u> in <u>The Complete Biblical Library,</u> (Springfield, MO: 1991), 13:100.

[58] Danker, θεότης.

[59] Charles Hodge, <u>Hodge's Systematic Theology,</u> electronic edition used by permission of DanielJ. Dyke, formatted by Oak Tree Software, Inc.

Godhead bodily" (Colossians 2: 9). In short, Oneness Pentecostals believe:

> ...the one true God is without parts or distinctions, and that Jesus is the full and final revelation of this one invisible God.[60]

Unfortunately, because of their emphasis on the Deity of Jesus, the Oneness view of '*Sonship*' is often misunderstood—even by those sympathetic to the Oneness message.

> Oneness theology teaches a sonship that is exclusively human. By virtue of his virgin birth he is the unblemished humanity that is finally given as a blood sacrifice for sin on the cross.[61]

Oneness Pentecostals deny the Trinitarian concept of "Sonship;" yet it is **inaccurate** to state that Oneness doctrine teaches the "Son of God" always and exclusively denotes the humanity of Jesus.

> Son of God *may* refer solely to the human nature or it may refer to God manifested in flesh—that is, deity in the human nature. Son of God never means the incorporeal Spirit alone, however. We can never use the term "Son" correctly apart from the humanity of Jesus Christ.[62]

In truth, Oneness Pentecostals teach that the title '*Son of God*' **_exclusively_** *encompasses the incarnation*. Thus, while the term *can stress* Jesus' humanity—it is also used with reference to Divinity *fused* with humanity (i.e. incarnation) but it is **never** used as a title of Deity *independent of the incarnation*.

Oneness Pentecostals believe Jesus is the "*Son of God*," but reject unbiblical terminology such as '*God the Son*' or '*eternally begotten.*' In fact, a threefold argument is used to show "Sonship" is **not** predicated on *eternal intra-personal relationships within God.* First,

---

[60] David A. Reed, In Jesus' Name The History and Beliefs of Oneness Pentecostals, in Journal of Pentecostal Theology Supplement Series, vol. 31., (Dorst DT, UK: Deo Publishing, 2008), 255.

[61] Ibid., 295. Reed is one of the most objective non-Oneness writers of post-modernity; yet, his statement in this regard is inaccurate. This may be—in part—due to poor articulation by Oneness believers. Indeed, for over 18 years—this writer has read Oneness publications and listened to several debates and this is often how "Sonship" is articulated.

[62] David K. Bernard, The Oneness of God, (Hazelwood, MO: Word Aflame, 1998), 98-99.

Oneness supporters argue the idea of an *"eternally begotten Son"* is contradictory. Indeed, the very word *"begotten"* means: *"to cause something to come into existence primarily through procreation or parturition;"*[63] thus, it is nonsensical to maintain one can be *eternally produced from a seed!*

Second, the Old Testament <u>never</u> refers to the Son of God as a hypostatic distinction of God. Rather, when used of the Messiah, *"Son of God"* is always *prophetic* or *proleptic*; thus, **anticipating** the incarnation. In fact, several Old Testament passages attributed to Jesus—are actually misconstrued and-or misapplied. For example in Daniel 3:25 Nebuchadnezzar declares:

> ...Lo, I see four men loose, walking in the midst of the fire, and they have no hurt; and the form of the fourth is like the Son of God (Daniel 3:25 KJV).

Many Trinitarian laymen believe the *"fourth-man"* refers to Jesus in his "pre-incarnate" state as the "eternal Son of God." However, the context of this verse reveals this is simply not the case. In the Hebrew text the word "God" is plural and there is **no** definite article (THE) before "Son" in **either** the Hebrew text or the Greek Septuagint. Hence, Nebuchadnezzar's declaration suggests the *"fourth man"* is like *"**a** son of God or gods."* Understood in this way—the pagan king is referring to an angel—a view supported by the Septuagint which plainly states the likeness of the "fourth" is as ἀγγέλουρ θεοῦ (an angel of God).[64]

The parallel readings of the Septuagint[65] follow the Hebrew text and identify the likeness of the fourth as υἱῷ θεός (a son of God). Yet, in verse twenty eight the <u>Hebrew,</u> <u>Greek</u> and <u>English</u> text agree that Nebuchadnezzar explicitly identifies the *fourth man in*

---

[63] Danker, γεννάω.

[64] Alfred Rahlfs, edt., <u>Greek Septuagint (LXX1)</u>, electronic edition, (Stuttgart, Germany: Deutsche Bibelgesellschaft, 2006).

[65] Alfred Rahlfs, edt., <u>Greek Septuagint (parallel texts) (LXX2)</u>, electronic edition, (Stuttgart, Germany: Deutsche Bibelgesellschaft, 2006).

the fire as an angel, saying the God of Shadrach, Meshach and Abednego:

> ...hath sent his angel...(KJV)
>
> דִּי־שְׁלַח מַלְאֲכֵהּ (who sent his angel)[66]
>
> ὃς ἀπέστειλεν τὸν ἄγγελον αὐτοῦ (who sent the angel of him)[67]
>
> ὃς ἀπέστειλεν τὸν ἄγγελον αὐτοῦ (who sent the angel of him)[68]

Third, according to Oneness Pentecostals—Scripture affirms the *Father-Son* relationship has a **substantial** origin *in human history*. While they agree the visible manifestation of the Son of God was God's eternal redemptive purpose—the *Father-Son* relationship was actuated **through** the incarnation. Psalm 2:7 teaches the 'Son' is <u>begotten</u> on a particular "<u>day</u>" and the writer of Hebrews expands upon this, saying:

> For unto which of the angels said he at any time, Thou art my Son, <u>This day</u> have I begotten thee? And again, I **will** be to him a Father, And he **shall** be to me a Son? (Hebrews 1:5).

The Greek text substantiates the translation '*I will*' and '*he shall*,' for both words are *future indicative verbs*.[69] Hence, the relationship between the Father and the Son is not *eternally ontological*—but is a result of the <u>historical incarnation</u>! This view is strengthened by the Apostle Paul in his epistle to the Galatians and this is evident in both the English and Greek Text.

> But when the fulness of the time was come, God <u>sent forth</u> his Son, <u>made of</u> a woman, <u>made under</u> the law (Galatians 4:4).

---

[66] Karl Elliger, William Rudolph and Adrian Schenker edt., *Daniel 3:28*, in <u>Biblia Hebraica</u>, (Stuttgart, Germany, Deutsche Bibelgesselschaft, 1983) electronic edition J. Alan Groves Center for Advanced Biblical Research 1991-2010. Translation through interlinear.

[67] Rahlfs, *"Daniel 3:95"* (LXX1).

[68] Rahlfs, *"Daniel 3:95"* (LXX2). Another equally misconstrued passage is Proverbs 8:25-30. Some assert this passage is speaking of the so-called *"eternal son of God."* However, the opening verses explicitly reveal this is a reference to <u>wisdom</u> and <u>understanding</u> **both** of which are personified in the feminine gender!

[69] Maurice A. Robinson and William G. Pierpont, <u>The New Testament in the Original Greek: Byzantine Textform 2005</u>, electronic edition.

ἐξαπέστειλεν ὁ θεὸς τὸν υἱὸν αὐτοῦ <u>γενόμενον</u> ἐκ γυναικὸς <u>γενόμενον</u> ὑπὸ νόμον[70]

This passage is believed to corroborate the incarnational view of Sonship because it does <u>not</u> teach God sent an *eternally begotten* Son into the world. Rather, the Apostle Paul specifically uses the Greek word γενόμενον twice—to describe the <u>type</u> of Son sent by God. This is significant for the primary definition of γενόμενον is:

> To come into being through process of birth or natural production...to come into existence, *be made, be created..*[71].
>
> *to come into existence; to be created, exist by creation...to be born, produced grow...*[72]

Moreover—Galatians 4:4 explicitly states the 'begetting' of the Son was **not** in eternity past, but that He was begotten ἐκ (*"from, out from..by means of..."*)[73] γυναικός (woman) and[74] ὑπὸ (*a marker of a controlling...institution..under the control of...*)[75] νόμον (*constitutional or statutory legal system*).[76] Thus, both Hebrews 1:5 and Galatians 4:4 clearly teach an incarnational view of Sonship and <u>not</u> the second-century doctrine of "Eternal Sonship."

While rejecting the ecclesiastical doctrine of eternal Sonship, Oneness Pentecostals do <u>not</u> deny the eternality of the Son. Yet, whereas Trinitarians believe the Son is an ontological eternally distinct hypostasis in the Godhead—Oneness supporters maintain the Son is the incarnation of the eternal one—*"...the Mighty God, The Everlasting Father..."* (Isaiah 9:6). Furthermore, because they

---

[70] Ibid., Galatians 4:4.

[71] Danker, γίνομαι.

[72] William D. Mounce, edt., γίνομαι, in <u>Mounce Concise Greek-English Dictionary of the New Testament</u>, electronic edition, www.teknia.com, 2011, formatted by Oak tree Software Inc.

[73] Barclay M. Newman, ἐκ, in <u>A Concise Greek-English Dictionary of the New Testament, Revised Edition</u>, electronic edition., (Stuttgart, Germany: Deutsche Bibelgessellschaft, 2010) Oak Tree Software, Inc.

[74] Danker, γυνή.

[75] Louw & Nida, ὑπό.

[76] Danker, νόμος.

believe the title "Son" is a incarnational designator—the eternality of the man, Christ Jesus is understood as <u>proleptic</u>—"That which anticipates a future event."[77]

Oneness theologians believe further support for a proleptic or prophetic anticipatory view of Sonship is revealed in the prologue of John's Gospel.

> In the beginning was the Word, and the Word was with God, and the Word was God (John 1:1).

Interestingly, Trinitarians use this passage to "*prove*" the '<u>Word</u>' (λόγος) is an *eternal hypostatic distinction* in God. Their method of interpretation is based on the model of eternal sonship—thus, purporting that John's use of θεόν (God) and θεὸς (God) refers to TWO distinct hypostases in God.[78]

The Oneness and Trinitarian view of John 1:1 forces one to ask: "*Which interpretation accurately conveys the message of John 1:1?*" The answer to this is discovered by examining the Greek Text of John's prologue.

> Εν ἀρχῇ ἦν ὁ λόγος καὶ ὁ λόγος ἦ πρὸς τὸν θεόν καὶ θεὸς ἦν ὁ λόγος
>
> in beginning was the word and the word pertains to God and God was the word.[79]

Those who support the Oneness view of this passage argue that there is no grammatical basis suggesting θεόν is a distinct entity or hypostasis from θεὸς.[80] In truth, the Greek and English text states

---

[77] Donald K. McKim, '*prolepsis,*' i n <u>Westminster Dictionary of Theological Terms</u>, (Louisville, KY: John Knox, 1996), 223.

[78] This is not usually expressed verbally; yet, the Trinitarian view of this text demands that the first use of God (θεον) be interpreted as the distinct hypostasis of 'THE FATHER,' while the second use of God (θεὸς) must be the distinct hypostasis of 'THE ETERNAL SON.'

[79] See pg. 84-87 for a more detailed treatment of John 1:1 and the translation of the phrase προς τον θεον as '*pertaining to.*'

[80] One might argue the definite article is used before θεόν (the God) but not before θεὸς (God) but this would not support Trinitarianism but would suggest there is **one** THE GOD and ?another? "GOD" who differs from THE GOD. Of course, this would be Scripturally in error.

the 'word' is with THE GOD and the 'word' is THIS SAME GOD! In fact, if **θεόν** refers to a *hypostatic distinction of God — the 'word' is this same hypostatic distinction*!

Most importantly—Oneness scholars believe the Trinitarian view of John 1:1 is rooted in a Greek philosophical understanding of the Logos that ignores the Hebraic milieu informing John's use of this word.

> The early Christians...were Jews. We must try to avoid describing the Godhead in Gentile terms. When the Greek Apologists started thinking like Gentiles, they became confused...We will not have to worry if we always remember to keep thinking like the early Christian did—to think 'Jewish.'[81]

There is no scholarly consensus regarding the specific Hebrew word forming the basis of the prologue's use of Logos. Yet, many Oneness and Trinitarian scholars believe the answer is revealed in the Hebrew word דָּבָר (dābār).[82]

Used as a verb, דָּבַר (dābar) focuses on the activity of speaking; yet, as a noun it is broader—encompassing speech, thought, reason and cause.[83] Moreover, theologically, this word denotes:

> an expression of the thoughts and will of God...the voluntative manifestation of Yahweh...NT usage agree with the OT insofar as "word of God" indicates the self-revelation of God in the spirit...[84]
>
> When dāvār is used for "word," it essentially means what Yahweh has said...the concept here is that the "word" is both

---

[81] Charles D. Wilson, *"The Religious Background of the Logos,"* in <u>Symposium on Oneness Pentecostalism 1988 to 1990,</u> (Hazelwood, MO: Word Aflame, 1990), 252.

[82] Frank Ritchel Ames, דָּבַר in <u>New International Dictionary of Old Testament Theology & Exegesis</u> (NIDOTTE) Willem A. VanGemeren, edt., electronic edition, (Grand Rapids, MI: Zondervan, 1997).

[83] David J. A. Clines edt., דָּבָר in The Concise Dictionary of Classical Hebrew, electronic edition, Oak Tree Software, 2009.

[84] G. Gerleman, דָּבָר in Theological Lexicon of the Old Testament (TLOT), Jenni-Westermann edts., electronic edition (Hendrickson, 1997).

the vehicle of communication and the thing signified at the same time.[85]

The substantive and theological use of דָּבָר (dābār) corresponds with the Classical Hellenic understanding of λόγος as "...*a word which...embodies a conception or idea*."[86] Thus, Oneness scholars maintain God's λόγος refers to His *reason* or *plan* but **also** includes the expression of His thoughts and plans.

> The Greek word logos means both the expression of a thought and the inward thought itself. Greek philosophers emphasized the logos as 'thought' or 'reason' while Jewish thinkers placed emphasis on the 'word,' or expression of inward thoughts. In John 1 the Logos is portrayed both as 'thought,' or plan of redemption in the mind of God, and the expression of that plan in the incarnation.[87]

The Hebraic foundation of John's use of λόγος is substantiated in John 1:14—which reveals God's eternal 'word' is *visibly personified or expressed* in the name and person of Jesus Christ. Thus, John's use of the λόγος in John 1:1-14 encompasses the idea of eternal **purpose** and historical **actualization**!

> And the Word was made flesh, and dwelt among us, (and we beheld his glory, the glory as of the only begotten of the Father,) full of grace and truth (John 1:14).

In truth, God's eternal λόγος of redemption that was actualized or personified through the incarnation was so **certain** that the man, Christ Jesus is the *eternal referent* of creation!

> ...Jesus Christ, who did not exist *actually* until he was born at Bethlehem, was the central figure of all creation. In other words, when God did the creating, he did it totally alone, but toward God, facing him in time, was the ideal figure, the envisaged image of one in God's mind whom God was to be.[88]

---

[85] Thoralf Gilbrant edt., דָּבָר The Old Testament Hebrew-English Dictionary Gimel-Zayin in The Complete Biblical Library: Old Testament, (Springfield, MO: World Library Press, 1996), 1746.

[86] Joseph Henry Thayer, Thayer's Greek-English Lexicon of the New Testament, electronic edition, hypertexted by Oak Tree Software Inc.

[87] Wilson, 230.

[88] Robert A. Sabin, "*Supposed Problems and Anomalies to Oneness Truth*," Special Oneness News & Journal, (Saint Paul, MN: Oneness Ministries

Support for this idea is revealed in Romans 5:14, which declares the first man, Adam *"...is the figure of him that was to come."* The word translated *'figure'* τύπος means both a *'copy'* and *'archetype' or pattern.*[89] These definitions are antithetical to one another and the context does not clearly reveal which meaning the Apostle Paul intends. This poses no difficulty for Oneness scholars—for they believe the ambiguity is *intentional* precisely because both meanings are intended! Indeed, the first Adam was the archetype or pattern of the second Adam—Jesus in a **substantial** or **tangible** sense. Yet, the first Adam is also a copy or pattern of the second Adam—for he was created on the basis of God's incarnation in the person of Jesus, the visible embodiment of the redemptive λόγος.

The Oneness view of the λόγος coincides with their perception of 'Sonship.' Indeed, both are integrally linked to the incarnation rather than ontological intra-relations within God.[90] In fact, they would argue God **did not need** a Son—but WE (fallen humanity) needed 'the Son' to reconcile the human family to God. This is the great redemptive truth taught in the Scripture!

> For **unto us** a child is born, **unto us** a son is given; and the government shall be upon his shoulder: and his name shall be called Wonderful, Counsellor, The Mighty God, Everlasting Father, Prince of Peace (Isaiah 9:6).

The word rendered *'unto'* is the Hebrew preposition לָ (lanu), which means *'to, for, in regard to...towards or reference to...'*[91] This clearly demonstrates that 'Sonship' is not germane to God's *'intra-relationships'* but is *with reference to* or *for the sake of* humanity! In other words, God's assumption of humanity—through the child born and son given is grounded in the salvific work of redemption

---

International, n.d.) 18. See Romans 4:17.

[89] Danker, edit, τύπος.

[90] Oneness theology rejects the idea that God's relational attributes necessitate eternal ontological distinctions in His being (see chapter 1).

[91] Francis Brown, S.R. Driver and Charles Briggs, A Hebrew and English Lexicon of the Old Testament, (Dania Beach, FL: Scribe, Inc.), electronic edition.

a n d <u>mediation</u>. While the soteriological work of 'the Son' in redemption and mediation is eternally purposed in God—the actualization of God's redemption has as substantial **historical** <u>point of origin</u> and a **eschatological** <u>point of realization</u>!

In Oneness theology the climax of experiential salvation results in the culmination of the redemptive mediatory work of 'Sonship.' This understanding is supported—in part—in the Apostle Paul's first epistle to the Corinthians.[92]

> Then cometh **the end**, when he shall have delivered up the kingdom to God, even the Father... For he must reign, till he hath put all enemies under his feet. The last enemy that shall be destroyed is death...And **when all things** shall be subdued unto him, then **shall the Son also himself be subject unto him** that put all things under him, **that God may be all in all** (1Corinthians 15:24-28).

The above passage provides a glimpse into the eschaton—and refers to the day when αὐτός ὁ υἱὸς ὑποταγήσεται *(lit. he the son <u>will be subject</u>)* to the one who put all things under his feet. The word rendered '*subjected*' (ὑποταγήσεται) is:

> to cause to be in a submissive relationship, to subject, to subordinate...[93]

Oneness scholars point out that this passage is problematic if one understands 'the Son' as an ontologically distinct hypostasis of God.

<u>IF</u> Paul's use of '<u>the Son</u>' in 1Corinthians 15:28 denotes a Divine hypostasis in the Godhead—it is strange that the verb '<u>subjected</u>' (ὑποταγήσεται) is written in the <u>passive voice</u>.[94] Indeed, unlike the Greek <u>middle voice</u>, which indicates <u>the subject</u> has self-interest or

---

[92] A more detailed examination of 'Sonship' and 1Corinthians 15:24-28 is addressed in *"The Scriptural Significance of the Right Hand of God"* in <u>Oneness Pentecostal Thematic Studies</u>, Vol. 3., by James Hogsten.

[93] Danker, ὑποτάσσω.

[94] Rex. A. Koivisto, <u>Morphological Tagging</u> for <u>The New Testament in the Original Greek: Byzantine Textform 2005</u>, electronic edition.

participates in the action of the verb[95] — in the passive voice *"the subject is represented as the recipient of the action. He is acted upon."*[96] Thus, according to the text, 'the Son' is **not** a participant in the subjection—but he—**himself**—is subjected!

Furthermore, it is evident 1Corinthians 15:28 is not referring to one *hypostasis of God* being made subject to another *hypostasis of God* because the purpose or goal of the Son's subjection is ἵνα ᾖ οʽ θεὸς (*in order that the God*) τὰ πάντα ἐν πᾶσιν (*be all in all*). This is nonsensical **if** the Son is a distinct person of the Godhead! Indeed, this would mean one of the *'hypostases'* i s **not THE** God or that there are two entities in spatial relationship—one of whom **is THE** God while the other is—something **other** than God! Thus, Oneness Pentecostals maintain that in 1Corinthians 15:28, the Son:

> ...refers to a specific role that God temporarily assumed for the purpose of redemption...When the reasons for the Sonship cease to exist...Sonship will be submerged back into the greatness of God...It is in this sense...Sonship will end.[97]

It is interesting to note that most Trinitarian expositors deviate from their usual position regarding the identity of 'the Son' when addressing 1Corinthians 15:24-28—adopting a Oneness view of this text.

> ...the language of the subordination of the Son to the Father is functional, referring to his 'work' of redemption, not ontological, referring to his being as such.[98]

> ...then Christ shall be subjected to God the Father. This simply involves the subjection of sonship.[99]

---

[95] Gerald L. Stevens, *Present Middle/Passive Indicative,* in New Testament Greek, second edition, University Press of America, 1997., electronic edition.

[96] A.T. Robertson, *The Passive Voice,* electronic edition.

[97] Bernard, The Oneness of God, 107-108.

[98] Gordon D. Fee, The First Epistle To the Corinthians, in The New International Commentary on the New Testament, (Grand Rapids, MI: Eerdmans, 1987), 760.

[99] Paul A. Hamar, *1Corinthians,* in The Complete Biblical Library vol 7. Romans-Corinthians, (Springfield, MO: World Library Press, 1986), 469.

In short, Oneness and Trinitarian scholars agree Paul's discourse on the subjection of the Son refers to the mediatory redemptive work of the glorified Messiah.

> The interpretation which affirms that the Son shall then be subject to the Father...it means the Incarnate Son, the Mediator, the man that was born and that was raised from the dead, and to whom this wide dominion had been give, should resign that dominion, and that the government should be re-assumed by the Divinity as God.[100]

In Oneness theology 1Corinthians 15:24-28 further confirms the temporal, salvific purpose of 'Sonship' and highlights the fallacy of using eternal ontological intra-personal distinctions as the foundation of 'Sonship.'

Oneness Christology does **not** teach the '*subjection*' of the Son is an ontological proposition; rather it is a functional declaration that is specifically related to the God's redemptive-mediatory work in the person and name of Jesus. Indeed, for Oneness Pentecostals the historical incarnation carries eternal consequences, in that humanity is now permanently incorporated into God's essential identity. Hence, the '*Lamb*'—*the human being within whom Yahweh resides*—remains as the visible image of the invisible God—and the glory of God will continually be apprehended in the face of Jesus Christ *throughout eternity* (Revelation 21:23; 22:3-4).

---

[100] Albert Barnes, Notes on the New Testament, (Grand Rapids, MI: Baker, 1950), internet resource, http://www.ccel.org. Adam Clarke also concurs with this view in his Commentary on 1Corinthians 15.

A Hebrew understanding of God's name[101]

Closely linked to their understanding of God and His identity in Jesus Christ, is the Oneness understanding of God's name. While focusing on 'The Name' may seem strange in post-modern Western society—it must be remembered that:

> ...among the ancient Semites the concept of a 'name' had a real bearing upon the functions and personality of the individual involved.[102]

In short, the Hebraic view of a name transcends familial labels of identification—encompassing the personality or characteristics of the '*bearer*' of the name. Scripture confirms this truth by recording instances where God changed the names of His servants to *reflect an inward change in the individual, his relationship to God or both.*[103]

The importance of a name is especially evident when examining the Scriptural revelation of God's name, which "...*signifies His self-revelation...His character, power, authority, and manifested presence...*"[104] In fact,

> The core of Oneness theology is the belief that God has revealed himself through his name, beginning in the OT. The Name is more than a human designation for divine reality. It is God's method of revealing his presence and character and the means by which one encounters him (Exod. 33:18-19).[105]

Oneness Pentecostals believe God used His own name as a form of *self-disclosure* and those who fail to recognize the revelatory use of God's name ultimately have a distorted view of His nature.

> The name...of God is the key to understanding the biblical doctrine of God...God's self-revelation in history is

---

[101] A more comprehensive treatment of this subject is found in A Oneness Pentecostal Christocentric Onomatology, by James D. Hogsten.

[102] R. K. Harrison, Introduction to the Old Testament, (Grand Rapids, MI: Eerdmans, 1969), 401.

[103] Abram's name was changed to Abraham, Sari was changed to Sarah and Jacob's name to Israel (see also Proverbs 22:1 and Ecclesiastics 7:1).

[104] David K. Bernard, In the Name of Jesus, (Hazelwood, MO: Word Aflame, 1992), 21, 25.

[105] Reed, "*Oneness Pentecostalism,*" 648.

accomplished by the giving of his personal name...God's name signifies the personal relation between God and his people, which is the supreme characteristic of biblical faith.[106]

The initial revelation of God's name is given in response to the query of Moses recorded in Exodus 3:13. The LORD answers his question by revealing the one personal covenant name that would distinguish Him throughout the Old Testament—and used over 6,000 times (Exodus 3:14-15). This name is composed of four Hebrew letters transliterated YHWH—and is commonly called the Tetragrammaton.[107]

The name YHWH is significant for two primary reasons, the first of which is that no other name for God in the Old Testament bears the designation of God's <u>everlasting memorial</u>. Second, YHWH is the **only name** linked to Israel's redemption and understood to be God's *salvific name* in the Old Covenant.

> ...the revelation of the name Yahweh on Horeb before the exodus from Egypt, emphasizes not only the aspect of God's indescribable and mysterious being in the revelation of the name but also the active and dynamic significance of God's work in his attention to his people...[108]

Most post-modern Christians are totally unaware that Scripture teaches God <u>has a name</u> and wants His people to know and revere His name! In fact, it is not uncommon to hear many professing Christians proclaim *"God has many names;"* thus, suggesting God's revelatory disclosure in Exodus 3:15 is simply *one among many names* for God. However, Scripture explicitly demonstrates that the revelation of the name יהוה (YHWH) in Exodus 3:15 is a pivotal event in Israel's salvific history.

---

[106] R. Abba, *"Name,"* <u>The Interpreter's Dictionary of the Bible</u>, George Buttrick edt., (Nashville, TN: Abingdon, 1962), 3: 500-1.

[107] The pronunciation is uncertain; yet, most believe 'Yahweh' accurately reflects the Divine name. In English Translations the appearance of '**the name**' is often designated by the upper-cased LORD.

[108] Ernst Jenni and Claus Westermann, "שֵׁם" <u>Theological Lexicon of the Old Testament</u>, electronic edition, (Hendrickson Publishers, 1997), prepared by Oak Tree Software Inc.

It was this name which God chose, for it is his only personal Name; the rest are titles. Now, the LORD took this moment to fully reveal the significance of the Name to Moses... This was that very special Name of God which was used by the Hebrews alone...[109]

The importance of the progressive revelatory use of God's name is affirmed in Exodus 6:1-3. This passage expressly links **'the name'** יהוה (YHWH) to the redemption of Israel—thereby demonstrating the uniqueness of this revelatory name of God.

I appeared unto Abraham, to Isaac, and to Jacob as God Almighty, <u>but by my name 'the LORD'</u> I was **not known** to them.[110]

There is considerable debate about the meaning of this verse due to the fact the name יהוה (YHWH) is used in the book of Genesis. Some scholars maintain that:

The words, "By My name Jehovah was I now [sic] known to them," do not mean, however, that the patriarchs were altogether ignorant of the name Jehovah...It was in His attribute as El Shaddai that God had revealed His nature to the patriarchs; but now He was about to reveal Himself to Israel as Jehovah...[111]

This view argues the meaning of Exodus 6:1-3 is that there was a qualitative difference between the patriarchs understanding of God's name and the revelation given to Moses in Exodus 3:14-15. In short, while the patriarchs had a rudimentary knowledge of the memorial name—they were unaware of its revelatory significance. However, those who were delivered from Egypt and entered into a covenant relationship with Yahweh at Sinai—*experientially knew*

---

[109] Stanley M. Horton, ed. <u>The Old Testament Study Bible: Exodus</u>, in <u>The Complete Biblical Library</u>, vol. 2, (Springfield, MO: World Library Press, 1996), 35.

[110] New English Translation, electronic edition, (Biblical Studies Press, 1996-2005). The following footnote explains its use of LORD: "*Heb 'Yahweh' traditionally rendered in English as 'The LORD.' The phrase has been placed in quotation marks to indicate the presence of the tetragrammaton.*"

[111] C.F. Keil and F. Delitzsch, <u>Commentary on the Old Testament</u>, Vol 1., (Peabody, MS: Hendrickson, reprint 1996), 303.

God through the revelation of His covenant-redemptive name יהוה (YHWH)—the <u>nationalized</u> memorial name of God!

Oneness Pentecostals recognize the theological significance of the revelatory name bequeathed to Moses and the Nation of Israel in Exodus 3:13-15. Yet, they do not believe the nationalized memorial name of יהוה (YHWH) is the culminate revelatory name of God.[112] In fact, following the declaration that יהוה (YHWH) is his memorial name *"forever,"* God continued to use His name as a vehicle of self-disclosure. However, there is a *difference* in the way God uses his name *subsequent* to the revelation of Exodus 3:14-15. The distinction is that **all** future revelatory disclosures of God's name incorporate the redemptive memorial name יהוה or יה (the shortened form of Yahweh) within them.[113]

Furthermore, Oneness scholars maintain that Scripture foretells of the *globalization* of God's name—that culminates <u>in</u> and <u>through</u> the Messiah.[114] Indeed, through the incarnation God's memorial name is visibly personified in the person and name of Jesus; thus, it is no coincidence the Hebrew name 'Jesus' contains *the memorial name and the meaning—YAHWEH is Salvation.*[115]

> Since Jesus etymologically embodies the name of Yahweh and the latter theologically anticipates the revealing of a future new name, the name of Jesus is regarded as the proper name of God for this age. It reveals the identity of Jesus and describes his function as Savior of the world.[116]

---

[112] Exodus 3:13-15 anticipates a future self-disclosure of the name, for "I AM" is a Hebrew *imperfect,* which *"essentially represents action that is incomplete..."* Allen P Ross, <u>Introducing Biblical Hebrew,</u> electronic edition (Baker Publishing Group), 2001, Oak Tree Software Inc.

[113] In short, subsequent 'name' revelations are *compound names*—that conjoin the memorial name with an attribute or quality God desires to reveal about Himself to the Nation of Israel (i.e. Exodus 15:26; 17:15).

[114] The global revelation of God's name is seen in several passages (i.e. Exodus 9:16; Malachi 1:11; Psalm 102:15). This is realized in the name of the Messiah (i.e. Isaiah 52:6, 10; Jeremiah 23:5-6 etc...).

[115] R. Laird Harris, edt., <u>Theological Wordbook of the Old Testament,</u> (Chicago, IL: Moody, 1980), electronic edition, Oak Tree Software Inc.

The Soteriological Application of God's Revealed Name

The doctrine of God's saving name is extraneous to most of post-modern Christendom; yet, Oneness Pentecostals believe the name has soteriological significance—via its application in the life of the believer. This is realized in the rite of water baptism wherein the culminate redemptive name of God—Jesus—is invoked over the baptismal candidate. In fact, Oneness Pentecostals argue that the monadic baptismal formula of '*Jesus name*' was a distinctive mark of the early church and an intrinsic part of conversion "*...without which they could not be said to have truly believed.*"[117]

Trinitarians often object to the monadic formula on the basis of Jesus' words recorded in Matthew 28:19 to baptize converts "*...in the name of the Father, and of the Son, and of the Holy Ghost.*" The majority of the Oneness Movement believes these words are authentic—but **do not** believe they are designed to teach the so-called *triadic baptismal formula*.[118] Indeed, they argue _every_ account or reference to water baptism subsequent to Pentecost, _explicitly_ or _implicitly_ supports the oral invocation of Jesus name (*i.e. Acts 2:38; 8:16; 10:48; 19:5*). In fact, Oneness Pentecostals argue that outside of Matthew 28:19, the words Father, Son and Spirit are never used in connection with the New Testament rite of water baptism.

> Although the Lord Jesus Christ commanded His original disciples to 'disciple all the nations, baptizing them in the Name of the Father, and of the Son and of the Holy Spirit' ...neither they nor the Church of the apostolic age ever literally

---

[116] Reed, "*Oneness Pentecostalism*," 648. (see Matthew 1:21; John 5:43; Acts 4:12; Philippians 2:9-11; Hebrews 1:4).

[117] James D. G. Dunn, Baptism in the Holy Spirit, (Philadelphia, PA: Westminster, 1970), 50.

[118] A minority of Oneness Pentecostals suggest "*of the Father and of the Son and of the Holy Ghost*" are interpolated. This view is primarily based on Eusebius' omission of these words when quoting Matt. 28:19. Yet, every extant Greek Manuscript contains the words; thus, substantiating their legitimacy.

repeated the words of that command in baptizing anybody, so far as the New Testament bears witness.[119]

Based upon the pristine application of Matthew 28:19—Oneness believers conclude that the words of Jesus are a command and **not** a liturgical rubric. Moreover, they maintain that merely repeating the words of Matthew 28:19 does not constitute obedience to the command. There are two reasons Oneness Pentecostals take this position—both of which are based on the syntax of the text. First, Matthew 28:19 does not advocate for the invocation of *three names* in baptism—but enjoins baptism in the *one singular name* "*of the Father, and of the Son and of the Holy Ghost.*" While one could argue that 'Father,' 'Son' and 'Spirit' are names because they are nouns—they are not proper nouns or proper names. Most importantly, they do not constitute the required *one singular name.*

Second, rather than being three proper nouns 'Father, Son and Holy Spirit' are descriptive nouns—that function as relational appellations of the one true God. This is especially clear when one understands each noun is in the Genitive case and each linked to the singular noun '*name.*' This is significant for in the Genitive:

> The sense of attribute is indeed the usual one with the genitive...the descriptive attributive genitive expresses quality like an adjective indeed, but with more sharpness and distinctness.[120]

The attributive genitive—sometimes referred to as the Hebrew Genitive, is "*...very common in the NT, largely due to the Semitic mindset of most of its authors.*"[121] Understood in this manner '*Father,*

---

[119] William Phillips Hall, Remarkable Biblical Discovery or 'The Name' of God According to the Scriptures, (St. Louis, MO: Pentecostal Publishing, 1951), 12. Hall's work was written in the 1920's and, although he was not a Oneness Pentecostal, his work was popular with early Oneness leaders.

[120] A. T. Robertson, Grammar of the Greek New Testament in the Light of Historical Research, electronic edition, (Wenham, MA: Gordon College, 2006), 496. Oak Tree Software Inc.

[121] Daniel B. Wallace, Greek Grammar Beyond the Basics, (Grand Rapids, MI: Zondervan, 1996), 86. This is especially noteworthy considering most scholars believe Matthew's Gospel is written to a Jewish audience

Son and Holy Spirit' would function as <u>attributes</u> of the one singular <u>name</u> in Matthew 28:19. However, the Genitives in this verse may be more accurately explained as a *possessive genitives* wherein:

> The substantive in the genitive possesses the thing to which it stands related. That is, in some sense the head noun is owned by the genitive noun...in these instances...the genitive noun *is animate and is usually personal;* the head noun, normally the kind of thing that *can* be possessed.[122]

The above view of the Genitive fits the grammar and context of Matthew 28:19, in that, the singular name *is owned* by the Father, Son and Holy Spirit. Yet, regardless of whether the Genitives in this verse are understood as *attributive or possessive*—the text emphasizes there is **one singular 'name'** that is <u>*simultaneously the name of the Father and of the Son and of the Holy Ghost.*</u> Thus, to properly obey this command—it is necessary to use the singular comprehensive <u>**name**</u> "...of the Father, and of the Son and of the Holy Ghost,"which Oneness Pentecostals identify as Jesus.

> Jesus is the one revelatory and proper name of God...The singular use of 'name' in Matthew 28:19 points forward to Jesus as the one name of the Father, Son and Holy Spirit...Matthew 28:19 is regarded as the command to baptize in the one name of the Father, Son and Holy Spirit, and Acts 2:38 provides the formula.[123]

---

and contains a variety of Hebraisms.

[122] Ibid., 81-82.

[123] Reed, *"Oneness Pentecostalism,"* 651.

The Name and the Atonement

Hebraic Monotheism, the Deity of Christ, the nature of 'Sonship' and the progressive revelation of God's name culminating in the name of Jesus has soteriological importance in Oneness theology. Moreover, the Oneness Pentecostal interpretation of these central Scriptural truths profoundly impact their view of the Atonement. There are several 'atonement models' within Evangelicalism; yet, each school of thought has a common motif, namely—that the Father sent someone other than Himself to secure redemption for humanity.[124]

There is no standardized atonement model embraced by the Oneness Movement—but they reject most Evangelical depictions of the atonement for three reasons. First, most of Christendom explains the atonement in a way that devalues Yahweh's role in reconciliation by making the Father aloof or uninvolved in the redemptive process. This is evident in literature and sermons that suggest '*God*' looked on the bloody scene of Cavalry from *'heaven'* and turned away from the suffering Son! Second, the idea that the 'spatially distinct' Father—was not a participant in redemption, lends itself to ditheism or tritheism.[125]

Third, several 'atonement models' (*i.e. penal substitution*) actually project God as engaging in child sacrifice. In fact, in recent years some Evangelical and Feminist theologians have argued that such models promote a type of divine child abuse!

> The cross of Christ, according to this model, becomes a manifestation of God's wrath and a paradigm of parental punishment...Atonement theology may urge images of the

---

[124] Wayne Grudem, Systematic Theology, (Grand Rapids, MI: Zondervan, 1994), 579-582. Atonement models mentioned by Grudem include: Penal Substitution; ransom to Satan; moral influence and governmental.

[125] This is the way the sacrifice of Cavalry is often presented. Indeed, in the popular film "The Passion of Christ" there is a scene with an arial view of the cross—and water is shown forming in the 'sky' to symbolize a 'tear' shed by the Father!

> grace of God, but...it can do so only at the expense of the abuse of the one perfect child...[126]

Some maintain this is an illegitimate accusation because Jesus willingly gave his life—whereas 'child abuse' always involves an unwilling victim and gratifies only the abuser.[127]

The idea of <u>divine child abuse</u> may be an overstatement; yet, one must admit that most descriptions of the atonement depict God as <u>actively</u> or <u>passively</u> engaging in child sacrifice. Oneness theology renounces such views—because Scripture expressly forbids child sacrifice to <u>false gods</u> or <u>Yahweh</u>. (i.e. Jeremiah 7:31; 19:5; 32:35 etc...). Jeremiah 32:35 is especially noteworthy, for it reveals:

> This sin, perhaps especially this sin, was a clear resistance of God's intentions for the people. God had *never even thought of such a possibility!* It may be that some among the readers claimed that these offerings were commanded by God...and hence the emphasis is placed on the point.[128]

Actually, Oneness scholars do **not** reject Evangelical portrayals of the atonement based on the '<u>model</u>' used. Rather, it is because most interpret the atonement in light of the doctrine of <u>eternal Sonship</u>, which ultimately results in a characterization that requires God to participate in <u>child sacrifice</u>—the very thing He proclaims **never** came to His mind! In contrast, the Oneness view of the atonement is grounded in <u>strict monotheism</u>, <u>begotten Sonship</u> and the <u>revelation of God's name</u>—resulting in a position that emphasizes Yahweh's <u>active</u> role or involvement in <u>human redemption</u>.

---

[126] Joel B Green, <u>Recovering the Scandal of the Cross</u>, (Downers Grove, IL: InterVarsity, 2011), 116.

[127] Steve Jeffery and Michael Ovey, <u>Pierced for Our Transgressions</u>, (Nottingham, England: InterVarsity, 2007), 230.

[128] Tence E. Fretheim, <u>Jeremiah</u>, in <u>Smyth & Helwys Bible Commentary</u>, vol. 15, (Macon GA: Smyth & Helwys, 2002), 465. Jeremiah 32:35 says *"...to cause their sons and their daughter to pass through the fire unto Molech; which I commanded them not, neither **came it into my mind, that they should do this abomination**..."*

Oneness theology asserts the *'sending of the Son'* is a reference to the <u>begotten Son</u>, the one **in whom** Yahweh was localized—**not** a distinct being <u>within</u> Yahweh. Jesus is <u>not</u> a *second hypostasis* of God or the *"second person of the Trinity,"* but the one God and Father tabernacled in human flesh to redeem humanity.[129] In fact, Oneness Pentecostals believe a proper view of the atonement begins with an understanding that—*in the name and person of Jesus*—Yahweh <u>becomes</u> *a man,* <u>suffers</u> *as man,* <u>experiences death</u> *as man,* is <u>buried</u> *as man,* <u>is</u> <u>resurrected</u> *as man,* and is <u>glorified</u> *as man.*[130] Furthermore, they contend this view **alone** successfully avoids a tritheistic conception of the atonement—wherein God is aloof and distant in the redemptive process.

---

[129] Hebrews 1:5; Galatians 4:4; 2Corinthians 5:19; Colossians 1:15; 2:9-10.

[130] 1Timothy 3:16. Oneness scholars typically avoid terminology suggesting God died on the cross. Yet, the reality of the incarnation necessitates that God—**as man**—experienced death in the person of Jesus. Of course, this is no less problematic for orthodox Trinitarians—who affirm Jesus is God. Thus, while difficult to grasp—if God was truly incarnate—then *at some level*—He experienced <u>human</u> <u>death</u> in Jesus Christ.

Oneness Theology and Historical Considerations

The growth of Oneness Pentecostalism has occasioned mixed reactions in Christendom—ranging from ambivalence to outright hostility. Moreover, most Evangelicals—even those sympathetic to the Movement—argue that the Oneness view of God's identity in Christ and their emphasis on the revelatory name of God is a recent innovation. Indeed, most insist these doctrines originated in 1913 and that the re-baptism of Frank Ewart and Glen Cook in 1914 represent:

> ...the first public baptism using that apostolic formula to receive its rationale from a more comprehensive theology of the nature and name of God.[131]

This statement is correct, but **only** in relation to the twentieth-century revival of Oneness theology. In fact, many of the Oneness doctrinal distinctives labeled unique and innovative by much of Christendom—are actually espoused by individuals and small groups throughout the reformation period.[132] For example, some segments of Anabaptists (A.D. 1500's) used the monadic formula of water baptism and opposed the doctrine of the Trinity. In fact, one of the songs written by the Anabaptist hymn writer "Haetzer' declares.

> I am he who created all things...I am not three persons, but I am one! And I cannot be three persons, for I am one...[133]

The seventeenth-century Quaker and founder of Pennsylvania William Penn was actually imprisoned for his work 'The Sandy Foundation Shaken' wherein he "...*denied the existence of three*

---

[131] Reed, *"Oneness Pentecostalism,"* 651.

[132] Space will not allow for an detailed examination ecclesiastical history but the Oneness view of the Godhead is evident even in the Dark Ages: (*i.e. A.D. 447 Pope Leo writes a letter condemning 'Sabellians'; A.D. 692 The Quinisext discusses how to re-admit 'Sabellians' back into the church; A.D. 950 Basilius the martyr taught the Father, Son and Holy Ghost were titles ascribed to God etc...*).

[133] George Huntston Williams, The Radical Reformation, Vol. XV., 3rd edition, (Kirksville, MO: Truman, 1992), 302.

separate persons in the Trinity."[134] Penn's rejection of the Trinity was not based on Unitarianism—for he firmly embraced the Deity of Jesus Christ and made this very clear in his letter to a Presbyterian colleague on January 4 1673.

> Must I therefore necessarily deny his Divinity, because I justly reject the Popish School of Personality? Hast thou never read of... Sabellius, that only rejected the imaginary personality of those times; who at the same instant owned and confessed to the Eternity and Godhead of Christ Jesus our Lord? It is manifest, then, that though I may deny the Trinity of separate persons in one Godhead, yet I do not consequently deny the Deity of Jesus Christ.[135]

Likewise, in 1876 Presbyterian minister John Miller expressed his view of God's nature in his work *'Is God a Trinity.'*

> God eternally, and before His incarnation, is to me, One Person; that God eternally, after His incarnation, is, as God, One Person; that, Spirit, Word, and Jehovah, He is but describing as the glorious Almighty...It would have been infinitely better never to load the faith with the Platonic Trinity.[136]

Miller, also maintained water baptism should be performed with the verbal invocation of Jesus name—using the <u>same rationale</u> as Oneness Pentecostals!

> In fact, why does it (Matt. 28:19) say 'name'? ...If Father, Son and Holy Ghost are hypostatically different...would eminently discredit the singular, 'name.' ...If it says, Baptize them in the name of the Father, the Son and the Holy Ghost, it means in the One Glorious Name (sing), enthroned as the Father, enshrined as the Son, and engrafted as the Holy Ghost.[137]

---

[134] Mary Maples Dunn and Richard S. Dunn, editors., <u>The Papers of William Penn</u>, Vol. 1 1644-1679, (PA: University of Pennsylvania Press, 1981), 73.

[135] William Penn, *'Letter to John Collinges,'* (November 22 1673) in <u>A Collection of the Works of William Penn</u>, (London, England: J.Sowle, 1726). PDF facsimile. Other Anabaptist descendants such as some 17th century Separatists (*i.e. sabellian particular Baptists*) embraced a Oneness view of God and some early Baptists allowed or exclusively used the monadic formula of water baptism.

[136] Miller, 17, 19.

[137] Ibid., 120-121.

Though not exhaustive—the above references demonstrate the Oneness understanding of God and baptism in the name of Jesus are **not** twentieth-century innovations.[138] Thus, the events of 1913-14 brought about the global restoration of these revelatory truths through the rise of the corporeal body of the Oneness Movement. Hence, the doctrines and practices of Oneness Pentecostalism are *"...neither a totally new innovation nor merely the reoccurrence of an ancient heresy."*[139]

---

[138] A more detailed examination of this topic will be provided the next chapter of this Volume.

[139] Reed, *"Aspects,"* 164.

Conclusion

Oneness Pentecostalism continues to be labeled as a 'cult' by some segments of Christianity; yet, is this designation justified? It is true the Movement is <u>heterodox</u> in regards to the historical creeds of Christendom. Yet, Oneness Pentecostals firmly defend the Deity of Jesus and believe salvation is found only in Him. This has come to the attention of some within the scholarly community who argue for accepting the Oneness Movement as a unique expression of Christianity—**not** an aberrant heresy.

> Heresy is a complex thing...It is my view that Oneness theology represents a 'rediscovery' of themes and practices which bear legitimacy from within the earliest Christian experience... Oneness commitment to baptism in Jesus' name can be supported by at least one significant strand of early Christian baptismal practice. And its theology of the Name bears some resemblance to early Jewish Christian theology...[140]

The Oneness Movement continues to grow in spite of opposition and is a witness to the spirit of restorationism and primitivism <u>originally embraced</u> by Pentecostalism. Indeed, like their forbears, Oneness Pentecostals believe God has used this Movement in the <u>rediscovery</u> of Biblical truth abandoned by much of Christendom. Moreover, they believe God <u>continues to use</u> their Movement to <u>completely restore</u> the original Apostolic Hebrew-Christian Faith of the New Testament. It is hoped the preceding pages has helped the reader gain a <u>better understanding</u> of the rational governing Oneness Pentecostal interpretation and a <u>better appreciation</u> of the unique Hebrew mode of thought that undergirds this theological position.

---

[140] David Reed, *"Oneness Pentecostalism: Problems and Possibilities for Pentecostal Theology,"* i n <u>Journal of Pentecostal Theology</u> 11 (October, 1997): 75-91.

James D. Hogsten

V

The Monadic Formula of Water Baptism

The Quest for Primitivism via a Christocentric-Restorationist Impulse

Introduction

Controversy regarding the proper baptismal formula enveloped much of the *'Finished Work'* camp of Pentecostalism from 1913 to 1916. Though often called the *'new issue'* by supporters and detractors—the following work demonstrates the use of the monadic formula of water baptism in the name of Jesus was **not** a new phenomenon. Rather, use of this formula is historically and theologically rooted in the Christocentric-restorationist impulse of the nineteenth century and was employed by various groups espousing the principle of primitivism—including those within the *'Second Work'* Holiness camp.

The revival of Jesus name baptism within Pentecostalism was a result of these <u>same influences</u> reignited through—*but not solely dependent on*—Durham's *Finished Work* doctrine. In other words, the historical framework for the Oneness Pentecostal revival of Jesus name baptism was already embedded in groups that sought to promulgate the principle of primitivism. In fact, one might argue that the development of Oneness Pentecostalism was the logical evolution of those who understood themselves to be God's eschatological people walking in the *"evening light"* of restoration.

The primary purpose of this study is to provide a *raison d'être* for Oneness Pentecostals insistence on baptism in Jesus name—from a historical and ecclesiological perspective. Thus, while it is true that the *'new issue'* did not become *'the'* issue until 1913-1916, the restorationist impulse of Pentecostal ecclesiology helped spawn this development of the Oneness Movement. This study does not address the many groups in ecclesiastical history that have taught baptism in Jesus name and/or embraced a Oneness view of God. Rather, it focuses on the historical influences leading to the restoration of the monadic formula within Pentecostalism in 1913-1914.

The Christocentric and Restorationist Impulse of the Nineteenth-Century

Doctrinal development never occurs in a vacuum separate from historical, sociological and theological presuppositions and the Pentecostal controversy surrounding the proper <u>formula</u> of water baptism and <u>nature</u> of God—is **no** exception to this rule. Indeed, both are grounded in the restorationist impulse and Christocentric thrust prevalent throughout nineteenth century revivalism.

> Nineteenth century revivalism immersed itself in Pietism that was Jesus-centered. Jesus became the central focus in the Full Gospel in both its four-fold and five-fold forms. It was Jesus who was invoked in testimony, prayer and song. This theme carried readily into the Pentecostal movement.[1]

The nineteenth-century Christocentric thrust was not confined to one segment of Evangelicalism, but spanned denominational lines and encompassed every aspect of worship. Indeed, nineteenth-century sermons, books and hymnology exhibit a *'Jesus centrality'* over and above that of previous centuries.[2] However, this 'Jesus centered' piety was especially pronounced within the Holiness movement. One of the greatest examples of this Christocentricism is found in the ministry of Phoebe Worall Palmer—arguably the most influential holiness promulgator of the nineteenth-century.

Palmer's ministry spanned more than forty years and her emphasis on the person and work of Jesus is revealed in personal letters, the hymns she composed and even her controversial *'altar theology,'* all of which placed Jesus as the centerpiece of devotion.[3]

---

[1] William Faupel, <u>The Everlasting Gospel</u>, in Journal of Pentecostal Theology, vol. 10 (Sheffield, England: Sheffield Academic Press, 1996), 283.

[2] Ibid., 188.

[3] Phobe Worall Palmer, *'Faith and Its Effects; or Fragments from My Portfolio,'* i n <u>The 19th Century Holiness Movement: Great Holiness Classics</u>, 4 Vols., (Kansas City, MO: Beacon Hill, 1998), IV, pp. 130-152. Palmer's letters emphasize that Jesus is the common ground of holiness, declaring: *'Even now we speak and think the same and cordially agree; United all in Jesus' name, in perfect harmony'* (p. 142). Her hymn, *The Cleansing*

Of course, Palmer was not alone in the exaltation of Jesus; indeed, A. B. Simpson, *the nineteenth century revivalist who influenced many early Pentecostal leaders*—succinctly expresses his Christocentricism in the words of Holiness hymn <u>Jesus Only</u>:

> Jesus only is our Message,
> Jesus all our theme shall be;
> We will lift up Jesus ever,
> Jesus only will we see...[4]

Stream, stresses the centrality of Jesus through the atonement (p. 152); Likewise, Palmer's *'altar theology'* explicitly teaches that Jesus is the altar of the Christian (p. 150).

[4] A. B. Simpson, *'Jesus Only'* i n <u>Wholly Sanctified</u>, (Harrisburg, PA: Christian Pub., 1982), 125. Simpson's influence on early Pentecostal leaders is unmistakable. Charles Parham visited A. B. Simpson's Christian and Missionary Alliance school in Nyack, New York (James R. Goff, Jr. <u>Fields White Unto Harvest</u>, pg. 60). Moreover, A. J. Tomlinson specifically mentions "Dr. Simpson," in his 1913 work <u>The Last Great Conflict</u> (pg., 156 in the reprint edition1984).

Primitivism and Jesus Name Baptism

The theological accentuation of Jesus coupled with the premise of primitivism and restorationism, provided fertile ground for the use of the monadic formula of water baptism in the nineteenth-century. The term Primitivism is a corollary of Restorationism and is defined as the effort or impulse to:

> ...restore the primitive or original order of things as revealed in Scripture, free from the accretions of church history and tradition.[5]

Evidence reveals that many nineteenth-century restorationists wrestled with the same issue that would later emerge as the 'new issue' in Pentecostalism. For example, Elias Smith, editor of the first religious newspaper—*The Herald of Gospel Liberty*—and a key leader in the New England branch of the 'Restoration Movement,' sought to separate himself from all creeds and denominational names—taking only the name 'Christian.'[6]

In his quest for primitivism, Smith and his followers appear to have embraced the monadic formula of water baptism. Indeed, in his account of a baptismal service recorded in '*The Herald*,' Smith says the Grand Master of Masons in Strafford submitted "*...to be baptized in the name of Jesus with his companion.*"[7] Likewise, this same issue of *The Herald* records that 300 attending a communion service in Portsmouth, NH—had been baptized in the name of Jesus Christ.[8] It is also of interest to note that Smith rejected the doctrine of the Trinity; yet, it is unclear if His understanding of God was Unitarian or a form of Oneness belief (i.e. modalism).[9]

---

[5] Daniel G. Reid, edt. Dictionary of Christianity in America, (Downers Grove, IL: InterVarsity, 1990), 940.

[6] Elias Smith, *The Herald of Gospel Liberty*, Sept. 1, 1808.

[7] Ibid., July 7, 1809.

[8] Ibid.

[9] Elias Smith, The Life, Conversion, Preaching, Traveling and Sufferings of Elias Smith, (Portsmouth, NH: Beck & Foster, 1816), 324. Since the time of the Reformation—those espousing a Oneness view of God have often been mistakenly classed as Unitarian by those who misunderstood

The Restoration Movement established by Elias Smith is not the only nineteenth-century group to question Trinitarianism and/ or the traditional triadic formula of baptism. For example, the 'General Baptists' originally adopted a position on the Godhead *"...that explained the deity as one person in three manifestations, rather than three persons in one God."*[10] Additionally, one of the central issues distinguishing 'Free Baptists' from 'mainline' churches was the baptismal formula. In fact, while acknowledging the validity of Matthew 28:19, Free Baptists pointed out that:

> ...not one example of using this particular formula occurs in all the practice of the Apostles. They baptized 'in the name of the Lord' Acts 10:48, 'in the name of the Lord Jesus' (8:16 and 19:5); at the Pentecost, even 'in the name of Jesus Christ' (2:38). Any one of these comprehended the full formula specified by our Lord in His commission.[11]

In their work, *'The Okefenokee Album,'* Francis Harper and Delma Presley provide a detailed description of life on *"Billy's Island,'* located on the Okefenokee Swamp.[12] This island, initially settled in 1850, became the home of Daniel and Nancy Lee in 1884.[13] Dave Lee—one of the Daniel and Nancy's fourteen children, maintains their family were identified with the Primitive Baptists, who were so called because *"...they retained the old ways of baptism by immersion in Jesus' name."*[14]

---

their teaching (i.e. William Penn). In fact, it is questionable as to whether the so-called 'Father' of Unitarianism (Michael Servetus) was—in fact, a Unitarian!

[10] Robert G. Torbet, A History of the Baptists, (Philadelphia, PA: Judson, 1950), 86.

[11] Oscar E. Baker, The Issues Distinguishing Free and Other Liberal Baptists, (Boston, MA: Morning Star, 1889), 20.

[12] Francis Harper and Delma E. Presley, The Okefenokee Album, (Athens, GA: University of Georgia, 1981), 29.

[13] C.T. Trowell, *"Okefenokee Folk: A kinder, or more hospitable people do not live,'* in The Natural Georgia Series: The Okefenokee Swamp, internet resource at www.sherpaguides.com/georgia/okefenokee swamp.

[14] Marvin Arnold, Pentecost Before Azusa, (Jackson, MS: Arno Pub., 1991), 11. Not all Primitive Baptists embraced the monadic formula, but given the fact that Baptist churches stress local autonomy—this is not

Controversy over the nature of God and the proper baptismal formula was quite extensive in the nineteenth-century. In 1876 the Presbyterian minister—John Miller penned his work entitled *'Is God a Trinity?'* which clearly teaches a Oneness view of God and supports the Jesus name formula of water baptism.[15] In fact, in a letter to Thomas Weisser, the American Baptist Historical Society confirms that during this time period *"...when triune baptism was discarded in favor of a single immersion, some pastors moved from Matthew's account to Luke's version of Baptism."*[16] Thus, one can see:

> Baptism in the name of Jesus Christ is no new phenomenon in the history of the church. Martin Luther encountered a dispute over the formula in his day. G.T. Stokes referred to certain Plymouth Brethren and other sects in Great Britain who used the exclusive formula of Acts 2:38...Some had used the formula for years, so its use was no drastic innovation.[17]

---

surprising.

[15] John Miller, Is God A Trinity?, reprint, (Hazelwood, MO: Word Aflame, n.d.), 86.

[16] Carl W. Tiller, *A Letter from the American Baptist Historical Society*, (Feb. 10, 1988). Quoted in Thomas Weisser, Jesus Name Baptism Through the Centuries, (Hazelwood, MO: Word Aflame, 1989), 41.

[17] Vinson Synan, Aspects of Pentecostal-Charismatic Origins, (NJ: Logos International, 1973), 159.

The Baptismal Formula and the Holiness Connection
1900-1905

With the close of the nineteenth-century, controversy regarding God's nature and the formula of water baptism seems to have abated. Yet, restoration ideology continued to dominate several segments of Christendom—that ultimately shaped the Pentecostal Movement. The ecclesiology of groups like the <u>Landmark Baptists</u> and restorationist ministries such as Alexander Dowie's '<u>*Zion*</u>' and Frank W. Sandford's '<u>Kingdom</u>' in Shiloh profoundly impacted the development of Pentecostalism.[18] In fact, two of the most prolific leaders of early Pentecostalism—Charles Fox Parham and A. J. Tomlinson—were directly influenced by Sandford's ministry.

Although Parham nor Tomlinson were *'members'* of Sandford's Kingdom—both spent time at Shiloh and were impressed with Sandford's ministry. In fact, in 1897 Tomlinson was baptized in the Androscoggin River by a 'Brother Gleason,' who was one of Sandford's *"Lieutenants."* Moreover, the teaching Tomlinson received at Shiloh so deeply affected him that, four years after his baptism, he would write *"...I feel all Shiloh is at my back pushing me on, I dare not go back on the teaching I received at Shiloh (Maine)."*[19]

A detailed analysis of Sandford's teaching and restoration efforts is beyond the scope of this study; yet his revival of *'Authoritative Baptism'* is worth noting. According to Sandford, the restoration of Authoritative Baptism was prompted by a message he received from the Lord on September 30, 1901 indicating *"...the time for a 'special baptism' had come and that it was to be held on the date signified—October 1, 1901."*[20] Interestingly, A. J. Tomlinson's diary

---

[18] Sandford was a colorful and dynamic leader who established *"The Holy Ghost and Us Bible School"* in Shiloh Maine. He was also the editor of the popular holiness periodical *"Tongues of Fire."*

[19] A. J. Tomlinson, <u>The Diary of A.J. Tomlinson</u>, Homer A. Tomlinson, edt., 3 Vols., (Queens Village, NY: 1948), 3:28.

[20] Frank W. Sandford, *'Authoritative Baptism,'* in <u>History and Times of the Kingdom</u>, Reginald Parker and Richard Sweet (edt.), 8.,

entry for October 1, 1901 confirms he was in attendance and that he entered the waters of baptism again and was immersed by Sandford Himself.[21] Tomlinson states the purpose of this baptism was for *"...the evangelization of the world, gathering of Israel, new order of things at the close of the Gentile age."*[22]

Tomlinson obviously regarded Sandford's restored baptism as significant, but he does not mention the formula Sandford used in the performance of this rite. Some evidence suggests Sandford may have used the monadic formula in this "special" restored baptism as opposed to the traditional triadic formula.[23] In his tract 'Authoritative Baptism,' Sandford maintains the authority for water baptism is revealed in Matthew 28:19; yet, he says:

> These are not three names, but *the one name* of the Trinity, hence, no commas should be used. What the Master said was, baptizing them into the name, not into the names of three persons, but into 'the name,' the one name, of the Father Son and Holy Ghost, hence, one baptism properly represents the *One Holy Name.*[24]

Sandford's explication of Matthew 28:19 closely resembles the argument used by Oneness Pentecostals when defending the monadic formula using this text. Yet, does Sandford provide any indication that he believed the comprehensive name of the Father Son and Holy Ghost is Jesus? In Sandford's explanation of Acts 19:1-5 he maintains the Apostle Paul:

> ...explained to them that the Messiah had appeared, and hence, they should be baptized in his name. 'And when they heard

---

www.fwselijah.com.

[21] Tomlinson, *Diary*, 31. *"I was baptized by Mr. Sandford in the Androscoggin River into the 'church of the living God.'"*

[22] Ibid.

[23] If Sandford used the monadic formula of Jesus name or a modified form of this formula—it might explain why Tomlinson was flexible concerning the formula for water baptism in the early years of his ministry. Of course, in his later years he developed a more hardened stance again the exclusive use of Jesus name in water baptism.

[24] Sandford, 7. (emphasis mine).

this, they were baptized into the name of Lord Jesus:' hence, as previously stated, they were baptized "twice."[25]

According to Sandford—Acts 19:1-5 shows John's baptism was *"supplemented at Ephesus by immersion in the name of Jesus Christ."*[26]

In addition, Sandford also used the motif of Acts 2:38; 10: 48 and 22:16 to support the essentiality of water baptism—stating that Baptism *"...is essential to the removal of sin"* and that *"nothing can wash away your sins but scriptural and authoritative baptism."*[27] Moreover, when describing a baptismal scene subsequent to his 1901 'revelation,' he states that the candidate for baptism came *"...to be buried in the name of her Lord."*[28]

Some may question Sandford's use of the monadic formula, but there is no debating that Charles Fox Parham verbally invoked the name of Jesus when baptizing converts.[29] Parham, spent six weeks at Sandford's complex and they conducted a month long revival crusade together in the fall of 1900.[30] Parham returned to Topeka in September—establishing his Bethel Bible School the following

---

[25] Ibid.

[26] Ibid. Sandford also maintains that *"Probably Aquila baptized Apollos in the name of the Lord."*

[27] Ibid., pg. 9-10.

[28] Ibid., 19. On June 1, 2004 this writer telephoned 'the Kingdom' and spoke with the great-grandson of Frank W. Sandford and also to the historical archivist, Timothy Murray. Neither Sandford or Murray was aware of any evidence suggesting Sandford used the monadic formula of water baptism. According to Murray, Sandford usually said *"into the name of the Father Son and Holy Ghost"* or *"in the name of Christ."* Murray also stated he was unaware of any of Sandford's works that would intimate his use of the name 'Jesus' in the rite of water baptism. When this author read the above quotes and mentioned—Parham's use of the monadic formula—he stated he could see how I would arrive at this conclusion, but he did not know of <u>any other</u> writings that supported this idea.

[29] Charles Fox Parham, <u>A Voice Crying in the Wilderness</u>, reprint 1910, (Lexington, KY: Pentecostal books.com, 2013), 18-21.

[30] James R. Goff Jr., <u>Fields White Unto Harvest</u>, (Fayetteville, AR: University of Arkansas Press, 1988), 60.

month—purposely modeled after Sandford's Shiloh.[31] According to Parham's testimony—it is here he received the revelation to use the monadic formula of water baptism.[32]

According to Parham, the Spirit of God actually impressed him to use the monadic formula of baptism earlier in his ministry, asking him the question:

> Have you obeyed every command you believe to be in the Word? I answered, yes; the question repeated, the same answer given. The third time the question was asked, I answered no, for like a flood the convincing evidence of the necessity of obedience rushed in upon us, how Peter said, Repent, and be baptized everyone of you in the name of Jesus Christ...these and other Scriptures were so convincing that the next day we were baptized by single immersion.[33]

Nevertheless, after this personal illumination Parham continued to intellectually struggle with the issue of '*triune immersion*,' and even encouraged some to be baptized in this manner.[34]

It was not until after opening Bethel Bible School that Parham's questions concerning water baptism were laid to rest.

> ...one day at the *Bible School*, we were waiting upon God that we might know the Scriptural teaching of water baptism. Finally, the Spirit of God said: 'We are buried by baptism into His death...' then how quickly we recognized the fact that we could not be buried by baptism in the name of the Father, and in the name of the Holy Ghost because it stood for nothing as they never died or were resurrected.[35]

While Parham claims this revelation was given <u>prior to</u> Sandford's restoration of 'authoritative baptism'—his rationale is very similar.

---

[31] Ibid., 63.

[32] In his work "<u>A Voice Crying in the Wilderness,</u>" (1902) Parham states his understanding of baptism in Jesus name took place '*about two years ago*' at the Bible School in Topeka Kansas. If this is correct this would be after Parham's personal association with Sandford had ended—and **before** Sandford's revelatory "Authoritative Baptism" in 1901.

[33] Parham, 21.

[34] Ibid., 21-22.

[35] Ibid., 23.

The Scripture nowhere states that God the Father died and rose again, or that the Holy Ghost died and rose again. The man Christ Jesus did die and rise again, hence one immersion in water correctly represents that event...[36]

Parham's position on the formula of water baptism was based on the Scriptural pattern of Acts and the necessity of personally identifying with the death burial and resurrection of Jesus as a part of being born of water and of the Spirit.

So if you desire to witness a public confession of a clean conscience toward God and man...you will be baptized by single immersion, signifying the death, burial and resurrection; being baptized in the name of Jesus, into the name of the Father, Son and Holy Ghost...[37]

Therefore when a person is buried with Christ in baptism he is baptized in to Christ's death; and as baptism by immersion in water, symbolizes Christ's burial and resurrection, so is he when he rises up out of the water to walk in newness of life, 'born of water.'[38]

In short, Parham's use of the monadic formula was not a protest against Trinitarianism nor did he believe the name of Jesus is the comprehensive name of God. In fact, though *"fully convinced"* as to the validity of the monadic formula of water baptism—Parham abandoned its use subsequent to the 'new issue' controversy—and repudiated the Oneness Movement.[39] Yet, Oneness leaders could use Parham's original restoration practice of baptism to augment the historicity of the monadic formula in early Pentecostalism.

Interestingly, other early twentieth-century radical Holiness groups appear to have encouraged use of the monadic formula of baptism. For example, the 1900 Constitution of the *Fire Baptized Holiness Association of America*, includes an interesting statement in its article on water baptism.

---

[36] Sandford, <u>Authoritative Baptism</u>, 5.

[37] Parham, *'Voice,'* 21.

[38] Charles Parham, *"Born of Water and the Spirit,"* in <u>The Gospel of The Kingdom</u>, Vol. 1, nd., 1908, (Alvin, TX: The Apostolic Faith).

[39] David K. Bernard, <u>A History of Christian Doctrine</u>, 3 Vols., (Hazelwood, MO: Word Aflame, 1999), 3: 21.

> As the question of water baptism has always been a subject of fruitless strife among carnal professors, we leave it entirely to the individual conscience and preference as to the mode by which the rite shall be administered, *but we insist upon the observance of the plain word of God, 'Repent, and be baptized everyone of you in the name of Jesus Christ for the remission of sins, and ye shall receive the gift of the Holy Ghost' (Acts 2:38).*[40]

This article is flexible with respect to the mode of baptism, but appears to indicate the monadic formula is compulsory![41]

Likewise, A. B. Crumpler's 'Holiness Church' displays a great deal of suppleness with respect to the mode of baptism. Yet, when addressing the formula, the 'Discipline' enjoins using the triadic formula, but maintains that subsequent to quoting Matthew 28:19, the administrator of baptism *"...may add any other invocation at his discretion."*[42] While there is no explanation given for the inclusion of this clause—several possible reasons exist that would be consistent with the historical questions surrounding the formula of water baptism.

First, the inclusion of the clause could suggest there was some sort of discussion in the organization over the proper formula of water baptism (i.e. Matt. 28:19; Acts 2:38). Second, the clause may represent a compromise for those desiring to use the monadic formula. Third, this could also suggest the church recognized both forms of baptism; yet, gave precedence to the triadic formula. Of course, regardless of the rationale—this clause allowed ministers to supplement the triadic formula with *'any other invocation;'* thus, suggesting a reference to the Acts 2:38 formula.

From 1903-1905 Parham's 'Apostolic Faith Movement' conducted evangelistic campaigns throughout the midwest—wherein he and

---

[40] The Constitution and General Rules of the Fire Baptized Holiness Association of America, (ns: 1900), 15-16., www.pctii.org.

[41] Strangely—the entire italicized section is omitted in the 1902 edition of the Constitution—without benefit of explanation!

[42] A. B. Crumpler, edt., The Discipline of the Holiness Church, (Goldburg, NC: Nash Brothers, 1902), 13. www.pctii.org/arc/1902html.

his ministers continued using the monadic formula of Jesus name in the rite of water baptism. In his Kansas crusade in 1903, Parham baptized nearly one hundred new converts in the name of Jesus, including a future leader of the Oneness Movement—Howard Goss.[43] While Parham's Apostolic Faith Movement ministered in the midwest—Alvin E Velie, a less renowned minister, conducted revival meetings in Florida, Wisconsin and Minnesota throughout 1904-1905.[44] Velie is significant—because it is said he used Acts 2:38 as the basis for baptizing converts in the name of Jesus.[45]

Clearly, the monadic formula of water baptism continued to be used by various individuals throughout 1900-1905 and there is evidence the formula was allowed in some of the Holiness groups at this time. Yet, there is no indication those who used the monadic formula understood this as salvific or believed the name "Jesus" is the comprehensive name of God. Furthermore, most of those using the monadic formula during this period of time were Trinitarian; thus, use of the formula was not linked to a denial of the doctrine of the Trinity.

---

[43] Fred J. Foster, Their Story: 20th Century Pentecostals, (Hazelwood, MO: Word Aflame, 1965), 50, 121. Goss would later be re-baptized during the Oneness controversy because, at the time of his initial baptism in Jesus name, he did not understand the name of Jesus to be the comprehensive name of God.

[44] Arnold, 10-11. Velie seems to have been responsible for the conversion of the Lee Family (on Billy's Island) in 1884. It is purported that he embraced the monadic formula of baptism, held a Oneness view of God and preached Pentecostal Spirit Baptism.

[45] Joe Nelson, *Telephone Interview, June 26th 2004*. Nelson substantiates the accuracy of Arnold's work regarding Alvin Velie's ministry. He also claims to possess an original work by Velie that provides details of his revivals in 1904-1905 and confirms his use of the monadic formula.

An Eclipse of the Spirit in Early Pentecostalism

During the initial global outpouring of God's Spirit (1906-1909) references to the formula of water baptism—*triadic or monadic*, are relatively sparse—for two reasons. First, while early Pentecostals were not ambivalent to water baptism—they did not embrace a sacramental view of this rite. In short, they believed baptism was important—but did not understand it as salvific in nature.

> We believe in water baptism, because Jesus commanded it after His resurrection...baptism is not a saving ordinance, but it is essential because it is a command of our Lord...[46]

Second, the restoration of Spirit baptism was the primary focus of the early Pentecostal revival. Indeed, the baptism of the Holy Ghost with the initial evidence of speaking with other tongues was a watershed experience that—*eclipsed every other doctrine and practice in Pentecostalism* . This is evident when examining popular early Pentecostal periodicals such as *The Bridegroom's Messenger* and *The Apostolic Faith*. In fact, the former has no direct references to water baptism through 1909 and the later, only a handful.[47]

In contrast, these early periodicals are replete with testimonies of Spirit Baptism and the occurrence of glossolalia. Moreover, the primacy of Spirit baptism and tongues speech is also confirmed by in written records of early Pentecostal leaders. For example the personal diary entries of A. J. Tomlinson from May-December 1908, contain twenty references to Spirit baptism and tongues; yet, only five references to water baptism with no reference to the formula.[48]

---

[46] William J. Seymour, edt., <u>The Apostolic Faith</u>, Vol., 1 No. 10., September, 1907, (Los Angeles, CA: The Apostolic Faith Mission), 2.

[47] Kim Alexander, *Matters of Conscience, Matters of Unity, Matters of Orthodoxy: Trinity and Water Baptism in Early Pentecostal Theology and Practice*, in <u>Second Joint Meeting of the Society for Pentecostal Studies</u>, (March 20, 2003) Wesleyan Theological Society, 1-4. Alexander reports seven direct references to baptismal services in the *Apostolic Faith* from 1906 to 1909 with no emphasis placed upon the formula.

[48] A.J. Tomlinson, <u>The Diary of A. J. Tomlinson 1901-1924</u>, Vol., 5 <u>The Church of God Movement Heritage Series</u> (Cleveland, TN: White Wing,

This is not to suggest there was no one advocating the monadic formula in Pentecostal circles at this time. Indeed, in 1907 after Seymour and Parham parted ways:

> Joshua Sykes established the Apostolic Church in East Los Angeles. He adopted the tenets of the Azusa Street Mission, with one significant difference. He baptized his converts in the name of Jesus Christ and did not invoke the traditional Trinitarian formula.[49]

Notwithstanding, most Pentecostals from 1906-1909 show little concern regarding the formula of water baptism. In fact, though Parham continued to use the monadic formula at this time—he no longer placed significant emphasis on this practice.[50]

2012).

[49] Cecil M. Robeck, Jr., <u>The Azusa Street Mission & Revival</u>, (Nashville, TN: Thomas Nelson, 2006), 189.

[50] This may reflect Parham's desire to maintain unity in response to the influx of ministers coming into the Apostolic Faith Movement who used the triadic formula.

Pentecostal Precursors for Reviving the Baptismal Formula Issue

1910-1915 is a time of growth and challenge in Pentecostalism that ultimately results in changing the face of the Movement.[51] The first challenge would be faced through the introduction of William Durham's 'Finished Work' teaching in 1910. This doctrine would have both positive and negative effects within Pentecostalism, both of which synergistically worked to bring about a renewed interest in the proper formula of water baptism—ultimately leading to the formation of the Oneness Movement.

The positive effect of Durham's teaching was its re-emphasis on the person and work of Jesus—which some believed was being supplanted by an *overemphasis* on the gifts of the Spirit.

> ...we must stick to our text, Christ, He alone can save. The attention of the people must be first of all, and always, held to Him...Any work that exalts the Holy Ghost or the 'gifts' above Jesus will finally land up in fanaticism. Whatever causes us to exalt and love Jesus is well and safe. The reverse will ruin all.[52]

> Keep your eyes on Jesus and not on the manifestations...if you get your eyes on manifestations and signs you are liable to get a counterfeit...[53]

> How often, alas! is He disappointed, for does He not too often see His children...taken up with manifestations and gifts, instead of keeping eyes and heart fixed on Jesus...[54]

Even if one does not agree with these assessments—there is little debate that Durham's 'Finished Work' message brought about an increased focus on Jesus.

---

[51] For example, by 1915 the Pentecostal Movement was divided into three camps: 'Second Work,' 'Finished Work' and 'Oneness.' The original *'missionary'* view of tongues was rejected and serpent handling became a frequent worship practice in some Pentecostal circles (*i.e. church of God*).

[52] Frank Bartleman, Azusa Street, reprint (Plainfield, NJ: Logos, 1980), 86. Bartleman wrote these words in 1906!

[53] William J. Seymour, edt., The Apostolic Faith, Vol., 1 No. 11., October-January, 1908., (Los Angeles, CA: The Apostolic Faith Mission), 4.

[54] A. A. Boddy, edt., "Consider Jesus" in Confidence A Pentecostal Paper for Great Britain, Vol., II No. 1. January 1909 (Sunderland, England), 12.

> People have been made to look to so many other things that Christ has largely been lost sight of. They have turned to theories and creeds, experiences, blessings, works of grace, states of feeling...and so many other things that their vision of the Blessed Christ of Calvary has been dimmed.[55]

The 'Finished Work' doctrine was not the sole catalyst for reviving the monadic formula of water baptism. Yet, its Christocentric emphasis created a *shift* in the Pentecostal salvific paradigm that lead to further Christological and Soteriological exploration.[56]

The salvific paradigm-shift is illustrated by two specific articles contained the July, 1910 edition of the *Voice in the Wilderness*. The first is entitled *"Message in Tongues Interpreted,"* which emphasizes the primacy of Jesus Christ, the power of His name and prophetically indicates the Lord will provide a further *revelation* of Himself to His people.

> There must be no glorying in names or orders or systems, only in MYSELF alone. All fulness is in ME, all power in MY gospel...I wait to reveal MYSELF...beyond all that you know...I have many things to say to you but you can not bear them now...I am working to...establish MY children...If the devil suggests to you to take any glory to yourself, refuse to receive the thought IN JESUS' NAME (emphasis original)[57]

The second article is a short defense of the 'Finished Work' doctrine that intimates a further soteriological shift by embracing *Acts 2:38 as the New Testament salvific paradigm!* This is important considering **both** articles are written three years *prior* to the '*new issue*' controversy within the movement.

> Surely our Lord knew what He was saying. Notice He did not say repentance, remission of sins, 'sanctification,' and the baptism of the Holy Ghost. Let's see what Peter preached on the day of Pentecost: 'Repent' and be baptized (in water) in the

---

[55] William Durham, *The Finished Work of Calvary*, i n Pentecostal Testimony, Vol. II., No. II, 1912, Chicago, IL., 3.

[56] Interestingly, in 1912 Durham changed the Masthead of his periodical Pentecostal Testimony from Acts 2:4 to Acts 2:38; thus, foreshadowing the coming Christological-Soteriological controversy in Pentecostalism.

[57] G. T. Haywood, edt., The Voice in the Wilderness, 2., (July, 1910), 1-2.

name of Jesus Christ for 'remission of sins,' and ye shall receive the 'gift of the Holy Ghost' (Acts ii, 38).[58]

Perhaps an even more direct link to Durham's teaching is seen in the ministry of Andrew Urshan, the Persian immigrant ordained by Durham in 1910.[59] This same year—Urshan began to examine the baptismal command of Matthew 28:19 in light of <u>its execution</u> in the book of Acts. Urshan maintained the apparent contradiction was resolved when:

> The blessed Lord showed me then and there, that 'The Lord Jesus Christ' is the ONE PROPER NAME of God for this gospel dispensation...that repentance and remission of sins should be preached everywhere in Jesus' Name ONLY.[60]

In response to this revelatory disclosure, Urshan *"...printed Acts 2:38 on the side of his baptismal tank and began to baptize all new converts into the name of the Lord Jesus Christ."*[61]

The Christocentric emphasis of the Finished Work teaching clearly accentuates the name of Jesus. In fact, "<u>The Bridegroom's Messenger</u>" reports on a Pentecostal meeting in a village of Nepal and specifically links the Finished Work with the name of Jesus.

> ...we witnessed joyfully to these dear unlettered peasants, not one of whom could read their own language. At the <u>mention of Jesus' finished work on Calvary</u>, one man started to oppose fiercely, but he was effectually silenced <u>in the name of Jesus</u>.[62]

Durham also ties the name of Jesus to the Finished Work doctrine.

> This is the continual order of things in the Acts of the Apostles. From the day the Holy Spirit fell on them...they declared that

---

[58] Ibid., 4.

[59] Bernard, *History*, 62. Durham mentions the opening of a Persian Pentecostal Mission on the North side of Chicago and says *"Brother Andrew Urshan is the pastor of this mission"* (Pentecostal Testimony, July, 1910 pg. 15).

[60] Andrew Urshan, <u>The Life of Andrew Bar David Urshan</u>, (Portland, OR: Apostolic Book Pub., 1967), 91. This was a unique understanding that would not gain wide acceptance until after 1914.

[61] Bernard, 63.

[62] Max Wood MoorHead, *"Visiting on the Border of Nepal,"* i n <u>The Bridegroom's Messenger</u> (Atlanta, GA: February 1, 1912), pg 1.

> there is salvation in <u>no other name</u>...they told those who were convicted, that if they would repent and be <u>baptized in the name of Jesus Christ</u>, for the remission of sins they would receive the gift of the Holy Spirit.[63]

There is little doubt Durham's teaching positively contributed to a renewed focus on the person and work of Jesus. Yet, his teaching also had a negative effect, which was manifested in the division this doctrine created within Pentecostalism.

> ...questions have arisen because of some of our leaders agains sanctification as a second work of grace. Divisions among Pentecostal saints have resulted from this teaching...we dare not charge God with these divisions; surely, "An enemy hath done this."[64]

> There were scarcely any divisions among the pentecostal people until Mr. Durham and others began teaching what they call "The finished work of calvary" doctrine...what is it today? Division, division, division![65]

As with any doctrinal dispute—much of the divisiveness of the Finished Work teaching was exacerbated by the manner it was *delivered* by supporters and *attacked* by opponents. Hence, some called for restraint on both sides of the question. For example, A. A. Boddy of Sunderland England offered a resolution to the controversy that stressed the need for unity among Pentecostal brothers and sisters.

> Recognizing the great need of unity in the body of the Lord...and noting the opportunities Satan is getting through sad divisions, we, by the help and grace of our Lord, do undertake...to refrain from condemning one another...to dissuade our beloved brethren and sisters in Pentecost from giving way to a spirit of harshness in those matters.[66]

---

[63] William H. Durham, *"The Two Great Experiences or Gifts,"* in <u>Pentecostal Testimony</u>, Vol. 1. No., 8., (Los Angeles, CA: 1911), pg., 5.

[64] Mrs. E. A. Sexton, edt., *"Doctrinal Teaching,"* i n <u>The Bridegroom's Messenger</u>, (Atlanta, GA: May 1, 1912), pg. 1.

[65] A. J. Tomlinson, *"Confusion of Scriptures Due to Natural and Mental Disarrangement,"* i n <u>The Church of God Evangel</u>, (Cleveland, TN: Evangel Publishing, July 27, 1914), pg. 2.

[66] Mrs. E. A. Sexton, edt. *"A Suggested Resolution,"* in <u>The Bridegroom's Messenger</u>, (Atlanta, GA: September 15, 1912), pg. 2.

Although the division wrought by the Finished Work doctrine was unfortunate—it produced a spirit of dissatisfaction and longing to return to the early Pentecostal restorationist impulse.[67] This would work to further a revival of the monadic formula and eventually lead to the rise of the Oneness Movement. History confirms Jesus name baptism and the Oneness view of God could develop independently of the Finished Work doctrine. Yet, this teaching provided fertile ground for the revival of a Christocentric and restorationist motif—two factors that **always** accompany the resurgence of these doctrines.[68]

The resurgence of restorationism is most perceptible after Durham's untimely death in 1912. Although his death was a great blow to 'Finished Work' Pentecostals—it brought a desire to heal divisions and return to the primitive days of Pentecostal power. In fact, many believed the Movement was on the threshold of a fresh revelatory breakthrough that would produce unparalleled unity and power. This conviction prompted the call for the "World-Wide Camp Meeting" to be held at Arroyo Seco in 1913.

> God has dealt definitely with us in regard to this camp meeting...Sister Etter...had already heard from heaven that God was going to gather His saints together in one place and deal with them, giving a unity and power that we have not yet known...it was God who was calling the camp meeting...[69]

The successful healing evangelist Maria Woodworth-Etter was the featured speaker during this month long crusade that would begin April 15th in Los Angeles, the memorable place of the first world-wide outpouring of God's Spirit. Sister Etter was convinced the Pentecostal movement was on the verge of a major

---

[67] Early Pentecostalism identified itself as a restoration movement; yet, for most of the Movement, this impulse seemed to wane after the Azusa outpouring (exceptions to this would be *ultra-restorationists* such as A. J. Tomlinson, General Overseer of the Church of God).

[68] As hitherto shown—these dynamics were present in the nineteenth century groups that taught these twin truths of Scripture.

[69] R. J. Scott, *'World-Wide Apostolic Faith Camp Meeting,'* in <u>Word and Witness</u>, 9.3 (March 20, 1913), 1.

breakthrough and that she was commissioned to help restore the God's people. Her message was prophetic and Christocentric as she proclaimed to the delegates in attendance:

> I am sent of God to unite His people here, in this part of His vineyard...we must love one another as little children and stop biting and abusing...we must know no man, save JESUS ONLY.[70]

The success or failure of this meeting is dependent on one's view of the outcome. Generally reports were positive—such as those found in '*Word and Witness*' and the *"The Latter Rain Evangel."*

> In many respects this was a wonderful camp meeting...there seemed to be a marked advancement in the unity of the saints. Brethren who had been hitherto divided over doctrinal differences were brought together in love on a basis of truth.[71]

> Wonderful deliverances have been experienced from incurable and long standing diseases...At first the meetings suffered because of lack of unity, but weeping and intercessory prayer caused a breaking up that brought the power of God upon the services mightily[72]

Others, were obviously critical of the meetings; in fact, Alex Boddy stated:

> Reports from the Camp Meeting at Los Angeles have been so contradictory and perplexing that it seems difficult to print anything...From Portland Oregon, comes an attacking letter of great bitterness, which calls the gathering "Compromise Camp," and criticises [sic] the healings. Mrs. Etter's great longing was to promote unity. She has found it difficult.[73]

Nevertheless, many of those attending these meetings believed God had visited them and opened up the revelatory truth of Jesus name baptism.[74]

---

[70] Alex A. Boddy, edt., <u>Confidence</u>, Vol. VI. No. 5 (London, England: Zion House, May, 1913), 100. Emphasis on 'JESUS ONLY' is original.

[71] '*Word and Witness,*' 9.6 (June 20, 1913), 4.

[72] *"Los Angeles Campmeeting,"* in <u>The Latter Rain Evangel</u>, (Chicago, IL: Evangel Publishing House, May 1913), pg. 13.

[73] Boddy, edt., *"Pentecostal Items.,"* <u>Confidence</u> Vol. VI. No 7. (London, England, Zion House, July, 1913), 145.

[74] A detailed examination of the events leading to this revelatory discovery is beyond the scope of this study. For more information

---

regarding this Camp meeting and the events leading up to the Jesus name revelation, one may consult a number of Pentecostal resources such as: Talmadge French, <u>Our God is One</u>; Stanley Burgess (edt), <u>The New International Dictionary of Pentecostal and Charismatic Movements</u>; Vinson Synan, <u>The Holiness-Pentecostal Tradition</u>., etc...

A Resurgence of Restorationism and the 'New Issue'

This study has demonstrated that it is inaccurate to claim that use of the use of the monadic formula of water baptism and the Oneness view of God **originated** among Pentecostals at the World Wide Apostolic Faith Camp Meeting in 1913. Rather, this event marked the beginning of a large scale systemization and global expansion of doctrines previously *regional, local or individual* in scope. Moreover, the doctrines comprising the 'new issue' did not appear as a united whole—but revealed or developed in stages, which some identify as:

> ...a concern to harmonize the two baptismal formulae...as a focus on the revelation of the name of God and...as a revelation of the nature of the godhead.[75]

Early Pentecostal literature confirms the accuracy of Faupel's *stages;* yet, also reveals the <u>foundation</u> upon which these stages are built. Indeed, each of Faupel's 'stages' are built on the principle of <u>primitivism</u>—a motif that permeates the writings of those who embraced and promulgated the 'new issue' of baptism in Jesus' name. Indeed, supporters firmly believed they were apostolic because they emulated the first-century church.

> ...Let us preach not OUR EXPERIENCE, but the WORD and let God be true though every man a liar. <u>Let us preach the Apostles' Gospel</u>—"repent and be baptised [sic] every one of you in the NAME of JESUS CHRIST for the remission of sins and ye shall receive the gift of the Holy Ghost,"[76]
>
> Glory, glory to the Lamb of God! Glory, glory for the cleansing flood! <u>I will follow where the saints have trod</u>, Baptized in Jesus' name.[77]

The above quotes reveal that supporters of Jesus name baptism interpreted this revelatory message in a restorationist context. In

---

[75] Faupel, 281. This specific study concentrates on the first of Faupel's stages because the latter was not fully developed until after 1919.

[76] WiniFred Westfield, *"What is Truth?"* in <u>Meat in Due Season</u>, Vol. 1, No. 9, Los Angeles, CA: December, 1915, pg. 2.

[77] Thoro Harris, *'Baptized in Jesus' Name,'* (copyright 1916) printed in <u>The Present Truth</u>, No. 1, Indianapolis, IN: 1916, 1. Emphasis mine.

fact, like early Pentecostals—they believed early church visibly apostatized—which necessitated a <u>restoration</u> and they believed this restoration effort culminated in the "Jesus Name" message!

> ...this passage (Isa. 28:20) describes every creed formed and every system of theology invented since the days of Constantine, when the "faith once delivered to the saints' was lost...God has been restoring this faith in a fragmentary manner in the last eight years...[78]

> In experience and teaching everything has been so abnormal... <u>since the calamity of the third century</u>. It is hard to pull out of it, back again to restoration....God is raising this standard to meet the oncoming, terrible stream of the Anti-Christ's opposition to the "name" and person, divinity of Christ.[79]

> In 1914 God made His final move to raise up a people to restore the One Body or Church of the Apostolic Age. The revelation on which the New-Issue (so-called) was formed, struck right at the very heart of the WOMAN...[80]

In truth, a proper view of the Jesus name message is impossible unless the ecclesiological and eschatological view of these early Pentecostals is understood. Indeed, their message—*like that of Spirit Baptism in 1901*—was comprehended in terms *uncovering or recovering essential truths of Scripture.*

> God has set His hand once more in the close of this age to recover to His people the faith once for all delivered to the saints.[81]

> Thanks be to God that in these days He is bringing us back to the true Pentecostal pattern, and many are receiving the

---

[78] Frank J. Ewart, *"The Last Great Crisis,"* in <u>Meat in Due Season</u>, Vol 1. No. 13, Los Angeles, CA: June, 1916.

[79] Frank Bartleman, *"Why I was Re-baptized, in the Name of Jesus Christ,"* in <u>Meat In Due Season</u>, Vol. 1, No. 9, Los Angeles, CA: December, 1915, pg. 1.

[80] Frank Ewart, <u>The Revelation of Jesus Christ</u>, (St. Louis, MO: Pentecostal Pub, n.d.), 27, 42. The 'WOMAN' is referencing the parable of leaven (Matthew 13:33) and Ewart identifies this woman as the Roman Catholic Church.

[81] Evang. F. Small, *'One Great Experience,'* in <u>The Present Truth</u>, No. 1, Indianapolis, IN: 1916, 4.

baptism with the Holy Ghost in the very act of obedience in immersion.[82]

The concept of restored 'truth' or receiving 'revelation' was a common theme in early Pentecostalism, but this language was not used to convey the idea of something **extra-biblical.** Indeed, Trinitarian and Oneness Pentecostals have always maintained that any legitimate subjective "revelation" must be substantiated by the objective word of God.

> By the word revelation in this narrative we mean, the Holy Ghost illuminating our hearts and minds to actually understand certain scriptures.[83]

> The most conspicuous aspect of the claim to revelation was that it never appealed to a medium beyond Scripture.[84]

Oneness Pentecostals used 'revelation' language in the same manner the Movement historically used this terminology.

> What once was so mysterious is now clear and plain...The Pentecostal light shows everything pup in true colors...Now the illumination is so great that Jesus, the Christ, is seen as the only centre around whom everything radiates...what once could not be understood...as the precious word of God, is now clearly understood by a revelation of the Spirit.[85]

Yet, despite its common usage—opponents of water baptism in Jesus' name argued that supporter were making *"...an issue out of modern revelations and humanly coined phrases."*[86]

In truth, those who accepted the validity of baptism in Jesus' name argued that they weighed current Pentecostalism against the early church and found the contemporary church wanting.

---

[82] G. B. Studd, *"One Baptism,"* in The Present Truth, No. 1, Indianapolis, IN: 1916, 2.

[83] Andrew D. Urshan, The Almighty God in the Lord Jesus Christ (Los Angeles, CA, 1919), 28.

[84] David A. Reed, In Jesus' Name in Journal of Pentecostal Theology Supplement Series, Vol., 31., (Deo Publishing, 2008), 170.

[85] J. O. Lehman, *"Pentecostal Revelation,"* in The Bridegroom's Messenger, Vol. 3., No. 70. (Atlanta, GA: September 15, 1910), 4. Emphasis mine.

[86] E. N. Bell, *"Editorial Explanation on Preliminary Statement which Appears Above,"* in The Weekly Evangel, 1 (May 22, 1915), 1.

Hence, like their forbearers—Jesus name Pentecostals *"...sought to continue the restoration of doctrine and practice started by the Protestant Reformers."*[87] Thus, while detractors maintained this *'new light'* was *'old darkness,'* supporters believed baptism in Jesus' name was a *"...forward step back to the New Testament."*[88]

> What the Pentecostal people have been raised up for, specifically speaking, is to obey the word og[sic] God just as it stands, and 'earnestly contend for the faith once for all delivered to the saints'[89]

> First the Holy Ghost, then the full merits of Jesus' blood, then the full revelation of Jesus, has been the order of restoration. All things are being summed up in Jesus...we are getting back to the simple powerful Apostolic order and gospel.[90]

Because of their commitment to Scripture—it is not surprising that early explications of the Jesus name message focus on harmonizing the command of Matthew 28:19 with its execution by the Apostles recorded in the book of Acts.

> ...to rightfully understand the commission of Jesus in Mt. 28:19, we must take the record of the only authentic church history in existence, the Acts of the Apostles.[91]

> When we first preached the mighty truth of baptism in the name of Jesus Christ...people...demanded an explanation of Matt. 28:19, and we referred them to the Apostle Peter, who under the Spirit's verbal inspiration gave the interpretation that the name of the Father and of the Son and of the Holy Ghost was Jesus Christ.[92]

> All the Scriptures...represent the apostles as teaching and commanding baptism in the name of the Lord Jesus...I consider

---

[87] Kenneth J. Archer, *Pentecostal Story: The Hermeneutical Filter for the Making of Meaning,* in <u>Pneuma,</u> 26.1 (Fall, 2004), 54.

[88] Talmadge French, <u>Our God is One,</u> (Indianapolis, IN: Voice & Vision, 1999), 50.

[89] Ewart, *The Last Great Crisis.*

[90] Frank Bartleman, *"Some Blessed Items of Truth,"* in <u>The Blessed Truth,</u> Vol., 3, No., 11 (Eureka Springs, AR, August 15, 1918), 1.

[91] G. T. Haywood, *Obey Peter or Jesus?* in <u>Meat in Due Season,</u> 1.6 (June 1915), 5.

[92] Frank J. Ewart, *"The Unity of God,"* in <u>Meat in Due Season,</u> Vol., 1, No. 13 (Los Angeles, CA, June, 1916), 1.

the Apostles to be the best interpreters on earth of what Jesus meant by Matt. 28:19.[93]

Glenn Cook offered a unique perspective as to the supposed incongruity of Matthew and Luke's record—suggesting the former is a *shrouded command* realized by those who possess the baptism of the Spirit.

> Matthew 28:19 was a veiled command and when Peter received the Holy Ghost the veil was lifted...Many have gone forth to disciple and baptize all nations without obeying the last command (*tarry for the baptism of the Spirit*) and for that reason have used the veiled formula instead of the one used by Peter and all the rest of the Apostles.[94]

In a similar vein, E. R. Bass indicated the revelation of the 'one name' of Matthew 28:19 was dependent upon Jesus' glorification and the outpouring of the Spirit.[95]

When one examines early Jesus name Pentecostal literature—it is clear the Jesus name formula was substantiated through an interpretive methodology that gave priority to the book of Acts. This is not because they believed Acts was more "inspired" than the rest of Scripture. Rather, like all early Pentecostals the book of Acts was the *hermeneutic filter* for understanding the doctrine and practice of the early church.[96]

> Nowhere in the Bible...is...baptism being performed in the formula of 'Father, Son and Holy Spirit,' throughout the Acts of the Apostles. If one single, isolated example of Christian Baptism could be found in the Bible...there would be some excuse for intelligent people adopting it.[97]

---

[93] E. N. Bell, *Safety in Counsel,* in <u>Word and Witness,</u> 12.10 (October, 1915), 1.

[94] G. A. Cook, *A Revelation,* in <u>Meat in Due Season,</u> 1.13 (June, 1916), 4.

[95] E. R. Bass, *"Be Baptized into the Name of Jesus Christ,"* in <u>The Present Truth,</u> No. 1., (Indianapolis, Indiana, 1916), 4.

[96] For an excellent resource for on early Pentecostal Hermeneutics and the methodology used by Oneness Pentecostals see: Kenneth J. Archer, <u>A Pentecostal Hermeneutic for the Twenty-First Century,</u> (JPTSup, 28; London; T & T Clark, 2004).

[97] Ewart, *The Revelation,* 16.

The only possible vindication of the Apostles' action in baptizing 'in the name of Jesus Christ' would seem to be the fact that Matt 8:19 was fulfilled in that baptism...The Book of Acts is the practical aplication[sic] of the Gospels....With the example set in the Book of Acts by the early church how would we be likely to baptize converts if we had never read Matt 28:19?[98]

The Apostles saw by divine revelation only one name (Acts 2:38) 'Repent and by baptized every one of you in the name of Jesus Christ,' etc. Here by divine revelation, is the name manifested, that is for the Father, Son and Holy Sprit...Philip and Paul also had the revelation as verified in Acts 19:5, 10:48, 8:16...So in that day the Holy Spirit flashed the revelation upon the apostles and they did accordingly.[99]

---

[98] Bartleman, *"Some Blessed Items of Truth."*

[99] John Schaepe, *"The One Name,"* i n <u>The Present Truth,</u> No., 1 (Indianapolis, IN, 1916), 6.

1914-1915 The 'New Issue' and the Ensuing Controversy

Perhaps if the message of water baptism in Jesus' name would have been understood simply in terms of 'a way' of emulating the Apostolic practice of the New Testament church—the controversy may have been short lived. This seems likely given the fact that the infant 'Assemblies of God' initially accommodated those who desired to use the monadic formula.

> The essential thing in Christian baptism is the burial, in obedience to the command of Christ...each minister or candidate should have the full liberty to be personally baptized with any words he prefers, so long as he stays within the Scriptures on the subject.[100]

Some may think this compromise should have satisfied both parties and facilitated an atmosphere of harmony. Yet, even if no hostile rhetoric was displayed on either side—the concepts of restorationism, primitivism and Pentecostal soteriology made such a compromise untenable. Indeed, much like the earlier controversy between the Holiness Movement and Pentecostalism, the 'New Issue' became a matter of "walking in the light."[101]

> When people walk up against light and will not obey and humble themselves, their next move is to wrest the Scriptures to justify themselves in their false position...[102]

Moreover, controversy between the two baptismal camps became inevitable—when supporters of the Jesus name formula

---

[100] Bell, *The Weekly Evangel*, 108 (Sep. 18, 1915), 1.

[101] Many Holiness leaders accepted the message of Spirit baptism after the initial outpouring at Azusa Street; however, others rejected the message as heretical. Those who accepted the message understood they were *'walking in the light'* and believed their very salvation depended on their obedience to the truth revealed in Scripture. Likewise, those who rejected the message understood this to be a deviation of truth; thus, their soul was at stake should they be carried away into false doctrine. Clearly, when a doctrinal controversy reaches this point—the two sides may continue in a <u>union</u>, but *unity is no longer possible*.

[102] Glenn A. Cook, *"Wresting the Scriptures,"* in <u>The Present Truth</u>, No., 1., (Indianapolis, IN: 1916), 6

began baptizing *new converts — **as well as** — those previously baptized in the traditional formula.* Unfortunately, some historians have misconstrued the <u>original</u> impetus governing the 're-baptisms.' For example, Vinson Synan maintains that Frank Ewart and Glen Cook believed Spirit baptism was:

> ...received **only in the immersion rite** and **only** if administered **in the name of Jesus**. As for the Trinitarian Pentecostals, the only way **to be saved** was to submit to re-baptism 'in Jesus' name' ...following their rebaptism they began a determined campaign to **reconvert** <u>and</u> rebaptize the entire Pentecostal movement.[103]

It is true Ewart and Cook embraced the salvific paradigm of Acts 2:38—believing it to be the *normative <u>Scriptural</u> pattern of salvation.* Yet, **neither** taught Spirit baptism was obtained **only** through the invocation of Jesus' name in water baptism. In fact, Ewart testified to receiving Spirit Baptism in 1908 and Cook in 1906[104] and there is no evidence either recanted this experience. On the contrary, even in 1947 Ewart's testimony remained constant.

> ...hearing of a large camp meeting at Portland, Oregon, [in 1908] we decided to go there...I prayed night and day for twenty-one days. At midnight, as the twenty-first day ended, I received a mighty infilling with the Holy Ghost....I spoke in several known languages.[105]

Clearly, Ewart and Cook's motive for baptizing each other in the name of Jesus was **not** to receive Spirit Baptism, but rather it was:

> ...guided by a self-conscious doctrine of the name...the practice received its rationale from a more comprehensive doctrine of the nature and name of God.[106]

---

[103] Vinson Synan, <u>The Holiness Pentecostal Tradition,</u> (Grand Rapids, MI: Eerdmans, 1997), 157. Emphasis mine. Ewart and Cook were the first to be re-baptized subsequent to the 1913 Camp meeting.

[104] See: G. A. Cook *"Receiving the Holy Ghost,"* <u>The Apostolic Faith</u> Vol. 1, No. 3 (Los Angeles, CA, November 1906), 2.; J Ewart *"A Baptist Minister's Experience,"* <u>The Bridegroom's Messenger</u> Vol. 4, No. 81. (Atlanta, GA., March 1 1911), 3.

[105] Frank Ewart, <u>The Phenomenon of Pentecost</u>, rev. edt., (Hazelwood, MO: Word Aflame, 2000), 12.

[106] Reed, <u>In Jesus' Name</u>, 144.

Moreover, while Ewart and Cook wanted the entire Pentecostal Movement to embrace Jesus name baptism—it is blatantly false to suggest they believed Pentecostalism needed to be *"reconverted."*

In truth, <u>most</u> early promulgators of the monadic formula were Spirit filled—prior to being baptized in Jesus' name; thus, they did not deny the salvific experience of those baptized in the triadic formula. However, in keeping with Pentecostal soteriology—they believed it was necessary to '*walk in the light*' of God's revelatory word—thus, baptism in Jesus' name was deemed essential.

> In order to be justified a man must be walking in every ray of light God sheds on his pathway...We must walk in the light as He is in the light for the blood to cleanse. I John 1:7...with light comes responsibility.[107]

> Acts 2:38...is God's prescription...There are no non-essential ingredients in it. You can no more cut out water baptism in the name of Jesus Christ than you can cut out repentance....Water baptism in the name of Jesus Christ is an imperative necessity both in Acts 2:38 and John 3:5.[108]

Even after their rejection of Trinitarianism—supporters of the Jesus name message gave a typical Pentecostal response regarding those who did not 'have light' on baptism in Jesus name and the Oneness of the Godhead.

> We need not worry about those who have died and gone one...they will stand before God for the light of their day and you and I for the light of our day...Those who have the light and refuse to walk in the light will have no chance in this judgement, they will be among those that obey not the gospel of our Lord Jesus Christ.[109]

Likewise—in answer to the question *"Are the unborn lost?"* G. T. Haywood responds:

> No, not by any means. They shall be given eternal life in the resurrection if they walked in all the light that was given them

---

[107] Harry Morse, *"Justification,"* <u>The Present Truth</u>, No., 1 (Indianapolis, IN: 1916), 6.

[108] L. V. Roberts, edt. <u>The Present Truth</u>, No., 1 (Indianapolis, IN: 1916), 7.

[109] H. E. Reed., *"The Birth of Water and Spirit,"* <u>The Blessed Truth</u> Vol. 3., No., 11 (Eureka Springs, AR: August 15, 1918), 2.

while they lived...Wesley, Luther, Whitefield...they lived up to the light of their day. We must live up to the light of our day. Their light will not do for us today...the evening time has come, and the true light now shineth.[110]

Other supporters of baptism in Jesus' name concurred; in fact, when Frank Bartleman gave his testimony *"Why I was Re-baptized in the Name of Jesus Christ,"* he said *"When I was baptized over twenty years ago my thought was to confess Christ. I was fully converted."*[111] Clearly—Jesus name baptism did not signify a 're-conversion,' for Bartleman—but he did consider it God's method of restoring the normative plan of *"...New Testament salvation."*[112] Thus, he believed it to be essential in this regard.

> 'Neither is there any other name under heaven that is given among men, wherein we must be saved' Acts 4:12. 'Repent and be baptized in the name of Jesus Christ, etc.' Acts 2:38. To ignore Jesus Name in baptism is to ignore His name in salvation. We cannot leave it out..[113]

E. N. Bell, the General Superintendent of the Assemblies of God, shocked constituents when he was re-baptized in Jesus' name in 1915. Like others, his rationale was not based on *re-conversion*, but it was an act of obedience to the word of God—prompted by the Spirit. *"When I saw this truth that the apostles taught baptism in the name of Jesus Christ, this fact...made me feel compelled to act."*[114] Bell also cites the twofold motivation of harmonizing the baptismal formulae and primitivism as the basis for his action.

Furthermore, Bell invokes the principle of *'walking in the light'* as a major impetus for his decision.

> The providence of God drove me to being baptized...God ...refused the anointing of His Spirit on all other subjects until I

[110] G. T. Haywood, <u>The Birth of the Spirit in the Days of the Apostles,</u> (Indianapolis IN: Christ Temple, n.d.), 12-13.

[111] Frank Bartleman, *Why I was Re-baptized in the Name of Jesus Christ,* in <u>Meat in Due Season</u>, 1.9 (December, 1915), 1.

[112] Ibid.

[113] Bartleman, *Some Blessed Items of Truth.*

[114] E. N. Bell, *Safety,* <u>The Weekly Evangel</u>, 108 (September 18, 1915), 1.

obeyed...All who think they can pray the power down while refusing to obey the voice of God are welcome to try it. I have tried it enough to know it won't work.[115]

For Bell—as well as others—baptism in the name of Jesus was a *salvific issue* because it was God's revealed *light!* Thus, while they did not necessarily pronounce condemnation on those who did not accept the message—they certainly believed their personal experience with God was in jeopardy if they did not obey!

Even Frank Ewart, who is often regarded as the chief architect of early Oneness Pentecostal theology, expressed similar thoughts on this issue. Certainly, Ewart preached the essentiality of Acts 2:38, but he did not believe those who embraced the triadic formula were automatically lost. Indeed, he speaks tenderly of his personal friend Alfred G. Garr—whose rejection of the Oneness message caused a painful rift in their fellowship—saying;

> Despite all these things, our love for each other survived and this divine love will be renewed in the glory where we will all see eye to eye and doctrinal differences will never again intrude.[116]

---

[115] Ibid.

[116] Ewart, *The Phenomenon*, 179.

1915-1916: Spirit Confirmation, Doctrinal Development and Painful Schism

Despite opposition, the message of Jesus name baptism gained momentum in 1915-1916. Indeed, following the re-baptism of the Canadian pastor Franklin Small—one proponent noted that *"The truth is spreading at a supernatural pace."*[117] In response to this trend, the October 1915 issue of *'Word and Witness'* refused:

> ...to publish reports containing references to baptism in a controversial spirit...All references to Acts 2:38 and Matt. 28:19 is [sic] considered to be out of order and will be cut out of all reports which we publish. We will report that so many were baptized in water, but will omit the scripture reference with a punch in it.[118]

The above action did little to dissuade Jesus name advocates—as several periodicals began to promulgate the *'new issue.'* [119]

Perhaps one of the major factors contributing to the success of the Jesus name message was the apparent validation this teaching received from the Spirit of God. For example, after preaching his first message on Acts 2:38, Frank Ewart and Glenn Cook conducted a revival in Los Angeles wherein Ewart notes:

> ...the vast majority of new converts were filled with the Holy Ghost after coming up out of the water...People visited us from all parts, were convinced, were baptized in Jesus' name and filled with the Holy Spirit in the water... after tarrying for years.[120]

Pentecostals have always considered the witness of the Spirit to be a significant confirmation of truth. Hence, it is not surprising Jesus name periodicals often included reports from the field emphasizing the Spirit's approval on the message of Acts 2:38.

---

[117] Frank Ewart, edt., *Pastor Frank Small Baptized,* in <u>Meat In Due Season,</u> Vol., 1., No. 9 (Los Angeles, CA: December, 1915), 2.

[118] E. N. Bell, edt., *Controversy Discouraged,* in <u>Word and Witness,</u> 12.10 (October, 1915), 4.

[119] Ewart's *'Meat in Due Season';* McAlister's *'The Good Report';* Haywood's *'Voice in the Wilderness';* Opperman's *'The Blessed Truth';* and L. V. Robert's *'The Present Truth'* promulgated the Jesus name message.

[120] Ewart, *The Phenomenon,* 99.

> At Tyndal, a near-by town to Winnipeg...God broke through in such power...Many also have embraced their privilege of being buried in the name of the Lord, and God confirmed His word by filling them with the Spirit according to the scriptures.[121]

> The street meetings are wonderful and crowds of hungry men and women follow into the hall. Many have repented of their sins and are applying for baptism in water, after which they will have hands laid on them and receive the Holy Ghost in the Bible order.[122]

One might be inclined to view the inclusion of such testimonies as a clever tactic designed to appeal to the emotions of readers; thus, swaying their opinion. However, Pentecostal publications have historically included testimonials as a means of validating the Pentecostal message.[123] In short, the Jesus name supporters were not unique in their use of testimonies to confirm that their doctrine and practice enjoyed Divine approval.

While positive reports concerning the 'new issue' came from the field—not everyone was convinced of its legitimacy. In fact, skepticism increased due to doctrinal developments coming out of the 'new issue' camp. Indeed, Jesus name advocates appeared to collapse the paradigm of salvation into one event—incorporating the elements of *water* and *Spirit* as components of the New Birth. In response, the *'Weekly Evangel'* issued a *'personal statement'* that declared:

> ...we reject, as totally unscriptural, the teaching that being born anew is the same as the baptism with the Holy Ghost.[124]

---

[121] F. J. Ewart, edt., *"From Winnipeg,"* <u>Meat In Due Season</u>, Vol. 1., No., 13 (Los Angeles, CA: June, 1916), 3.

[122] F. J. Ewart, edt., *"Our Trip North,"* <u>Meat In Due Season</u>, Vol. 1., No., 9 (Los Angeles, CA: December, 1915), 4.

[123] Examples of this can be seen in the *'Apostolic Faith'* periodical from 1906-1909; *The Church of God Evangel,* 1910-1920; *The White Wing Messenger,* 1923-present. Testimonials were used to confirm a variety of doctrines such as Spirit Baptism, Divine Healing, Sanctification etc...

[124] *Weekly Evangel,* 108 (September 18, 1915), 2. The Evangel does not attack the essentiality of water or Spirit baptism—but objects to the idea that the New Birth encompasses Spirit Baptism.

Literature coming out of the 'Jesus name' camp reveals the objection of the *Evangel* was not without merit. Yet, it should be noted that several future leaders of the Jesus Name Movement began wrestling with Soteriological issues linking water and Spirit baptism with New Testament salvation prior to the above statement.

> Now if we are brought into the body by the new birth, then we conclude that the new birth and the baptism of the Holy Ghost are synonymous; or else there is a baptism into the body through the new birth, and a baptism of the Holy Ghost...but this would be in direct contradiction of the Word of God which says there is one baptism.[125]

Likewise, one month before his historic re-baptism in the name of Jesus, F. J. Ewart wrote concerning New Testament salvation

> Jesus preached the gospel of the kingdom to Nicodemus... prospectively. The New Birth...was not made manifest in its full significance until the day of Pentecost...When the convicted crowd at Pentecost asked Peter what they were to do, his answer was 'Repent, and be baptized every one of you unto the remission of sins, and ye shall receive the gift of the Holy Ghost.' These two...were always in evidence in the early church where God's normal plan was carried out. At Pentecost people were baptized in the name of Jesus Christ as a means of obtaining the gift of the Holy Ghost.[126]

By 1915 advocates of the Jesus name message were beginning to coalesce in their view that the 'new birth' is a comprehensive and inclusive term incorporating the elements of both water and Spirit baptism.[127] Moreover, they believed the salvific pattern for the 'New Birth' was found in Acts 2:38. In an article written by George

---

[125] G. T. Haywood, *"Baptised [sic] Into the Body,"* in <u>The Good Report</u>, Vol. 1., No. 7., (Los Angeles CA: December, 1, 1913), 3. While Haywood's conclusion does not reflect his view subsequent to being baptized in Jesus' name—it demonstrates he is already thinking in this direction nearly **two years** before the height of new issue controversy.

[126] F. J. Ewart, *'The Gospel of the Kingdom,'* <u>The Good Report</u>, Vol. 1., No. 10. (Los Angeles, CA: March 1, 1914), 2.

[127] The majority of Pentecostals understood the 'new birth' as a synonym for justification. However, Jesus name Pentecostals specifically linked Jesus' discussion of the New Birth in John chapter three (especially vrs., five and nine) with the event of Pentecost (Acts 2:4, 38).

Farrow, he stated that Peter's response to the question given in Acts 2:37 is the only answer one should give to those inquiring the way of salvation.[128]

Supporters of the Jesus name message did not discount the salvific experience of Trinitarian Pentecostals or deny their own previous experience. Rather, they **were** challenging the movement to return to the normative preaching and teaching of the pristine church, which Pentecostalism claimed to be a continuation of!

> It's our silly ideas and limitations of God that is in the way... there is but one promise and that is the new birth...Don't preach experiences—Preach Christ!...Just tell them to repent and be baptized in water in Jesus' name ang [sic] God will fill them with the Holy Ghost.[129]

Those embracing the 'new issue' believed the Acts 2:38 paradigm of salvation was simpler and certainly more Scriptural. They did not deny the doctrines of justification, adoption, regeneration or sanctification—but believed these benefits were afforded to those who obeyed the Gospel as explicated in Acts 2:38.

> Repentance, water baptism in the name of Jesus Christ and the reception of the Holy Ghost are the three great acts of faith, by which the sinner is idtentified [sic] with Jesus Christ...[130]

> The conclusion is irresistible... namely that the one gospel...set forth Repentance and water baptism in the name of Jesus Christ to be the Divinely appointed means of identifying the sinner with his Saviour, in His death burrial[sic] and resurrection.[131]

By 1916 there was a definite escalation of doctrinal development in the 'new issue' segment of Pentecostalism—increasing division among Finished Work Pentecostals. Even some of those who

---

[128] George Farrow, *God's Sign on Normal New Testament Salvation* in <u>Meat in Due Season</u>, 1.6 (June 1915), 2.

[129] William E. Booth-Clibborn, *Suddenly,* i n <u>Meat in Due Season</u>, 1.13 (June 1916), 4.

[130] F. J. Ewart, *Identification with Christ,* in <u>Meat in Due Season</u>, 1.13 (June 1916), 4.

[131] F. J. Ewart, *"Baptism is it for the Remission of Sins?"* <u>Meat in Due Season</u>, Vol. 1., No., 21, (Los Angeles, CA: August, 1917), 3.

supported the use of the monadic formula repudiated the 'new issue' due to their position on the nature of God and His identity in the person and name of Jesus Christ.

> The last issue of the paper bridged the gulf that had sprung up between us and many of our fellow Ministers who had been baptized in the name of Jesus...they had withdrawn from our fellowship.[132]

This year also marked an end of fellowship between supporters of the Jesus name message and the infant Assemblies of God. In August, 1916 the *Weekly Evangel* announced the upcoming fourth General Council of the Assemblies of God—encouraging:

> ...all Pentecostal Assemblies, no matter by what name they may be called, who stand for...the principles of UNITY and COOPERATIVE FELLOWSHIP to send representatives to this **Great Open Bible Council.**[133]

The purpose behind the 'Great Open Bible Council' was to:

> ...consider together the great problems now confronting the Pentecostal Movement, some of which are confusing doctrines which affect the fundamentals of the Faith...[134]

Unfortunately, supporters of the Jesus name message discovered the open invitation was limited only:

> ...to those who were in perfect harmony with the operation of the General Council...for that reason we were not permitted to partake in any doctrinal discussions that took place...Several others were denied the privilege because it was known that they were standing for the 'Revelation of Jesus Christ, and baptizing in His name'...there was a spirit of drifting into another denomination manifested when they began to draw up a 'creed' which they termed 'fundamentals.'[135]

---

[132] Ibid., 2. The departure Ewart refers to was based on the acceptance of the Oneness view of the Godhead as opposed to the doctrine of the Trinity.

[133] J. W. Welch and J. R. Flower, *"Come to the Fourth General Council,"* The Weekly Evangel, No., 153., (St. Louis, MO: August 19, 1916), 8-9.

[134] Ibid.

[135] G. T. Haywood, *St. Louis Council,* in The Voice in the Wilderness, 19. (1916), 1.

From its inception, the General Council of the Assemblies of God maintained it was not *"...a human organization that legislates or forms laws and articles of faith and has jurisdiction over its members."*[136] In fact, according to E.N. Bell *"All the council can do is consider methods of cementing together the hearts of the Pentecostal people in one effective service."*[137] Yet, it is interesting to note the Constitution was slightly altered in 1915—stating the Assemblies is not

> ...a human organization that legislates or forms laws and articles of faith and has **unscriptural** jurisdiction over its members.[138]

In less than 7 months the 1914 'Preamble and Resolution of Constitution' was altered and by 1916 the General Council had abrogated its original premise—by making the *"Statement of Fundamental Truths"* the basis of ministerial fellowship.

> ...the Credential Committee is hereby instructed to ask each applicant of the ministry...whether he recognizes and accepts the truth in the Statement of Fundamentals...This Committee is hereby instructed to issue credentials to those who agree and to refuse to those who seriously disagree; and that in the case of minor disagreements, the committee is instructed to use its own discretion in the matter...[139]

The majority of those in attendance believed the "Fundamentals" solidified doctrinal orthodoxy. However, those supporting Jesus

---

[136] Minutes of the General Council of the Assemblies of God, (Hot Springs AR: April 1-12, 1914) 4.

[137] E. N. Bell., edt., *'Power to Legislate,'* i n The Christian Evangel, 65 (Findlay, OH: October, 31, 1914), 3.

[138] Combined Minutes of the General Council of the Assemblies of God, Held at Hot Springs AR April 2-12, 1914 and the Stone Church Chicago IL, Nov. 15-29, 1914, pg 4. Emphasis mine. The word 'unscriptural' was added but it seems no one noticed—in fact, the minutes state that the council made a *"re-affirmation of our position and standing upon the SAME preamble and resolution adopted at Hot Springs."*

[139] Minutes of the General Council of the Assemblies of God, (St. Louis, MO: October 1-7, 1916), 14. The "Statement of Fundamentals" included a section entitled The Essentials as to the Godhead which contained 10 subsections that made it impossible for anyone affirming the Jesus name message to accept.

name baptism and the Oneness of the Godhead understood this as a message to:

> press on...without the camp, bearing his reproach, for here we have not a continuing city, but we seek one to come.[138]

Despite their continual claim to the contrary—the 1916 General Council of the Assemblies of God clearly introduced a creedal statement concerning the nature of God.[139] Only eternity will reveal what might have taken place if the General Council had not taken this step. In truth, like Rebekah—the Assemblies of God found *"the children struggled within her"* and that *"two nations"* were in her womb (Genesis 25:22-23). Those who supported the Jesus name message were younger and forced to leave the house of their birth. However, like Jacob of old—they were convinced the message of Jesus name baptism and the Oneness of God represented the **birthright** and **blessing** of the Father. Moreover, they would argue the Spirit of God confirmed this fact as revival and re-baptisms continued unabated from 1916-1920!

---

[138] Haywood, *Council*, 1.

[139] The Trinitarian ministry certainly believed the 10 point sub-section on the Godhead was necessary—but to say this is not a creedal statement is somewhat disingenuous. First, the very language used to describe God's nature in this section is derived from the historic ecclesiastical creeds. Second, most items in the "Fundamentals" are simple doctrinal statements that affirm historic Pentecostal teachings—while the Essentials as to the Godhead contains 10 subsections using Roman Catholic creedal terminology. Third, in 1920 section 13 The Essentials as to the Godhead was placed as an addenda to section 2—renamed 'The Adorable Godhead' in 1927 (see Glenn Gohr, *"The Historical Development of the Statement of Fundamental Truths,"* Assemblies of God Heritage, Vol. 32., (Springfield, MO: Flower Pentecostal Heritage Center, 2012, 61-65).

<u>Conclusion and Reflection</u>

This study has sought to demonstrate that—while the primary proponents of the monadic formula of Acts 2:38 in the twentieth-century have been Oneness Pentecostals—the Jesus name message was not their innovation. Indeed, the modern history of this message can be traced in the nineteenth and early twentieth century restoration movements. Moreover, Oneness Pentecostals could easily point back to the early forbears of Pentecostalism as a means of validating water baptism in the name of Jesus Christ.

In addition—the writer has demonstrated that the link between use of the monadic formula of baptism in the nineteenth-century and its resurgence in 1913-14 Pentecostalism is a Christocentric restorationist impulse. While this impulse is evident in the earliest years of the Movement (1906-1909) it was eclipsed by the doctrinal recovery and experience of Spirit baptism with the evidence of speaking in other tongues. This would change in 1910 as a result of the positive and negative impact of Durham's 'Finished Work' theology. In short, while the Jesus name message was not entirely dependent on Durham's teaching—it provided the conditions that historically favored the re-appearance of the monadic formula.

The Oneness Pentecostal message of Acts 2:38 continues to challenge Pentecostalism to return to its restorationist roots. The danger of forsaking this 'landmark' is readily apparent by the 'identity crisis' enveloping much of post-modern Pentecostalism. In fact, it could be the Oneness Movement has avoided this predicament to a greater degree—because they have retained more elements of restorationism than any other segment of the Movement.

Lastly, the information in this section also challenges Oneness Pentecostals to examine the attitudes and rhetoric manifested towards those who do not embrace or fully comprehend the Jesus name message. This writer uncompromisingly believes in the Acts 2:38 message and the Oneness view of God's identity in the person and name of Jesus Christ. However, he is keenly aware that many supporters of this great message have drifted from the amiable spirit manifest in Apostolic forbears. It would do well for post-modern Oneness Pentecostals to prayerfully consider the attitudes of pioneers like Frank Ewart and Howard Goss—both of whom fully embraced truth; yet, expressed genuine love and respect towards those who rejected this great message. Indeed, presenting this revelatory message with such a conciliatory posture will reap eternal dividends!

Glossary

Abandonment of the Faith: An ecclesiological position that asserts the primitive church had a complete understanding of the faith but organically apostatized from this faith in fulfillment of Biblical prophecy. This view is in contrast to the belief that the church progressively developed into the faith after the death of the Apostles. Those who embrace this position believe the doctrinal controversies of the late second through fourth centuries reveal this deterioration, which culminates with the adoption of the Nicene creed in A.D. 325.

Alogian: This word literally means *"against Logos."* It is used of second-century groups that rejected Logos Christology. Some Alogians may have denied the deity of Christ and rejected John's Gospel. However, some of them simply rejected the apologists *interpretation* of the Logos used in John 1:1-14 (i.e. Monarchians).

Apologists: Highly educated second-century Gentile converts that were schooled in Greek philosophy. The Apologists impacted the historical development of Christianity by successfully syncretizing Greek philosophy with Biblical Christianity. Their intent was not to assault the Faith—but to make Christianity more palatable to the Greek audience. Unfortunately, in so doing, they introduced innovative doctrines unknown to the pristine church.

Apostasy: A revolt or abandonment of the Faith—personally or corporately. In reference to the visible church—Scripture uses the term "The Apostasy" (2Thess 2:2-3) which appears to refer to the Church's defection or departure from the faith which many believe occurred subsequent to the first century

Atonement (Evangelical): The teaching of 'how' God reconciles fallen humanity to Himself. There are a variety of views regarding the atonement in Christendom; yet, most share the central theme that God sent someone other than Himself to procure salvation. Post-modern explanations of the Atonement often render the Father aloof or uninvolved in the redemptive process and depict God engaging in—child sacrifice.

Atonement (Oneness): In Oneness theology—God sent the Son, but not a distinct eternal hypostasis. Rather, the 'Son' is the one born of a woman—the incarnation of the one true God and Father. The

Oneness understanding of the Atonement emphasizes God's active involvement in the process of redemption—teaching that God was localized in the Son for the procurement of salvation.

Christendom: The visible professing church encompassing every denomination confessing Christianity.

Christocentric: A term that simply means Christ-centered.

Christology: The study of the person, nature and work of Jesus Christ.

Creeds: Any humanly devised doctrinal or propositional statement used as a basis for determining 'fellowship' between believers.

Dabar: The Hebrew term meaning 'word.' In the Old Testament it refers to the creative power of God—the purpose and plan of God expressed in divine utterance. Since Yahweh's 'Dabar' is His expression, some passages personify Dabar, but **never** as a distinct hypostatic being in God. This Hebrew word is a primary basis for John's use of the Greek term 'Logos' in John 1:1.

Distinction (Eternal): The idea that the Father-Son distinction is based on eternal intra-personal hypostases in God's nature.

Distinction (Incarnational): The idea that the Father-Son distinction is a consequence of God's assumption of humanity in the person and name of Jesus. In this view, the distinction between 'God' and 'Jesus' is understood in terms of God's simultaneous existence within and beyond His incarnate state.

Ecclesiology: The study of the nature and work of the Church.

Ecclesiological Presuppositions: The idea that one's perception of the church—especially in the area of a visible corporeal apostasy—influences one's interpretation of the historic doctrinal struggles of the second through fourth century. Those espousing the theory of an embryonic faith tend to view the doctrinal struggles as God's way of bringing the church *into* the faith. In contrast, those who believe in a corporeal apostasy maintain the historic ecclesiastical controversies demonstrate that the church departed *from* the faith.

Echad: The Hebrew cardinal numeral one.

Ecumenical Councils: In Protestant branches of the Church this usually refers to the historic councils up to and including A. D. 454.

Elohim: The intensive plural word rendered "God" or 'gods' in Scripture. It is used to designate Israel's God over 2,500 times in the Old Testament. Some Trinitarians argue this word 'proves' there is an inherent 'plurality' in God's nature; however, several Hebrew words are plural in form but singular in meaning but are not indicative of an 'internal' plurality (i.e. 'water' and 'face').

Epistemology: Literally, this is the study of knowledge but it is used in theology to refer to the foundation upon which a proposition or theory is formed.

Etymology: The study of the origin and development of a word. Etymology is often used to show the 'historical relationship' between two words. Oneness Pentecostal theology uses this to demonstrate the etymological relationship between the name of Jesus and the memorial name of God—YHWH (Exodus 3:15).

Evolving or Embryonic Faith: An ecclesiological theory that teaches the early church was primitive in their doctrinal understanding of the Faith; hence, God used the doctrinal controversies of the late second through fourth centuries to reveal the complete Faith.

God: A term that means 'Deity.' When used in reference to the God of Scripture—it does **not** refer to a one "hypostasis" of God, but the supreme Deity.

God the Father: In Trinitarianism this refers to <u>one</u> hypostasis in the Deity. In Oneness Theology it simply refers to the one true God who is 'Father' by virtue of creation and in the begetting of Jesus.

God the Son: A Trinitarian term used to refer to the second person or hypostasis of God. It is believed this distinct hypostasis is the Divinity resident in the person of Jesus.

Hashem: Literally "the name." This word is used in Scripture with reference to the Tetragrammaton—the personal covenant name of God. The name is a means of God's self-revelation—and a vehicle of His dynamic presence.

Hebraic Monotheism: The belief that there is one God with no eternal hypostatic distinctions in his nature. This view of God was held by ancient and second temple Judaism—and is sometimes referred to as strict or absolute monotheism.

Hebrew-Christian Monotheism: The position of the pristine Christian church, which embraced Hebrew monotheism; yet, taught that Jesus was incarnation of the one God Yahweh. In post-modern Christianity this position is embraced by Oneness Pentecostals.

Hebraic Thought: The idea that Scripture is primarily grounded in Hebrew contours of thought and not Hellenistic thinking.

Hellenization: The process wherein Greek philosophical modes of explaining the faith supplanted the earlier—Hebrew or Semitic thought of the church.

Heterodoxy: Literally *"another orthodoxy."* The word is generally used of groups that are at variance with creedal Christianity, but not necessarily in conflict with Scripture.

Heresy: Evangelical traditions define heresy two ways. First, any belief or doctrine at variance with the Scripture. Second, any belief or doctrine at variance with Scripture and the historic creeds of Christendom.

Hermeneutics: A system of interpretation (i.e. literal, allegorical, historical etc...)

Hippolytus: An apologist whose particular contribution is found in his work "Refutation of All Heresies." He was an opponent of the Monarchian view of God and confirms the widespread influence of this teaching. He writes against 'Noetus' and identifies at least three Bishops of Rome who supported the Monarchian view of God rather than the pre-Trinitarian view he espoused.

Hypostasis: A term referring to a shared existence of spiritual or corporeal entities. In Trinitarian theology it refers to any one of the 'persons' of the Godhead.

Hypostatic distinction: Refers to the three eternal distinctions within the one God.

Ignatius of Antioch: Bishop of Antioch and early Ante-Nicene Father. Although his writings are not devoted to an explication of God's nature, they reveal a closer affinity to the Monarchian view of God than the position advocated by the apologists.

Imago Dei: The image of God. There are a variety of views regarding how this term is used in Scripture.

Impassibility: The idea that nothing external can affect God—thus, making Him incapable of suffering. This philosophical idea is a bulwark of Logos Christology and was used by the apologists to attack those who taught that God suffered in the person of Jesus Christ. Of course, such a view presupposes Jesus is something 'other' than God.

Incarnation: Literally an *embodiment in the flesh*. Christian theology uses this term in reference to God becoming a human being in the person of Jesus Christ. Trinitarians maintain the *'second person'* or *'hypostasis'* of God was incarnate in Christ. Oneness theology argues the one God Yahweh—who is identified as 'Father' was incarnate or embodied in Jesus—while simultaneously retaining His existence as transcendent Spirit.

Interpolation: Inserting words *'into'* a text.

Jesus (Divinity): In Trinitarian theology Jesus' divinity is grounded in an ontological relationship with the Father as an eternal hypostasis in God's being. Thus, the Deity resident in Jesus is the second hypostasis of God.

Jesus (Divinity): In Oneness theology Jesus' is Divine because He is the localization, personification or incarnation of the one true God. Thus, the Deity resident in Jesus is **not** a hypostasis *of* God, but the one indivisible Spirit of the Father manifest in human flesh.

Jesus (The Name): In Trinitarian theology the name Jesus is the human name of the Messiah—the Christ of God.

Jesus (The Name): Oneness theology emphasizes the etymological relationship between the name Jesus and the memorial name Yahweh. The name 'Jesus' is *theophoric* for it *contains* the memorial name and carries the meaning "Yahweh is salvation." The name 'JESUS' is the culmination of God's progressive revelatory use of

His name. Indeed—"Jesus" is understood as the comprehensive name of God in the New Covenant—the one singular name of the Father and of the Son and of the Holy Ghost.

Logos: Literally meaning 'word.' In Semitic understanding it refers chiefly to oral communication wherein the mind finds expression or utterance. It is the Greek equivalent to the Hebrew word 'Dabar' in the Old Testament. In Trinitarianism the *Logos* refers to the 'second person' or hypostasis in the Godhead. In Oneness theology the 'Logos' is the expression of God that is made visible tangible in the person of Jesus Christ—the 'Logos' made flesh.

Logos (Eternality): In Trinitarianism the eternality of the Logos is understood as a tangible pre-existent relational state in God's being as the second person or hypostasis in the Godhead. This distinct hypostasis is believed to be incarnate in Jesus.

Logos (Eternality): In Oneness theology the Logos is the eternal expression of God—encompassing His salvific plan and purpose to assume human identity in the person of Jesus Christ. This expression or 'Logos' is visibly actualized in and through the incarnation event. Thus, the Logos is eternal but **not** a hypostatic distinction in God's being.

Logos Christology: A second-century doctrine of the Apologists that maintains the 'Logos' of John 1:1 refers to a distinct hypostasis in God's being. This teaching is an amalgamation of Plato and Philo's doctrine of God—which teaches the supreme Deity needed an intermediary to communicate with humanity. Philo identified this intermediary as the 'Logos' or *deuteros theos* (the second God). Justin Martyr introduced this concept into Christian thought—identifying the 'Logos' as Jesus. Origen systemized this teaching, and linked it to his innovative doctrine of *eternal Sonship*.

Mishneh Torah: Code of Religious law authored by Maimonides.

Mitzvot Aseh: The 'positive commandments' of the Mishneh Torah.

Monadic Formula: This formula of water baptism is accomplished through the invocation of the name "Jesus" only. Proponents of this formula argue that Matthew 28:19 is not a liturgical rubric—but a command to baptize in the singular name of the Father, and of the Son and of the Holy Ghost. Based upon the book of Acts, it is believed this singular name is Jesus and therefore the only way to properly obey the command of Matthew 28:19 is to invoke God's culminate name—**Jesus**—in water baptism (Acts 2:38; 8:16; 10:48; 19:5; 4:12 etc..).

Monarchianism: The name assigned to groups who rejected the second-century 'Logos Christology' to protect the 'Monarchy' of God.

Modalistic Monarchianism: A form of Monarchianism that denied there is an ontological plurality of distinct hypostases in God. Hence, they taught the Father, Son and Holy Ghost are relational aspects of the one true God. Moreover, they identified Jesus as the incarnation of the one God and Father—thus, the Deity in Jesus is the undifferentiated Spirit of God. Modalism is sometimes referred to as Patripassianism or Sabellianism.

Monolarty: The exclusive worship of only one God.

Monotheism: The belief that there is only one God. In Hebraic thought this oneness is both numerical and in essence.

Mystery of God: Trinitarian theology teaches the 'mystery' is God's eternal existence in three distinct hypostases. In Oneness theology the mystery of God refers to the incarnation—God localized in humanity without sacrificing his existence as transcendent Spirit.

Onomatology: Literally the *study of a name*. In Jewish theology—the development of a 'Divine' onomatology is seen in the revelation of God's personal covenant name YHWH. In the New Testament God's name is personified in the person and name of Jesus—the culminate name of God in the New Covenant.

Ontological: Relating to the essence or nature of being.

Origen of Alexandria: The second-century apologist credited with the systemization of '*Logos Christology*.' He integrated his view of the 'logos' into Christology via his doctrine of *eternal Sonship*—that renders Jesus as deuteros theos (the second god).

Perichoresis: A term used in Trinitarianism to refer to the mutual indwelling or interpenetration of the three hypostases of God. It is formed from the words '*peri*' (around) and '*choreau*' (dance) and sometimes called "the divine dance." Oneness theologians believe this is an unbiblical concept that borders blasphemy and is simply an attempt to rescue Trinitarianism from overt tritheism.

Philo: The Alexandrian Jew noted for his allegorical interpretation of Scripture. Although not a Christian—His understanding of the Logos was accepted and incorporated into Christian doctrine by the second-century apologists. Yet, his view of the logos is derived from Plato's teaching of an second deity in his metaphysical work entitled 'Timaeus.'

Primitivism: A corollary of restorationism that refers to the effort or impulse to restore the original order of things as revealed in the pristine church of the Bible. It is a hallmark of Pentecostalism.

Progressive Revelation of God's Name: The teaching that God used his name as a form of self-disclosure beginning with the revelation of His personal covenant-redemptive name YHWH (Yahweh) in Exodus 3:13-15. The revelatory use of God's everlasting memorial name culminates in the person and name of Jesus.

Restorationism: The idea that the original church apostatized and needed to be restored rather than reformed. All early Pentecostals espoused this belief and recognized their Movement as God's last days vehicle for restoring Apostolic Christianity.

Revelation: Pentecostalism uses this term to refer to a Scriptural illumination by and through the Spirit—wherein truth, previously hidden, is made manifest to believers. Pentecostals do not use this term to denote subjective extra-biblical revelation—but revelation that can be examined and judged by the objective word of God.

Shema: Literally "HEAR!" This is the first word of Deuteronomy 6:4—the cornerstone of Jewish and Christian Monotheism.

Social Trinity: The idea that God is a 'society' or 'community' of persons or three distinct centers of consciousness enjoying intra-personal relationship with one another. There are several strands of Social Trinitarianism; yet, each share the common theme of an eternal relationality in God's essential being.

Sola Scriptura: Literally *"Scripture Alone."* The watchword of the Reformation period and the only legitimate means of determining orthodoxy.

Son of God: In Trinitarian theology: a title of Divinity that refers to the second 'person' of the Godhead—the eternal Logos. It is used interchangeably with the title *"God the Son"* because the distinct hypostasis of the Logos—is localized in Jesus; yet, simultaneously exists transcendently.

Son of God: In Oneness theology this is an incarnational title referring to God's assumption of humanity in the person and name of Jesus Christ. The term *can* emphasize the humanity of Jesus or *humanity united with Divinity*—but is never used to denote Deity alone nor does Scripture **ever** employ the title *'God the Son.'* Jesus is the "Son" by virtue of the fact that God took on an additional simultaneous existence in the human Messiah while retaining His transcendence.

Sonship (Begotten): The teaching that Jesus is the "Son" by virtue of the incarnation—for Yahweh is the casual agent of His conception. In this view, Sonship is not predicated on an eternal relationship in God's being, but has a distinct tangible beginning in *Salvific history* for the purpose of redemption and mediation and will have an eschatological culmination and fulfillment.

Sonship (Eternal): The teaching that Jesus is the 'Son' by virtue of His ontological relationship in God—as a distinct hypostasis. According to this teaching—the Son is eternally generated from the Father.

Tetragrammaton: The four-lettered personal covenant name of God in the Old Testament. It is transliterated YHWH and the name God called his everlasting memorial name.

Tertullian: Second-century apologist often called the *"Father of the Trinity,"* though his view does not reflect current Trinitarianism. Tertullian was an outspoken opponent of the Monarchian view of God; yet, admits they constitute the 'majority of believers'. His polemic against "Praxeas" shows the 'Oneness' view of God was the dominate understanding of the Godhead in his geographical area and that they opposed his pre-Trinitarianism based on what they believed was the historic *'rule of faith.'*

Triadic Formula: This formula of baptism views Matthew 28:19 as a liturgical rubric and that baptism is accomplished by repeating the words *"in the name of the Father and of the Son and of the Holy Ghost"* over the baptismal candidate.

Yachid: The Hebrew word meaning *unique* or *only*. It is a derivative of 'yachad,' which carries the meaning of *united* or a *unit*.

YHWH (Yahweh): The memorial name of God used over 6,000 times in the Old Testament. This is not just '*one name among many*' but the personal covenant-redemptive name of God in the Old Covenant. Scripture anticipates the globalization, localization and personification of God's name in and through the human Messiah.

Selected Bibliography

Akin, Daniel L. Edt. A Theology for the Church. Nashville, TN: B&H, 2007.

Alexander, Kimberly. *Matters of Conscience, Matters of Unity, Matters of Orthodoxy.* Paper for Joint Meeting of the Society for Pentecostal Studies. March 20, 2003.

Archer, Kenneth J. *Pentecostal Story: The Hermeneutical Filter for the Making of Meaning.* Pneuma. 26:1. Fall, 2004.

Assemblies of God. Combined Minutes of the General Council of the Assemblies of God. Hot Springs AR. April 2-12 and Chicago IL. Nov. 15-29, 1914.

_____. Minutes of the General Council of the Assemblies of God. Hot Springs AR. April 1-12, 1914.

_____. Minutes of the General Council of the Assemblies of God. St. Louis, MO: October 1-7, 1916.

Bacchiocchi, Samuel. From Sabbath to Sunday. Rome, Italy: Gregorian University, 1977,

Baker, Oscar E. The Issues Distinguishing Free and Other Liberal Baptists. Boston, MA: Morning Star, 1889.

Bartleman, Frank. Azusa Street. Plainfield, NY: Logos, 1980.

_____. *Some Blessed Items of Truth.* The Blessed Truth. Vol. 3. No. 11. Eureka Springs, AR: August 15, 1918.

_____. *Why I was Re-baptized in the Name of Jesus Christ.* Meat in Due Season. Vol. 1. No. 9. Los Angeles, CA: December, 1915.

Bass, E. R. *Be Baptized into the Name of Jesus Christ.* The Present Truth. No. 1. Indianapolis, IN: 1916.

Baukham, Richard. Jesus and the God of Israel. Grand Rapids, MI: Eerdmans, 2008.

Berchman, Robert M. <u>From Philo to Origen: Middle Platonism in Transition</u>. Chico, CA: Scholars Press, 1984.

Bernard, David K. <u>A History of Christian Doctrine</u>. 3 Vols. Hazelwood, MO: Word Aflame, 1995.

_____. <u>In the Name of Jesus</u>. Hazelwood, MO: Word Aflame, 1992.

_____. <u>Oneness and Trinity A.D. 100-300</u>. Hazelwood, MO: Word Aflame, 1991.

_____. <u>The New Birth</u>. Hazelwood, MO: Word Aflame, 1990.

_____. <u>The Oneness of God</u>. Hazelwood, MO: Word Aflame, 1983.

Boddy, A. A. *Consider Jesus.* <u>Confidence</u>. Vol. II. No. 1. Sunderland England: 1909.

Boyd, Gregory A. <u>Oneness Pentecostals & the Trinity</u>. Grand Rapids, MI: Baker, 1992.

Brown, F., S.R. Driver and C.A. Briggs. <u>Enhanced Brown-Driver-BriggsHebrew and English Lexicon</u>. Electronic edition. Oak Harbor, WA: Logos Research, 2000.

Bruce, Frederick Fyvie. <u>The Acts of the Apostles: The Greek Text with Introduction and Commentary</u>. Grand Rapids, MI: Eerdmans, 1990.

Burgess, Stanley. Edt. <u>International Dictionary of Pentecostal and Charismatic Movements</u>. Grand Rapids, MI: Zondervan, 2002.

Burridge, Richard A. and Graham Gould. <u>Jesus Now and Then</u>. Grand Rapids, MI: Eerdmans. 2004.

Buttrick, George. Edt. <u>The Interpreter's Dictionary of the Bible</u>. Nashville, TN: Abingdon, 1962.

Clibborn-Booth, William E. *Suddenly*. In <u>Meat in Due Season</u>. 1.13 June, 1916.

Colle, Ralph Del, *Oneness and Trinity: A Preliminary Proposal for Dialogue with Oneness Pentecostalism* in Journal of Pentecostal Theology. 10., April, 1997.

Cook, Glenn A. *A Revelation.* Meat in Due Season. Vol. 1 No. 13. Los Angeles, CA: June, 1916.

_____. *Receiving the Holy Ghost.* The Apostolic Faith. Vol. 1. No. 3. Los Angeles, CA: November 1906.

_____. *Wresting the Scriptures.* The Present Truth. No. 1. Indianapolis, IN: 1916.

Counet, Patrick Chatelion. *The Divine Messiah Early Jewish Monotheism and the New Testament.* In The Boundaries of Monotheism. Leiden, Netherlands: Brill, 2009.

Cowely, A. E. edt., Gesenius' Hebrew Grammar. Electronic edition., Oak Tree Software.

Crumpler, A. B. Edt. The Discipline of the Holiness Church. Goldsburg, NC: Nash Brothers, 1902.

Danielou, Jean. The Theology of Jewish Christianity. Philadelphia, PA: Westminster, 1964.

Danker, Fredrick William. A Greek-English Lexicon of the New Testament and other Early Christian Literature. Third edition. Electronic. Chicago, IL: University of Chicago, 2000.

Davids, Peter H. The Epistle of James. In The New International Greek Testament Commentary. Grand Rapids, MI: Eerdmans, 1982.

DelCogliano, Mark. *The Interpretation of John 10:30 in the Third Century: Anti-Monarchian Polemics and the Rise of Grammatical Reading Techniques.* In Journal of Theological Interpretation. 6:1. Winona Lake, IN: Eisenbrauns, 2012.

Duck, Ruth C. Praising God: The Trinity in Christian Worship. Louisville, KY: John Knox, 1999.

Duggar, Lillie. A. J. Tomlinson: Former General Overseer of the

Church of God. Cleveland, TN: White Wing, 1964.

Durham, William H. *The Finished Work of Calvary*. Pentecostal Testimony. Vol. II. No. II. Chicago IL: 1912.

_____. *The Two Great Experiences or Gifts*. Pentecostal Testimony. Vol. 1. No. 8. Los Angeles, CA: 1911.

Dunn, James D. G. Baptism in the Holy Spirit. Philadelphia, PA: Westminster, 1970.

_____. Christology in the Making. Grand Rapids, MI: Eerdmans, 1989.
_____. Jesus and the Spirit. Grand Rapids, MI: Eerdmans, 1997.

Dunning, Ray H. Grace Faith & Holiness. Kansas City, MO: Beacon Hill, 1988.

Easton, M.G. Easton's Bible Dictionary. Nashville, TN: Thomas Nelson, 1897.

Erickson, Millard J. Christian Theology. Grand Rapids, MI: Baker, 1998.

_____. God in Three Persons. Grand Rapids, MI: Baker, 1995.

Estep, William R. The Anabaptist Story. Grand Rapids, MI: Eerdmans, 1996.

Eusebius. The Church History of Eusebius. The Nicene and Post-Nicene Fathers of the Christian Church. Albany, OR: Sage Digital Library, 1996.

Ewart, F. J. *A Baptist Minister's Experience*. The Bridegroom's Messenger. Vol. 4. No. 81. Atlanta, GA: March 1, 1911.

_____. *Baptism is it for the Remission of Sins?* Meat in Due Season. Vol. 1. No. 21. Los Angeles, CA: August 1917.

_____. *From Winnipeg*. Meat in Due Season. Vol. 1. No. 13. Los Angeles, CA: June, 1916.

_____. *Identification with Christ*. In <u>Meat in Due Season</u>. 1.13. June, 1916.

_____. *Our Trip North*. <u>Meat in Due Season</u>. Vol. 1. No. 9. Los Angeles, CA: December 1915.

_____. *The Gospel of the Kingdom*. <u>The Good Report</u>. Vol. 1. No. 10. Los Angeles, CA: March 1, 1914.

_____. *The Last Great Crisis,* <u>Meat in Due Season</u>. Vol. 1. No. 13. Los Angeles, CA: June 1916.

_____. *The Unity of God*. <u>Meat in Due Season</u>. Vol. 1. No. 13 Los Angeles, CA: June, 1916.

_____. <u>The Phenomenon of Pentecost</u>. Hazelwood, MO: Word Aflame, 2000.

_____. <u>The Revelation of Jesus Christ</u>. St. Louis, MO: Pentecostal Pub. n.d.

Farrow, George. *God's Sign on Normal New Testament Salvation*. <u>Meat in Due Season</u>. 1.6. June, 1915.

Faupel, William. <u>The Everlasting Gospel</u>. In <u>Journal of Pentecostal Theology</u>. Vol. 10. Sheffield, England: Sheffield Academic Press, 1996.

Fee, Gordon D. The First Epistle to the Corinthians. In <u>The New International Commentary on the New Testament</u>. Grand Rapids, MI: Eerdmans, 1987.

Ferguson, Everett. <u>Backgrounds of Early Christianity</u>. Grand Rapids, MI: Eerdmans, 1993.

Flynn, David Michael, *The Oneness-Trinity Debate on the Early Church*. In <u>Toward Healing Our Divisions</u>. Springfield, MO: Society of Pentecostal Studies. March 11-13. 1999.

Fortman, E. J. <u>The Triune God</u>. Philadelphia, PA: Westminster, 1972.

Foster, Fred J. Their Story: 20 th Century Pentecostals. Hazelwood, MO: Word Aflame, 1965.

French, Talmadge. Early Interracial Oneness Pentecostalism. Eugene, Oregon: Picwick, 2014.

_____. Our God is One. Indianapolis, IN: Voice & Vision, 1999.

Frend, W.H.C. The Early Church. Minneapolis, MN: Fortress, 1994.

Fretheim, Terence E. Jeremiah. In Smyth & Helwys Bible Commentary. Vol. 15. Macon, GA: Smyth & Helwys, 2002.

George, Timothy. Galatians. In The New American Commentary. Vol. 30. Nashville, TN: Broadman & Holman, 1994.

Gilbrant, Thoralf. Edit., The Old Testament Study Bible. In The Complete Biblical Library. Springfield MO: World Library Press, 1996.

Gill, Deborah Menken. *The Pastorals*. In The Full Life Bible Commentary to the New Testament. Grand Rapids, MI: Zondervan, 1999.

Gohr, Glenn. *The Historical Development of the Statement of Fundamental Truths*. Assemblies of God Heritage. Vol. 32. Springfield, MO. Flower, 2012.

Gomes, Alan. Unmasking the Cults. Grand Rapids, MI: Zondervan, 1995.

Gonzalez, Justo L. A History of Christian Thought. 3 Vols. Nashville, TN: Abingdon, 1987.

Green, Joel B. Recovering the Scandal of the Cross. Downers Grove, IL: InterVarsity, 2011.

Grenz, Stanley J. Theology for the Community of God. Grand Rapids, MI: Eerdmans, 1994.

Grudem, Wayne. Systematic Theology. Grand Rapids, MI:

Zondervan, 1994.

Hall, J. L. *Cults, Orthodoxy and Biblical Christianity*. In <u>Symposium on Oneness Pentecostalism 1988-1990</u>. Hazelwood, MO: Word Aflame, 1990.

Harnack, Adolf. <u>History of Dogma</u>. Gloucester, MS: Peter Smith, 1976.

Harper, Francis and Delma E. Presley. <u>The Okefenokee Album</u>. Athens, GA: University of Georgia, 1981.

Harris, Laird R. edt. <u>Theological Wordbook of the Old Testament</u>. Chicago, IL: Moody, 1980.

Harrison, R. K. <u>Introduction to the Old Testament</u>. Grand Rapids, MI: Eerdmans, 1969.

Hatch, Edwin. The Influence of Greek Ideas on Christianity. Gloucester, MS: Peter Smith, 1970.

Haywood, G. T. *Baptised[sic] Into the Body*. <u>The Good Report</u>. Vol. 1. No. 7. Los Angeles, CA: December, 1913.

_____. <u>The Birth of the Spirit in the Days of the Apostles</u>. Indianapolis, IN: Christ Temple, n.d.

Hegesippus. *Concerning the Martyrdom of James, the Brother of the Lord*. In <u>The Ante-Nicene Fathers</u>. Vol. 8. Albany, OR: Sage Digital Library, 1996.

Hertz, Joseph H., trans. The Thirteen Principles of Faith of Maimonides. in <u>The Authorized Daily Prayer Book</u>. Revised edition, New York, NY: Bloch, 1948.

Hippolytus. <u>Philosophumena</u>. <u>Ante-Nicene Fathers</u>. Grand Rapids, MI: Eerdmans, 1993.

_____. <u>Philosophumena</u>. IX. F. Legge Translation. New York, NY: Macmillian, 1921.

_____. <u>The Refutation of All Heresies</u>. In <u>Ante-Nicene Fathers</u>. Vol. 5. Electronic edition.

Hodge, Charles. <u>Systematic Theology</u>. Vol. 1. New York, NY: Charles Scribner & Sons, 1883.

Hoffman, Daniel. *The Authority of Scripture and Apostolic Doctrine in Ignatius of Antioch*. In <u>The Journal of Evangelical Theological Society</u> March 1985.

Horbury, William. *Jewish and Christian Monotheism in the Herodian Age*. In <u>Early Christian and Jewish Monotheism</u>. New York, NY: T&T Clark, 2004.

Horrell, J. Scott. *Toward a Biblical Model of the Social Trinity* in <u>Journal of the Evangelical Theological Society</u>. 47/3. Louisville, KY: Evangelical Theological Society, 2004.

Horton, Stanley M. Edt. <u>The Old Testament Study Bible: Exodus</u>. <u>The Complete Biblical Library</u>. Vol. 2. Springfield, MO: World Library Press, 1996.

Howard, David M. *Philistines* in <u>Peoples of the Old Testament</u>. Grand Rapids, MI: Baker, 1994.

Ignatius. *Letter to the Ephesians*. <u>Ante-Nicene Fathers</u>. Vol. 1. Grand Rapids, MI: Eerdmans 1993.

_____. *Letter to the Magnesians.*

_____. *Letter to the Romans.*

_____. *Letter to the Smyrnaeans.*

_____. *Letter to the Trallians.*

Jeffery, Steve and Michael Ovey. <u>Pierced for Our Transgressions</u>. Nottingham, England: InterVarsity, 2007.

Jenni, Ernst., edt. <u>Theological Lexicon of the Old Testament</u>. Electronic edition. Oak Tree Software, 1997.

Jones, Rufus M. <u>The Church's Debt to Heretics</u>. New York, NY: George H. Doran, 1924.

Keil, C. F. and F. Delitzsch. <u>Commentary on the Old Testament</u>. 10 Vols. Peabody MS: Hendrickson, reprint 1996.

Kelly, J.N.D. <u>Early Christian Doctrines</u>. New York, NY: Harper, 1960.

Koehler, Ludwig and Walter Baumgartner. <u>The Hebrew and Aramaic Lexicon of the Old Testament</u>. Leiden, Netherlands: electronic edition, 2000.

Kraabel, A. T. *The Disappearance of the 'God-Fearers.'* in <u>Numen</u>. Vol. 28 December 1981. Brill.

Kydd, Ronald A. N. <u>Charismatic Gifts in the Early Church</u>. Peabody, MA: Hendrickson, 1984.

_____. *Jesus, Saints and Relics: Approaching the Early Church Through Healing*. <u>Journal of Pentecostal Theology</u>. 2. April, 1993: 91-104.

Larson, Martin A. <u>The Story of Christian Origins</u>. Washington, D.C: New Republic, 1977.

Lehman, J. O. *Pentecostal Revelation*. <u>The Bridegroom's Messenger</u>. Vol. 3. No. 70. Atlanta, GA: September 15, 1910.

Levine, Lee I. <u>The Ancient Synagogue: The First Thousand Years</u>. New Haven, CN: Yale 2005.

Lightfoot, J.B. <u>Biblical Essays</u>. London, England: Macmillian, 1904.

_____. <u>The Apostolic Fathers</u>. Grand Rapids, MI: Baker 1981.

Lint, Gregory A. edt., <u>The Old Testament Hebrew-English Dictionary: Aleph-Beth</u>. in <u>The Complete Biblical Library</u>. Springfield, MO: World Library Press, 1996.

Longnecker, Richard N. *The Christology of Early Jewish Christianity* <u>Studies in Biblical Theology</u>. Second Series 17., Naperville, IL: Alec R. Allenson, 1970.

Louw, Johannes P. and Eugene A. Nida edts., <u>Greek-English</u>

Lexicon of the New Testament Based on Semantic Domains. New York, NY: United Bible, 1989. Electronic edition.

Lust, J. E. Eynikel and K. Hauspie. A Greek-English Lexicon of the Septuagint. Stuttgart, Germany. Deutsche Bibelgesellschaft, 2003. Electronic edition.

Macchia, F. D. *Pentecostal Theology* in The New International Dictionary of Pentecostal and Charismatic Movements. Grand Rapids, MI: Zondervan, 2002.

Martyr, Justin. *Dialogue with Trypho.* Ante-Nicene Fathers. Vol. 1. Grand Rapids, MI: Eerdmans, 1993.

_____. *The First Apology of Justin.*

Mattingly, Gerald L. *Moabites* in Peoples of the Old Testament. Grand Rapids, MI: Baker, 1994.

Metzler, Norman. *The Trinity in Contemporary Theology: Questioning the Social Trinity,* in Concordia Theological Quarterly. 67:3/4. Fort Wayne, IN: Concordia Theological Seminary July/October 2003.

McClain, S. C. Highlights in Church History. Reprint. Hazelwood, MO: Word Aflame, 1990.

McDowell, Josh and Don Stewart. Understanding the Cults. San Bernardino, CA: Here's Life Publishing, 1983.

McGiffert, Arthur C. A History of Christian Thought. New York, NY: Scribner & Sons, 1954.

McGrath, Alister E. Reformation Thought. Grand Rapids, MI: Baker, 1993.

McKim, Donald K. Edt. *Perichoresis.* In Westminster Dictionary of Theological Terms. Louisvile, KY: John Knox, 1996.

McQuilkin, Robertson. Understanding and Applying the Bible. Chicago, IL: Moody, 1992.

Miller, John. Is God a Trinity? Reprint. Hazelwood, MO: Word

Aflame, 1975.

Moore, George Foot. Judaism. 3 Vols. Peabody, MA: Hendrickson, 1997.

MoorHead, Max Wood. *Visiting on the Border of Nepal.* The Bridegroom's Messenger. Atlanta, GA: February 1, 1912.

Morse, Harry. *Justification.* The Present Truth. No. 1. Indianapolis, IN: 1916.

Morris, Leon. The Epistle to the Romans. Grand Rapids, MI: Eerdmans, 1994.

Mozley, J.B. The Theory of Development. Reprint. Biblo Bazaar 2009.

Newman, Barclay M. A Concise Greek-English Dictionary of the New Testament. Stuttgart, Germany: United Bible Societies. Electronic edition.

Newman, John Henry Cardinal. *An Essay on the Development of Christian Doctrine.* Sixth Edition reprint 1878. Project Gutenberg 2011.

Nygren, Anders. *Agape and Eros* in The Altruism Reader: Selection from Writings on Love Religion and Science. Conshohocken, PA: Templeton, 2008.

Olson, Roger E. The Story of Christian Theology. Downers Grove, IL: InterVarsity. 1999.

Palmer, Phoebe Worall, *Faith and its Effects.* The 19th Century Holiness Movement: Great Holiness Classics. 4 Vols. Kansas City, MO: Beacon Hill, 1998.

Pamphilius, Eusebius, *The False Prophets of the Phrygians.* In Nicene and Post-Nicene Fathers. Vol. XIV. www.ccel.org.

Parham, Charles Fox. A Voice of One Crying in the Wilderness. 1902. Kindle edition, 20012.

Parker, James. *The Incarnational Christology of John.* In Criswell

Theological Review. 3:1. Criswell College, 1988.

Patterson, Eric and Edmund Rybarczyk. The Future of Pentecostalism in the United States. New York, NY: Lexington Books, 2007.

Penn, William. *Letter to John Collenges* (November 22, 1673). in A Collection of the Works of William Penn. London, England: Sowle, 1726.

Phillips, Wade H. God the Church and Revelation. Cleveland, TN: White Wing, 1986.

_____. The Church in History and Prophecy. Cleveland, TN: White Wing, 1990.

_____. Quest to Restore God's House. Vol. 1. 1886-1923. Cleveland, TN: CPT Press, 2014.

Philo. The Works of Philo. Translated by C.D. Yonge. Peabody, MS: Hendrickson, 1993.

Pierce, Larry. Edt. Hebrew and Greek Lexicon Aids. In The Online Bible Millennium Edition. Ontario, Canada: The Online Bible Foundation, 2003.

Plato. Timaeus. Translated by Francis M. Cornford. Indianapolis, IN: Bobbs-Merrill, 1959.

Pseudo-Clementine Literature. Recognitions of Clement, in Ante-Nicene Fathers. Vol. 8. Albany, OR: Sage Digital Library, 1996. 1:43.

_____. The Epistle of Clement to James.

_____. The Epistle of Peter to James.

Purkiser, W.T. Exploring Christian Holiness. 3 Vols. Kansas City, MO: Beacon Hill, 1983.

Rahlfs, Alfred. Edt. Septuaginta: Greek Septuagint. Stuttgart, Germany: Deutsch Bibelgesellschaft, 2006. Electronic edition

2012. Oak Tree Software Inc.

Reed, David. *Aspects of the Origins of Oneness Pentecostalism*. In Aspects of Pentecostal-Charismatic Origins. Plainfield, NJ: Logos, 1975.
_____. In Jesus' Name: The History and Beliefs of Oneness Pentecostals. In Journal of Pentecostal Theology Supplement Series Vol. 31. Dorst DT, UK: Deo Pub. 2008.

_____. *Oneness Pentecostalism*. In The Dictionary of Pentecostal Charismatic Movements. Grand Rapids, MI: Zondervan, 1988.

_____. *Oneness Pentecostalism: Problems and Possibilities for for Pentecostal Theology*. In Journal of Pentecostal Theology. 11. October, 1997.

Reed, H. E. *The Birth of Water and Spirit*. The Blessed Truth. Vol. 3. No. 11. Eureka Springs, AR: August 15, 1918.

Reid, Daniel G. Edt. Dictionary of Christianity in America. Downers Grove, IN: InterVarsity, 1990.

Roberts, L. V. The Present Truth. No. 1. Indianapolis, IN: 1916.

Robertson, A.T. A Grammar of the Greek New Testament in the Light of Historical Research. Nashville, TN: Broadman, 1934.

_____. Robertson's Word Pictures. In The Online Bible For Windows. Ontario, Canada, The Online Bible Foundation, 2002.

Robinson, Maurice A. and William G. Pierpont., edts. The New Testament in the Original Greek: Byzantine Textform. Electronic edition, 2005.

Sandford, Frank W. *Authoritative Baptism*. In History and Times of the Kingdom. Reginald Parker and Richard Sweet edt. www.fwelijah.com

_____. Seven Years With God. Reprint. Mont Vernon, New Hampshire: Kingdom Press, 1957.

_____. The Art of War for the Christian Soldier.

Reprint. Amherst, New Hampshire: Kingdom Press, 1966.

Schaff, Phillip. <u>History of the Christian Church</u>. Vol. 1. <u>Apostolic Christianity A.D. 1-100</u>. Online edition. <u>www.ccel.org</u>.

_____. Edt. <u>Religious Encyclopedia or Dictionary of Biblical, Historical, Doctrinal and Practical Theology</u>. Vol. 2. New York, NY: Funk & Wagnalls, 1883.

_____. *The Nicene Creed: Expanded A.D. 381*. in <u>Creeds of Christendom with a History and Critical Notes</u>. Vol. 1. www.ccel.org

Schenker, Adrian., edt. <u>Biblia Hebraica Stuttgartensia</u>. Stuttgart, Germany: Deutsche Bibelgeselschaft, 1933. electronic edition.

Schmaus, Michael. <u>Dogma 4: The Church its Origin and Structure</u>. London, England: Sheed & Ward, 1972.

Schoenberg, Shira. *The Shema*. <u>Jewish Virtual Library</u>. Online edition. www.jewishvirtuallibrary.org. 2012.

Scott, Julius J. *Church of Jerusalem in Acts: The Final Scene*. Unpublished paper presented at <u>The National Meeting of Evangelical Theological Society</u>. Philadelphia, PA: 1995.

_____. *Did the Jerusalem Christians Flee to Pella? Evidence from Biblical, Historical, Archaeological and Critical Studies*. Unpublished paper presented to <u>Wheaton College Archaeology Conference</u>. Wheaton IL: Novemeber, 1998.

Scott, R. J. *World-Wide Apostolic Faith Camp Meeting*. <u>Word and Witness</u>. Vol. 9. No. 3. March 20, 1913.

Segraves, Daniel Lee. <u>Andrew D. Urshan: A Theological Biography</u>. Ann Arbor, MI: ProQuest, 2011.

Sexton, E. A. *A Suggested Resolution*. <u>The Bridegroom's Messenger</u>. Atlanta, GA: September 15, 1912.

_____. *Doctrinal Teaching*. <u>The Bridegroom's Messenger</u>. Atlanta, GA: May 1, 1912.

Seymour, W. J. edt. The Apostolic Faith. Reprint in The Azusa Street Papers 1906-1909.1997.

Simpson, A. B. Wholly Sanctified. Harrisburg, PA: Christian Pub, 1982.

Small, Frank. *One Great Experience*. The Present Truth. No. 1. Indianapolis, IN: 1916

Smith, Elias. The Herald of Gospel Liberty.

_____. The Life, Conversion, Preaching, Traveling and Sufferings of Elias Smith. Portsmouth, NH: Beck & Foster, 1816.

Snow, Eric V. A Zeal for God not According to Knowledge. Lincoln, NE: 2005.

Spicq, Ceslas. Edt. Theological Lexicon of the New Testament. Hendrickson Pub, 1994. Electronic Edition. Oak Tree Software Inc.

Spurling, R. G. The Lost Link. Turtletown, TN: Church of God Pub, 1920.

Stevens, Gerald L. New Testament Greek. Second Edition. University Press, 1997.

Swanson, J. Dictionary of Biblical Languages with Semantic Domains. Electronic edition, Oak Harbor, WA: Logos Research, 1997.

Synan, Vinson. Aspects of Pentecostal-Charismatic Origins. NJ: Logos International, 1973.

_____. The Holiness-Pentecostal Tradition. Grand Rapids, MI: Eerdmans, 1997.

Tabbernee, William. Fake Prophecy and Polluted Sacraments. Leiden, Netherlands: Brill 2007.

Talbert, Charles H. The Development of Christology During the First Hundred Years. In Supplements to Novum Testamentum

140. Leiden, Netherlands, Brill. 2011.

Tertullian. *Against Praxeas*. Ante-Nicene Fathers. Vol. 3. Grand Rapids, MI: Eerdmans, 1993.

Thayer, Joseph Henry. Thayer's Greek Lexicon. Electronic edition. Oak Tree Software Inc.

Thomas, E. J. *Tertullian: Adversus Praxean*. In Review of Theology and Philosophy. Vol. 3. Edinburgh, Scotland: Otto Shulze, 1908.

Thompson, J.A. Deuteronomy: An Introduction and Commentary. Tyndale Old Testament Commentaries. Downers Grove, IL: InterVarsity, 1974.

Tomlinson, A. J. Historical Annual Addresses. 3 Vols. Cleveland, TN: White Wing, 1970.

_____. The Diary of A. J. Tomlinson. 3 Vols. Queens Village, NY: 1948.

_____. The Diary of A. J. Tomlinson. Vol. 5-6. in Heritage Series. Cleveland, TN: White Wing, 2012.

_____. *Confusion of Scriptures Due to Natural and Mental Disarrangement*. Church of God Evangel. July 27, 1914.

Toon, Peter. The Development of Doctrine in the Church. Grand Rapids, MI: Eerdmans, 1979.

Torbet, Robert G. A History of the Baptists. Philadelphia, PA: Judson, 1950.

Touger, Eliyahu, trans., The Mishneh Torah (English-Hebrew). Moziam publication online edition at www.chabad.org.

Towner, Phillip H. The Letters to Timothy and Titus. In The New International Commentary on the New Testament. Grand Rapids, MI: Eerdmans, 2006.

Trowell, C. T. *Okefenokee Folk*. In The Natural Georgia Series: The Okefenokee Swamp. www.sherpaguides.com

Urshan, Andrew. The Life of Andrew Bar David Urshan. Portland, OR: Apostolic Book Pub, 1967.

VanGemeren, Willem A., edt., New International Dictionary of Old Testament Theology & Exegesis. Grand Rapids, MI: Zondervan, 1997. Electronic edition.

Vinyard, Denise W. edt., The New Testament Greek-English Dictionary. 5 Vols. In The Complete Biblical Library. Springfield, MO: World Library Press, 1986.

Wake, William. Forbidden Books of the Original New Testament. Reprint. Project Gutenberg Ebook.

Wallace, Daniel B. Greek Grammar Beyond the Basics. Grand Rapids, MI: Zondervan, 1996.

Wardle, Timothy Scott. Continuity and Discontinuity: The Temple and Early Christian Identity. Doctoral Dissertation. Duke University, 2008.

Weisser, Thomas. *Was the Early Church Oneness or Trinitarian?* Symposium on Oneness Pentecostalism. Hazelwood, MO: Word Aflame, 1986.

Wells, Ronald A., History Through the Eyes of Faith. San Francisco, CA: Harper Collins, 1989.

Whiston, William. *Ignatius' Epistle to the Magnesians.* In Primitive Christianity Revived in Four Volumes. London, England: 1711.

Willoughby, Bruce E. *A Heartfelt Love: An Exegesis of Deuteronomy 6:4-19* Restoration Quarterly. Vol. 20., Wenham, MA: Gordon College 1977.

Wilson, Charles D. *The Religious Background of the Logos.* In Symposium on Oneness Pentecostalsim 1988 to 1990. Hazelwood, MO: Word Alfame, 1990.

Wilson, Marvin R. *The Contour of Hebrew Thought.* In Restore. Atlanta, GA: Restoration Foundation, n.d.

36662493R00146

Made in the USA
Middletown, DE
18 February 2019